For Love of the World

UNIVERSITY

OF IOWA PRESS

IOWA CITY

ESSAYS

ON

NATURE

WRITERS

For
Love
of the
World

SHERMAN

PAUL

University of Iowa Press, Iowa City 52242

Copyright © 1992 by the University of Iowa Press

Printed in the United States of America

Design by Richard Hendel

Printed on acid-free paper

96 95 94 93 92 C 10 9 8 7 6 5 4 3 2 1
96 95 94 93 92 P 10 9 8 7 6 5 4 3 2 1

Library of Congress Cataloging-in-Publication Data
Paul, Sherman.
    For love of the world: essays on nature
  writers/by Sherman Paul.
        p.   cm.
      ISBN 0-87745-383-7, ISBN 0-87745-396-9 (pbk.)
      1. American literature—History and
  criticism.   2. Natural history—United States—
  Historiography.   3. Nature in literature.
  I. Title.
  PS163.P38 1992   92-6160
  810.9'36–dc20   CIP

Contents

vii   Preface

THOREAU

3   *Thinking with Thoreau*

13   *From Walden Out*

22   *Three Reviews*

LEOPOLD

37   *The Husbandry of the Wild*

54   *Aldo Leopold's Counter-Friction*

LOPEZ

67   *Making the Turn: Rereading Barry Lopez*

BESTON

111   *Coming Home to the World: Another Journal for Henry Beston*

NELSON

135   *The Education of a Hunter: Reading Richard Nelson*

163   *A Letter from Richard Nelson*

EISELEY

179   *Back and Down: Loren Eiseley's Immense Journey*

MUIR

221   *Muir's Self-Authorizings*

🕸 *Preface*

These essays treat the standing problem of our relatedness to nature that Emerson, thinking of his own work in the great succession of thought, said "has exercised the wonder and study of every fine genius since the world began." Nature writers are their subject because they now have a certain exemplarity whose increasing importance we confirm by giving them increasing attention. Inevitably they put the problem of our relation to nature in the most primary and direct way. Even as they confront it, they clarify its twofold aspect: how to reenter the world, participate in it, and recover respect for it, and how to express the experience and significance of encounters of this kind without, by means of language itself, displacing the world.

These essays belong to our moment in history, when, according to George Kateb in his essays "Thinking about Human Extinction," nothing is more essential than our reattachment to earthly existence, even "existence as such." This, to my mind, is spoken for best in the monosyllabic phrases of George Oppen: *This in which; That it is.* Kateb ponders our fate and the fate of the earth because of the imminence of nuclear destruction. But it seems to me that ecological destruction of a nonnuclear kind is equally imminent and that nature writers, whose witness is informed by many of the perspectives we need, have much to teach us. I know no better fable for our time—for the restoration we must begin—than Jean Giono's *The Man Who*

Planted Trees or recall in a lifetime of reading books of more immediate summons than *Walden*, *A Sand County Almanac*, and *Silent Spring*.

I find that the titles that suggest themselves either before or during the writing of a book are both constitutive in their intuitive naming and heuristic, veritable *working titles*. I have had several in mind all along: *Worlding*, from Richard Pevear, to stand for works that "belong to the world" as against those that are alienating; *Omen[s] of the World*, the subtitle of Stephen Owen's *Traditional Chinese Poetry and Poetics*, which treats a poetics, to some extent fulfilled in the work of both contemporary poets and nature writers who give priority to "the bright countenances of physical things"; and *In the Grain of Things*, which appropriates a phrase of Gary Snyder's *The Practice of the Wild*. All these titles indicate a concern with (and for) the world and the requisite turning outward, the "miraculous dimension," according to George Oppen, who also noted that worlding is descendental, "To get down / Never the effort to go up."

At one time, I put aside my working titles for a descriptive title, *Six Nature Writers and Maybe a Seventh*. This would have allowed me to stop and replace the last, the proposed meditation on Muir, with another selection of entries from my journal. I appreciate the confirmation of those who favored this formal diversity, but I am glad that I went on to Muir. In writing about him I found, at the very end, a more significant title, out of Hannah Arendt, that speaks alike for the writers I have written about and for myself. I have kept the initial installment, "Thinking with Thoreau," as a token of my journal and because it places me here at Wolf Lake, where most of what is gathered in this book was written. It is properly introductory because many of the essential themes are considered here and situated in my life and thought. The journal, in any case, is in the meditative mode of much of the book and what follows may be said to continue the meditation it sets in motion. For everything here is a thinking with Thoreau—and with Emerson, who long ago first engaged me and with whom, in treating the manifold uses to which he put the idea of correspondence, I began to consider some of the problems, to cite the subtitle of my book on Emerson, of *Man and Nature in American Experience*. I recall now that my thinking with Emerson and Thoreau was prompted by what I had learned of Cartesianism, by a revulsion that measured an equally strong attraction to writers who, for love of the world, repudiated its epistemology and began the work of what Morris Berman calls "the reenchantment of the world." Thus, with so much of the end in the beginning, I am not surprised to find myself at last turning to nature writers and writing about them in my now permanent place in the woods.

The installments of this book were written over a period of several years, and some of them were occasional, in response to requests. In a very real sense, I owe these essays to others: to Wendell Glick, who, when reviving the *Thoreau Quarterly*, asked me to write about *Walden* and *Cape Cod*; to Douglas Wilson, who, two years before the celebration of the Leopold centennial at Knox College, put me to work on a lecture on *A Sand County Almanac*; and to Robert W. Lewis, editor of the *North Dakota Quarterly*, who allowed me to co-edit a special issue on nature writers to which I contributed the essay on Beston and for which, when no one seemed ready to do it, I began to write the essay on Richard Nelson published here. The essay on Barry Lopez was not solicited and was published when and where it was, in my *Hewing to Experience: Essays and Reviews on Recent American Poetry and Poetics, Nature and Culture*, because Paul Zimmer, director of the University of Iowa Press, welcomed it and waived cost for fitness. The essays on Eiseley and Muir, and the one on Nelson, were written with a book in mind and, as with the essay on Lopez, are longer than the others because meditation, my freely undertaken morning work, resists limitation. The generosity of others also accounts for what I reprint: David Hamilton, editor of the *Iowa Review*, accepted what I wrote on Leopold; and Dale Kramer, an editor of the *Journal of English and German Philology*, took the reviews of the books I had chosen to review, the recent studies of Thoreau that kept me thinking about Thoreau and moving in the direction of this book.

Should the reader wish to read these installments historically, that is, as a sequence of writers in a tradition of nature writing, I list them here by date of birth:

Henry David Thoreau, 1817–1862
John Muir, 1838–1914
Aldo Leopold, 1887–1948
Henry Beston, 1888–1968
Loren Eiseley, 1907–1977
Richard K. Nelson, 1941–
Barry Lopez, 1945–

But I have arranged the installments in the order of composition, beginning, fortunately, with Thoreau, about whom, in this instance, I wrote in the early 1980s, then Leopold, who focused my attention on nature writing in 1985 and enabled me, from 1987 on, to consider other nature writers in more rapid succession. This sequence is preferable, I think, because it respects the wandering way and temporality of thought. To follow this sequence is, as Merleau-Ponty says, to take a nonlinear path and enter "an experience which gradually clarifies itself, which gradually rectifies itself and proceeds by dialogue with itself and with others." This way of proceeding explains the repetitions that occur when it is necessary for thought to take its bearings and why, when possible, I append the response of the writer whose work I address. Richard Nelson's letter, for which I am especially grateful, both clarifies and rectifies what I have written and, as an example of dialogic criticism, reminds me that my voice is only one in the conversation and requires the amendment of other voices. I find it inexplicable now, not having a letter of this kind from Barry Lopez, that I did not ask for one.

Many libraries generously assisted me, those of the University of Iowa, the University of North Dakota, Bemidji State University, the University of Wisconsin, Yale University, the University of Pennsylvania, and the University of the Pacific. I am especially indebted for material on Eiseley to Gail M. Pietrzyk, archivist, the University Archives and Record Center of the University of Pennsylvania; for material on Leopold to James Liebig of the University of Wisconsin Archives; and for material on Muir to Daryl Morrison, department head, Holt-Atherton Special Collections, the University of the Pacific, and to Scott MacPhail, the Beinecke Rare Book and Manuscript Library, Yale University. To Nina Leopold Bradley I owe the privilege of visiting the Leopold Memorial Reserve. With others already mentioned, the following friends have sustained me: W. H. Rueckert, H. Dan Peck, Jim Summerville, Edward Brunner, William Decker, Mark Luccarelli, Gary Snyder, Tom Lyon, John Tallmadge, Don Scheese, Kevin Oderman, and Richard Blevins. My debt to Michael Olson, a *courrier de bois*, is incalculable, and so, as always, is my debt to Jim.

S.P.
Wolf Lake
July 1991

Thoreau

Thinking with Thoreau

[The following passages, in some way bearing on Thoreau, have been excerpted from Here/Now, *a journal I kept during the summer of 1980. My situation in a cabin by a lake in Minnesota—my life in the woods—was not wholly unlike Thoreau's and the keeping of a journal was clearly indebted to his practice. I am not an inveterate journal keeper and without forethought began to keep this journal in response to a crisis in my life—an interior crisis occasioned by the summer's work of building an addition to the cabin. After twenty years this wooden tent would become a house, habitable in all seasons, and to everyone who passed by to observe the transformation it raised the inevitable question of retirement. The journal, I found, did admirable therapeutic work, enabling me to review the many years of summer occupancy and, in Williams' words, to begin to begin again. Though it is meditative, it was not premeditated. I wrote it without revision as, in Olson's formulation, "language as the act of the instant" and not "language as the act of thought about the instant." In doing this, I discovered something else about the many previous seasons and present season: that Thoreau had*

become so much a part of me and my life that I was thinking with Thoreau.]

You must change your life. (Du musst dein Leben ändern.) Rilke says this on beholding an archaic statue of Apollo, on recognizing the summons—the imperative—of ancient Greece. But I make it almost as soon as I turn on to Route 80 and begin the *journey* north. (Adding *north* now reminds me of Basho. For good reason?) Journeying is a mode of change: You go from one place and, hopefully, one state of mind to another. In our case from city to country, from civilization to nature (does this distinction still apply?), from a less to a more physical, "real" (why the quotation marks?) life, to immediate (less mediated) experience. We do this every year, to break the circuits of the year's teaching and restore the generativity of mind and body, so quickly used up in what too often are only unilateral relationships. Why not say it? The increasing bureaucracy and the cannibalism of students. It is salutary to simplify, as Thoreau says, though he was not troubled as much as we are by the media that mediate our lives. (A mediated life is not worth living.) To get free of that! There is seldom any news of moment on weekends, even less during the summer, and it disarms crises to read about them a few days late. Anyway, if there were *news*, be sure your neighbors would tell you. So not having these conveniences clears the air, affords quiet and time—an unmeasured space of life.

Life is change; one changes willy-nilly. Yet even our changes, like those cited, are routine, a phase of rhythmic pattern, systole and diastole. Rilke had something else in mind, as Olson also did when he alluded to him in "This," the bullfight poem in which death, not Greece, makes changing one's life imperative. The will to change. One wills change only in extremity, to create the necessary disequilibrium of life. And when I begin the trip, when that physical change is under way, I feel such discontent, such dissatisfaction with myself (my self) I recall Rilke's injunction. *I want to change my life.* I have felt this before. Do I feel it now, enough to think of Rilke, because we have begun to remodel the cabin for year-round living? To be here year-round would change my life. Would that accomplish the change from householder to forest sage I have often contemplated, so long admired in the wisdom of the Orient?

Intrusive sounds disturb, noises that demand you notice them, that fill all the space and thereby dominate you. The soughing wind, the bird calls, even the crows' caw and the hammer rap, are *of* the space, elements within it, and so, as Thoreau found, may belong to the grand relation of sound and silence.

Where there is no silence, the people perish.

How could I resist the aphorism? Facing me, as I look up, is a window-sized poster in the Sierra Club Format Series that pictures what I might well look out on. If Henry Schmidt—he was over seventy-five years old then—had remembered to put a window in that wall; he built the study in his garage over the winter and assembled it here. If there hadn't been a forest fire in the forties. I'm sure it was quiet then. The photograph, a visual image of silence, just trees and fog, no people, is by Eliot Porter, who, with Ansel Adams, has given us our images of wilderness, pristine sacred space; and the caption, taken from Thoreau, is the motto of the wilderness movement: "In wildness is the preservation of the world." Thoreau didn't say *wilderness*, he said *wildness* because he had had some experience of the (howling) wilderness (how he relished the openings of lakes and clearings!) and because more than the actual wilderness itself he valued its psychic correlative: *wildness*, the instinctual; *wildness* as *willed-ness*, the expression of will, in the interest of keeping open one's vital, instinctual life. The will to change: In that, paradoxically, is the *preservation* of the world. *World*, from OE, *woruld*, human existence.

Wild, world, from OE, and also *friend* and *neighbor. Wood,* too. With *sough,* you'd think OE preempted life in the woods. OE, *widu, wudu,* wood, tree; and *wōd,* insane? Am I, a planter of trees, mad about them, those friends, from OE *frēon,* whom I love, to whom I am attached, who dwell *at nigh,* constitute my neighborhood?

Inhabiting. That's what we're doing, have been doing all these years since the first summer when, not having heard from the Schmidts, we drove in with our camping gear and to our surprise saw the cabin wholly surrounded by trees and brush (bush: wilderness) down an access (hardly a road) on a slight ridge overlooking the lake . . .

Of the dictionary definitions of *inhabit*, I prefer the last, "*vi, archaic*: to have residence [dwell] in a place." That's not the same as "to occupy as a place of settled residence." The archaic meaning insists on the importance of *place*. By inhabiting space you *create* place. Dwelling-in, living-in is transformative. When you say you have *a* place, you should mean *the* place.

We are invaders, too, unless our seasonal coming-and-going is likened to that of the birds. By way of Bachelard I have taken over the idea of *nesting*, though now, at this stage of life, it's the sheltering roundness, the intimate space, not the reproductive aspect, that applies. Yet there is a generational aspect: We are making this place a place for others, not just ourselves. For others, at another time of life, since such places are most welcome to small children and city-scarred adults. This is not exactly a cottage by a lake, the summer playground of adolescents, and it is too remote for any but those with the desire to come to it. Someday we will be able to live here year-round, but no one is likely to make a living here, not on this sandy soil, in this cold climate. You can't make a living off (of) the place, and only a marginal living by working in town. You could get your fuel (and warm yourself getting it, as Thoreau remarked) and vegetables and berries; fish, too, if you fished, meat if you hunted and trapped. This place will serve someone with a guaranteed annual income—as in the Goodmans' paradigm three, where the option is freedom from the luxury economy. Or someone on pension, like us.

Seasonal. Income determines it, and so defines it in terms of city and country. If you add up the summers, we have spent five full years here. But only by living and working elsewhere. And this is not a simple matter of either/or but a complex matter of both/and. My sense of culture shock is renewed each year by the long drive up, by the increasing visible evidence as we move north of diminished life (the culture of poverty and the poverty of culture). What we do in the summers is invaluable. But winter would be another matter, wouldn't it? I'm not thinking of the cold . . .

The Idea of Landscape and the Sense of Place. The title of John Barrell's book makes distinctions, of great historical importance, between concept and percept, observing from without and participating from within. Though he doesn't use *space* as the polar word to *place*, as in the title of Yi-Fu Tuan's recent book, the fascination of "landscape"—certainly for Americans in the great age of landscape painting and viewing when painting taught one what to view—was with space, and spaciousness: with the liberation of visually searching out space in the joyful security of knowing it "composed," readily conformed to aesthetic expectations and was as ready to conform to economic ones. Space seen is not the same as space sensed. The latter is *place*. Thoreau, himself given to romantic viewing, knew the difference and practiced it by wedding the mind to Nature, by knowing, as he said, by "direct intercourse and sympathy." He knew with all of his senses—"he will smell, taste, see, hear, feel better than other men"—and knowing in this careful, attentive, intimate way, he familiarized space, made it *familial*, or place. His journals report this lifetime work of familiarization. *Walden; or, Life in the Woods* (he wished to omit the subtitle but it has stuck) fables a representative action of human history and of nineteenth-century America; clearing the wilderness, building a homestead, beginning to farm. The Homestead Act. And primarily because it involved homesteads, space may be said to have been conquered. Thoreau's distinction is that in the course of doing these things he also created a sacred space, the place of places. Walden is cosmologically central, but this clearing beside Wolf Lake and most homesteads are not. I was about to say in defense that Thoreau's greatest achievement was an act of imaginative arrogation (arrogant imagination, isn't that the romantic hubris?), but I believe otherwise, that only an imagination of cosmos, of cosmological scope, will transform our places, make us at home where finally we most wish to be, in the universe.

Primordial Acts. Clearing, building, farming (gardening). Emerson puts it in a more sophisticated way than Thoreau; his eye is on the village, not his woodland by the pond, and he knows that place is generational. He says that we should build a house, plant a tree, beget a child. He probably meant fruit trees, since there was no need to plant other kinds and he was an orchardist. He did not sanction Thoreau's experiment perhaps because he considered Walden a place away from home and not a homeplace. Did he realize the extent to which Thoreau achieved cosmicity or dismiss it as brag? And did Thoreau finally leave Walden—as he frequently did during his stay there—because it was not *everything* a place should be?

When we came up that first summer, woods and brush surrounded the cabin. We were the first occupants of a quarter-mile of lakeshore wilderness a resort owner had platted (and plotted) for sale. We chose three lots at the end of the road—also because they were the deepest and best wooded, with more pine and varieties of trees. Later, as our conception of place grew and others began to build nearby, we purchased the quarter-mile strip of woods behind us which joined the eighty acres we acquired farther back. Initially, clearing was the essential task. Not trees—or only when electricity came in—but brush, a head-high tangle that was almost impenetrable. Working outward from the cabin, I attacked this on all sides with a sickle, an inexpensive tool, one of my favorites, still in use, having outworn the file with which I sharpened it. With this tool, I have become adept, hacking even inch-thick stems with one clean stroke. It is a tool with which to lay about, a primitive tool, I now recall, for a primitive fury. By using this tool, I can say that I came to know almost every stem and stalk on the place. Talk of familiarity! I knew brush where Thoreau knew beans, but in my case with no harvest of tropes. It rained every day that summer, and I knew mosquitoes too—knew them as the Jesuits tell of them so woefully in their *Relations*. To expedite matters I purchased at fourth-hand a sickle-bar mower. I think of this formidable machine as a tank, partly because it was heavy and cumbersome with high awkward handlebars and partly because the gasoline engine mounted at the top would occasionally flare up. It did good service but went the way of machinery: Parts could not be procured and it could no longer be repaired. The motor has been salvaged, and for years it has been sitting behind this hut—I was hoping to get someone to make parts for it but now I will take it to the dump.

I used to endure the cold but by degrees have begun to think insulation. When I first occupied my hut, which in size is comparable to Thoreau's, it was as airy as his. (Why didn't I work there in the afternoons? Was I so fixed to a morning routine?) By not putting in an east window, Henry Schmidt forced me to leave the door open for light—and open to the mosquitoes, since mounting a screen door was one of the things he left for me to do. I surmounted that, but for a long time—for many seasons—endured the open door and the chilly air. I dressed heavily, and on ritual occasions—Father's Day, birthday—I was thoughtfully (compassionately) given a handwarmer, useful at late fall football games, and a catalytic heater of the kind used in tents. I never thought of improvements; those I have made have been at the instigation of others, who I sometimes think spend the long winters here thinking up things for me to do in the brief summer. Jerry proposed wiring the hut: He would make the connections if I dug in the wire. In this way I acquired both light and heat, the latter supplied, frequently in insufficient quantities, by an electric dairy heater.

Why is it I choose small spaces for studies? The study at home is the smallest room in the house and has necessitated taking over another, larger room across the hall. My hut here is ten by twelve feet. Perhaps I want what may well be the place of places to be snug? Bachelard does not consider studies in *The Poetics of Space* probably because the spaces that most concern him belong to childhood. Much of my adult life has been spent in studies. Yes: in two senses.

In this beginning to begin again are we building in Heidegger's sense, creating a *location*, making a *space*, a *clearing*, an *open*, in which the fourfold—earth, sky, divinities, and mortals—may *gather*, come to *dwell*, have their *dwelling*? Of all the essays I have read recently in *Poetry, Language, Thought*, none has spoken so directly to me and found me so responsive as "Building Dwelling Thinking." Yet Heidegger, himself a deconstructionist, overlooks the destructiveness of building, and this does not accord with his recognition of *dwelling* as *sparing, preserving, nurturing*. But certainly he is right when he says that we must be capable of dwelling before we can (truly) build. For then the buildings we erect will be complemented by the *building that cultivates growing things*. *Bauen*, to build, derives from *bhu*, to be, to grow. A dwelling place is a place where one grows things. It is also a place one grows into and from; it is the place one is, has being.

Jim Summerville, in Nashville, recently reminded me that down there some people are quietly marking the fiftieth anniversary of *I'll Take My Stand*. He did not mention Berry, who more than anyone I know has kept Southern Agrarianism alive. He has done this as much by his example as by modifying it, by eliminating the defensive regionalism and pressing the national claims of agrarianism. His misgivings about political action and his sense of the human situation ("these separate problems are merely aspects of the human problem, which never has been satisfactorily solved") are those of the Southern Agrarians, but his moral stance is Thoreau's, that the problems and their solution are, at bottom, personal, and social reform begins (and ends) at home. We create the energy problem (and the building of the nuclear power plant he protests) and we can solve it by reducing our energy needs, by gardening, for one thing.

Is this a response to delay, to the fact that the weather, among other things, keeps the workmen away and such a workman as we have, a college-educated young man doing the back-filling, is doing it, literally, shovel by reluctant shovel? and at his whim? reminding us by the way he works and what he knows about welfare and other kinds of payment of those in his generation whose most practiced skill is the rip-off? Who would have thought such skills would be discovered here in the last outpost of rugged individualism? But, then, life in the woods is now often a way of life correlative with rejection of the society—no, the *demands* of the society—whose bounty one readily takes, whose bounty makes it possible. In *Communitas*, the Goodmans say of the third paradigm of rural, subsistence living, that it serves the end of freedom: One chooses to live marginally, at the margin, in order to free oneself from the luxury economy and thereby pursue one's own (usually) creative ends. But from what I have seen those who have chosen the marginal life are seldom Thoreaus. To choose a marginal life is not necessarily to choose a life, to have something purposeful to do, and lacking this wouldn't life in the woods lose its attraction and become dismal, as dismal as one's interior landscape? Life in the woods is not an end in itself: You must have a life and want to live it there, knowing that thereby you may have more life. Doesn't the fact that this is not the rule explain resentment, the frequency of gratuitous acts like that of the other night, when someone smashed Farrell's iron gate?

I read this morning in David Miller's dissertation on the iconology of Dismal Swamp about the popular sentimental image of the secluded lake or pond in the early nineteenth century: "It stood for the never-never land of the soul's mystic yearnings." Such lakes and ponds belonged only to the imagination; they were ungraspable, images of redemption. Doesn't this make Thoreau's attempt to realize the ideal at Walden all the more remarkable? And Yeats' "Innisfree"? Isn't that a sentimentalizing of *Walden*? And *this* lake?

I am rereading Wendell Berry's *The Unsettling of America*, a jeremiad of the first order, which makes me realize, as with Lasch and Mumford, that the most radical (to the roots) and revolutionary (turning, turning back) perspective today is conservative (conserving). Nothing less than saving the earth and the human legacy of our culturation, the immemorial affair of land and life, of the culture that once respected agriculture. Speaking of houses, which are very much on my mind, Berry locates in the household the habits of consumption that make us so destructive of the world. He says that "the modern house is not a response to its place, but rather to the affluence and social status of its owner." That answers to what I noted earlier of houses being built here but doesn't exactly exonerate me. Berry defines place in relation to work and responsibility: You live where you work. Our cabin might be said to express the conservation ethic of the wilderness movement: It modified nature as little as possible and provided shelter for the enjoyment of sacred space. It was only a wooden tent, as we are reminded by our attempts to keep out wind and water, to make it more substantial. Still, we alter and add to it, don't abandon it or build from scratch because, for us, it is of the place, "organic." We have done nothing to the cabin for twenty years—just added a porch. And our outbuildings are the response to need, to the work made possible by settling in a wooden tent. Studying and gardening, varieties of nurturance. Our addition, with its expensive, dressy triplepane windows, its better building, is "modern" and "suburban," though its modesty (it is inset and of lower roofline than the cabin) and tie-in with the cabin (by uniform cedar siding) perhaps subdue that impression. Both buildings are very much the products of the carpenters who built them, in that respect are local. Now the addition of a large kitchen over a basement fitted to the functions of storing and canning food is the direct result of land use. We have moved beyond but not abandoned the wilderness ethic, incorporated it—if our buildings tell the story—in an ethic of land use, of caring for and building up the soil, of planting trees, of gardening. Our gardens could easily sustain us, and perhaps they will if—again, the future—we *ever* live here and have the strength and energy to do so. "This is no country for old men." Except Scott Nearing! Shouldn't the enterprise toward which we advance be the lifework of the young? The extent to which this is impossible suggests to me a meaning Thoreau never had in mind when he wrote that "America is still unsettled and unexplored." We may have missed "America" entirely.

Did I say earlier—has this been the drift of my summer's thought—that the marginal life isn't worth living? I must amend that: I meant that the land here, land such as ours, will not support it, that there is very little one can do—perhaps raise berries, or bees—that will supply the needed cash. We cannot raise tobacco or make maple sugar. When I overlooked the landscape from the Chippewas' vantage the other day, I thought of how few there had been in this vast woodland and of how few even then this woodland had supported. Of course there are farms, many of them in the state of marginality that concerns Berry, and what he says of *margins* applies to them and in its way to us. No one since Thoreau has made so much of margins—and in our time recognized its connection with survival:

It is of great importance to understand that the marginal possibility, the marginal place, and the marginal humanity that I have been describing are reinforced by a marginal way of thinking—until now a sort of counter-theme in our history, so far always subordinate to the theme of exploitation, but unbroken and still alive. This is the theme of settlement, of kindness to the ground, of nurture.

Yes, American criticism, because from the beginning it has been concerned with culture (of immediate references) and with settlement (place), speaks from the margins and is a marginal way of thought. It talks at the boundaries (David Antin) between Nature and Culture, Wildness and Civilization. And it reminds us that not in wildness alone but in margins is the preservation of the world.

The new measure of success? Am I supplying at least as much or more energy of my own than I buy? Another context for Thoreau's injunction to simplify.

The measure of success: When I pause in my shoveling and look out over the lake, now dark with scud, and note the reeds (the natural beauty of natural things, this landscape), I know that what I build must conform to this, belong to this composition.

From Walden Out

"We wished to associate with the Ocean until it lost the pond-like look it wears to a countryman." This remark in the penultimate chapter of *Cape Cod* reiterates the opening paragraph of the book and shows how far the excursion has advanced. The essential act involves sight, the look of things, or, if you will, a change in views, which of course involves a changed opinion of what is viewed. *Cape Cod* is a travel book in which travel is, variously, discovery, adventure, meditative walking, and seeing, the last of most importance to those nineteenth-century travelers in search of the picturesque, of scenery, of *views*. Thoreau's initial sentence seems to offer that visual inducement: "Wishing to get a better view than I had yet had of the ocean, etc." What follows suggests that the view will be worth the trouble, especially to inlanders like himself; it even suggests, in the allusion to *Moby-Dick* ("the ocean . . . covers more than two-thirds of the globe"), a strange new world, "another world," as fabulous as heaven. However, in the play on "fresh" and "salted" it apprises us of lost innocence, and Thoreau, in providing his credentials, notes that he was *accustomed* to make excursions to the ponds but "latterly [pun] I have extended my excursions to the seashore." Walden Pond is familiar, and what recommends *Walden* is the familiarization by which it becomes place and answers to the most intimate necessities of self. But the sea is not familiar—is *unaccustomed*, without custom. And *seashore* is exact, a boundary of opposites, the boundary of his experience, the farthest extent of his excursions in behalf of views. At the beginning, then, Thoreau reminds us to view *Cape Cod* in the perspective of *Walden*. And vice-versa.

Note the change in statement. He now capitalizes "Ocean" and speaks of associating with it. He will get a better view of it by being with it, not merely by seeing it, and even so it will not become familiar. Ocean, by this time, has become Okeanos, "Deep-running Ocean" in the citation from Homer, a reminder that, then and now, "'the Ocean is the origin of all things.'" Immemorial, unchanging, primordial, it is that which, as Heraclitus says, all things are (in Charles Olson's words, "Okeanos the one which all things are and by which nothing / is anything but itself, measured so"). "When once we began to look," Thoreau says in an account of the ocean's immensity, "we could see what proportion man and his works bear to the globe. . . . we looked off, and saw the water growing darker and darker and deeper and deeper the farther we looked, till it was awful to consider." Awful (aweful) to consider a bottom that in effect is bottomless because "out of sight"; awful because, as the Veda reminds him, there is nothing to cling to—nothing hopeful like the green weed at the bottom of Walden Pond, only seaweed fifteen hundred feet long for which he finds no correspondence; no deep, as Emerson would have it, opening on another deeper deep. And the "distant shore," recalling the spiritual haven evoked in the chapter on the shipwreck, is at best a distant hope, as distant, in fact, as heaven, which Sir Humphrey Gilbert is quoted as saying is as near by sea as by land, a claim Thoreau repudiates by saying, "I saw that it would not be easy to realize," the pun here doing good service. What he does realize, and merely from the vantage of the shore, is enough: that the sea is an other that is not fallen or ruined, lending itself to picturesque vistas, but source; that "we, too, are the product of seaslime"; that the sea is also "a vast *morgue*"; that it is the wildest of wilds, water, unlike that of Walden, that bears no relation to his shore. Like Hart Crane, who takes over Melville's view in "At Melville's Tomb," he, too, sees "the dice of drowned men's bones"; like Crane, watching the kids play on the beach in "Voyages," he knows "the bottom of the sea is cruel"—"naked Nature," he says, is "inhumanly sincere." Though he doesn't give us the correspondences as Whitman does in "As I Ebb'd with the Ocean of Life," the evidence he supplies suggests that he has realized that the "sobbing dirge of Nature" is also for himself and that the self that makes correspondences is no match for the sea.

This transformation is the result of taking more than a single view, of having that "breadth of view which is almost equivalent to motion." It involves seeing the *restless* sea and, just as important, hearing its *ceaseless* roar—having as one the testimony of the distant and intimate senses. It involves the radical transformation of giving over the habits of viewing incorporated in landscape painting: the predisposition, from a fixed and advantageous position, to find composed before one the very landscape one has, a priori, in mind. There are no grand views of this kind in this guidebook, no special vantages, like the Catskill House. This deliberate avoidance is most extraordinary in a travel book. What we have instead is Thoreau's concern with "the whole of it," that is, with an all-inclusive view made up of innumerable views or glimpses, one (try to imagine it) that puts him not in a spectatorial position at the focal point, whether of a canvas or the stage of a proscenium theater, but in the center of an illimitable circle, within a field of experience, a participant in the arena, the theater of life (where, as here, the drama is almost always tragic and the sea is the chorus?). It involves giving over the view (opinion) that nature can be so readily and pleasantly composed. "Breadth of view," answering to the purposes of Thoreau's excursion, also suggests acquiring, as Thoreau does, a wealth of information about what one sees, of letting that come into one's view. If *Cape Cod* does not give us the whole of it—it is, finally, too shore-bound for that—it gives us an unusual breadth of view. And it remains a still-serviceable guidebook because of its unusual view and its exemplification of a present way of seeing.

When Thoreau puns on his name, he invites us to consider his material imagination, the imagination which, according to Gaston Bachelard, characteristically works with one of the four elements: earth, air, fire, and water. "Thor-eau," it seems, spells it out, though we should not overlook the first syllable in eagerness to seize the last. Still, Thoreau's most important books, *A Week*, *Walden*, and *Cape Cod*, are those in which water is the conspicuous element. Bachelard treats water in *Water and Dreams*, but in my recollection of this wonderful book dreaming is not as important as death, though the dreaming may be of death, as the brilliant analysis of Poe's imagery reminds us. Neither *A Week* nor *Walden* especially calls up Poe—nor Melville and Whitman. But *Cape Cod* does, by virtue of the fact that getting a better view of the ocean is tantamount, as the first chapter indicates, to getting a better view of death. Beginnings and endings in *Cape Cod* are not exclusively matters of discovery and settlement; voyaging (and shipwreck), discovery, and settlement are metaphors, ways of viewing life and its prospects.

One of the most important things about *Cape Cod* is that it unsettles Thoreau's views and has no settled view. In it, to borrow from his own etymological account of the name, the root of the matter is *to take hold of a thing* and to retain one's faith in seeds. He grapples with *death*—as fact and idea—and perhaps in contemplating the seeds of the shipwrecked *Franklin* (providentially named after a doer of good works and a believer in benign Providence) is better satisfied, takes a better view of death, than in the eloquent but forced passage in the first chapter, where death is transfigured, "shipwrecked into life again." I think this transcendental-Christian view is sentimental, too easily come by—a desperate resistance to what he has shown death objectively predicates. It is a stock response Thoreau subsequently questions. Later on he tells Channing, his companion, that he "did not intend this for a sentimental journey," and when he finds the French crown piece inscribed with the legend *Sit Nomen Domini Benedictum*, he remarks, "a pleasing sentiment to read in the sands of the seashore."

The journey in search of the picturesque is usually a sentimental journey. That Thoreau's is not is attested by the absence of such views as those of other excursions, "Saddleback" in *A Week*, for example, and by the fact that he proceeds by deconstructing such delectable views as he gives us. ("Delectable" comes to mind because I sense in *Cape Cod* the presence of Bunyan's *Pilgrim's Progress*.) Maybe when we reach the end (which is a beginning) and look out to sea, we can say of the sea as certainly as Thoreau says of the wreckage on Grampus Rock, "I saw it." His book, after all, is itself a gathering of wreckage and accords with what he says of the sea: "There is no telling what it may not vomit up. It lets nothing lie." The sea compels us to recognize the truth of things, and so does *Cape Cod*. Melville equates truth with landlessness, Thoreau with restlessness.

Travel is restless, inconsequent, and improvisatory. It is a kind of vagrancy, not in behalf of the extravagant so much as the unexpected, occasions that petition the attention. The significance is literally in the sign, in what Thoreau sees, the sights he pays attention to. The symbolic meaning with which he habitually completes seeing is not as important here as what the objects themselves predicate or the meaning they gather by accumulation, by repeated seeing. Under these conditions the mind is open and receptive, less inclined to give than to receive meaning. It takes a considerable journey, long exposure, to receive the meaning(s) of the sea; several excursions, in fact, and these, we feel, are not enough. Thoreau can never, as in his own backyard, anticipate Nature. He is, so to speak, out of his element. The role of perceiver, accordingly, is minimized. He is not a sovereign spectator, the monarch of all he surveys. The "I" is inconspicuous, now "eye" (and ear), and it is often subsumed in the "we." Inquiry solicits the speech of others, others' views; and Thoreau himself is only one of several "characters" in a story of wayfaring more picaresque (he and Channing are taken for bank robbers) than picturesque. If the book is amiable, perhaps this is the reason. In enacting the visual drama of Emerson's "Circles"—here is the abandonment, here the eye is the first circle, the horizon the second—the process, as Thoreau observes it, is lateral, not ascendant. He has extended his scope (his *landskope* view) but not necessarily advanced an Idea. The "whole of it" does not receive a covering generalization. All of which is to say that *Cape Cod* is not a fable of the will.

At the start, plan yields to accident, itself a significant turn of events. News of the shipwreck of the *St. John* summons the travelers to Cohasset, but in Thoreau's case the motive is not merely curiosity or morbid sentiment. He refers later on to an earlier experience of shipwreck, that of the *Elizabeth* on Fire Island, where he had gone to recover, among others, the body of Margaret Fuller. This shipwreck undoubtedly informs Thoreau's view of the *St. John*, or perhaps I should say that the shipwreck of the *St. John* recalls the earlier shipwreck, which involved him personally. Had that earlier journey to the beach been a sentimental journey? Was the present journey a test? "The Shipwreck" gives *Cape Cod* its themes, reminds us that everything, human culture itself, is founded on death. In *Cape Cod*, the book of nature is also the book of culture: Death mediates them.

The subsequent journey enables Thoreau to put the earlier shipwreck in perspective. He does get a better view of death than he had yet had. And *viewing* is directly involved because the context is the mirage he experiences on the beach ("Objects on the beach, whether men or inanimate things, look not only exceedingly grotesque, but much larger and more wonderful than they are"). Yet what he now recalls seeing on the beach at Fire Island is not disclaimed, and death, as *death*, is given its due: "They ['some bones with a little flesh adhering to them'] were alone with the beach and the sea, whose hollow roar seemed addressed to them, and I was impressed as if there was an understanding between them and the ocean which necessarily left me out, with my snivelling sympathies. That dead body had taken possession of the shore, and reigned over it as no living one could, in the name of a certain majesty which belonged to it." The only questionable word here is "hollow," which even so may be to the purpose in suggesting and denying "hallow." Here fact flowers into truth. These words ring true where the extended metaphor on spiritual passage in "The Shipwreck" does not.

Death is the ultimate other, a realm of its own. The sea and the beach, also other, are familiar with it. So death, accordingly, possesses it, *belongs* there. The living are left out, excommunicated, if one may be permitted a pun that calls up Thoreau's remark that he would like communication with the sublime. Sympathy is unavailing, and understanding, too. Though Thoreau is a wrecker taking much of his material from the beach and though he is responsive, the sea is not. It will not communicate with him. It is as unanswering as the icy seascape of Crane's "North Labrador" and denies the possibility of correspondence. In the chapter on the shipwreck the ubiquitous verb is one of seeing, and what is interesting here, where views are expected, is that none, finally, composes. Nature, on this shore and almost everywhere on this cape, refuses to be picturesque, which is to say that it will not be shaped by human imagination and answer to its expectations. Correspondence does not avail, death cannot be translated, transformed. It is ineffable, as Wittgenstein teaches us: Some things cannot be said, only shown. Moreover, it is real and resists the apocalyptic desire of the mind. *This*—not the perception of the insubstantiality of the world that Emerson, for one, considered sublime—makes for awe, terrifies in this spectacle. To speak, as Thoreau does, of the vastness and immensity of the sea is to speak also of the lack of human measure or "meaning." In this way, Thoreau defines the sublime as against the beautiful. When, with artfulness, he concludes "The Shipwreck" by juxtaposing the sublime and the beautiful, it is to the end of discounting the beautiful and of showing the cracks in its representation of reality. His object here and throughout the journey is to let reality reveal itself, to give a truer representation of it.

Thoreau *admits* death, lets the other enter his work. He recognizes it as real, terrible, immutable. And isn't he admitting its presence in his own life, readying himself for death?

In "The Shipwreck," Thoreau provides a measure of the sympathy he is said to lack by reporting the callous response of others. At the same time, he challenges their view that they have seen "the whole of it." Nothing is seen from a prospect, not even the funeral, and though Thoreau says it was not an impressive scene, he does not, as he might have, fully describe it, present it as a view. He offers instead a canvas without a center, a detailed, close-up inspection of the things he sees as he walks about among them. The impression is kaleidoscopic. The most frequently occurring object is the box, the "rough deal" box (pun?) which, it seems, disturbs him most. Later on, when he describes the charity house, he reminds us of it by concluding that the house was "not a *humane house* . . . but a sea-side box." Still later, the phrase "boxed up" tells his fears, and coming on the stagecoach so soon after the boxes on the beach may give this comic episode, itself concerned with views, a macabre turn: Like Thoreau, you see very little when boxed up.

What strikes me most on this reading is Thoreau's respect for *adéquation*. The term is Francis Ponge's for a literary equivalence that respects the thing and lets it stand forth. *Adéquation* is not to be confused with *correspondence*: It is not a symbolic mode but an activity in words that is literally comparable to the thing itself. Here is an example from "The Beach": "Though for some time I have not spoken of the roaring of the breakers, and the ceaseless flux and reflux of the waves, yet did they not for a moment cease to dash and roar, with such a tumult that if you had been there, you could scarcely have heard my voice the while; and they are dashing and roaring this very moment, though it may be with less din and violence, for there the sea never rests." It also seems to me that each chapter tries to find a mode adequate to, approximating, matters at hand. Thoreau is not thoroughly Pongean, though he, too, exploits puns and practices etymology and uses historical and scientific materials; he does not always make verbal equivalents. But he understands that language is a representation of reality and may be variously, approximately used to that end. There is exceptional variety, and the book doesn't "keep," even though thematically it has threads and structurally follows the chronology of a journey. It is a daybook, each day offering its different weather and views; and it is truer to the case to speak of modulation rather than progress, a rhythm of inland and shore, and often of humor and seriousness, that brings us freshly to the beach again and again, where most of the viewing takes place and our sense of the sea deepens. (This incremental grasp is Pongean.) When there is only sea to be seen we are at the end of the journey.

Thoreau himself likens the making of the book to gathering wreckage. This is appropriate to his sense of reality, to the fact that throughout he respects what the sea casts up, takes what he finds, and gives over the compulsion to unify, the transcendental push for meaning, which results, as Emerson knew, from the tyrannizing desire of the mind for unity. I value this book—and its author—because, in fidelity to truth of this kind, he did so little to compose it. His better view is composite, inclusive, the book in toto. In this way he gives us a proper sense of "the whole of it." And by respecting the limits of language, he humbles us.

Cape Cod denies the truth of views. Thoreau knows that viewing is always from a perspective, as in the comic instance of the Wellfleet Oysterman's tobacco juice. He knows that viewing is observational and uninvolved and gives over the predilection for it. He enters the field of experience and, as he says (the puns again doing good service), is "wholly absorbed by this spectacle and tumult." *Cape Cod* does not give us any views comparable to Fitz Hugh Lane's luminist seascapes. It accords more with Herbert Gleason's photographs of Cape Cod, only a few of which may be said to be romantic. But even so, Gleason's photographs give us little of the Cape Cod that Thoreau's words give us; they miss the sublime altogether. Thoreau deprecates his own work when he says, "In it there is no roar, no beach-birds, no tow-cloth."

Thoreau's water, though an element inflicting death, is not like Poe's, *dead water*. It is alive with life and is the agency of life's accidents. It brings the seeds of the *Franklin* to shore, a compensatory result that helps us understand Thoreau's remark on accidents of discovery (all in terms of America) that "led to real, if not compensatory discoveries." In a historical sense the journey along the cape goes back in time, puts present, fashionable, commercial America behind us, and recovers, in finally reviewing the history of discovery, America's origins, beginnings. Here, as in *Walden*, Thoreau uses time (not natural, cyclical but historical, linear time) to deny it, uses time to resist death—uses art to resist death. And so Thoreau's book is about beginnings as well as endings, about renewal as well as death. There are such mediating images as seeds and seaweed, the latter gathered for compost.

What is remarkable in *Cape Cod* is Thoreau's respect for the accidental, his view of a universe in which human purpose ("the intervention of man") fails, or if it succeeds does so in some unfathomable fashion. This is what he takes in his larger view, and discovery belongs in it because discovery is a mode of being that risks randomness.

Thoreau's sense of disappointment in America and his concern with discovery as renewal call up Charles Olson's desire to refound America at Gloucester. No one after Thoreau knows the history of discovery, founding, fishing, and settlement as well as Olson does nor so fully takes over the implicit project of the book—and in respect to viewing, too, since Olson had to overcome the romantic way and enter the field. Thoreau visited Cape Ann, the other arm of Massachusetts Bay, but chose to discover Cape Cod because walking there, he explained, was more convenient. (What, one wonders, would he have made of Dogtown and the granitic upthrust of this cape? Would his book have been a rocky rather than sandy one? Or was it that having seen rocks at Katahdin, he didn't need to *see* rocks anymore?) Olson does not mention *Cape Cod*, though one can learn quite as much from it about human culture as from Carl Sauer's *Land and Life*. It is unlikely that Olson didn't read it—not unlikely that he overlooked it. Perhaps he did not think of it because he thought, as he says in his notebooks, that Emerson and Thoreau were "misleading men" (they "acted as if they were in on the original creation & made some corrections"). Yet in another entry on "problems of culture" he is closer to the Thoreau of *Cape Cod* when he places Thoreau with Melville and sets both over against James and Eliot, who, he finds, wanted "frames . . . in which they could fit themselves."

Cape Cod, as Thoreau acknowledges, is sometimes "heavy" going. Sometimes its humor is forced and thin. But, to employ a good Olson word, this book gives his work "size" and puts him in the company of writers like Whitman, Melville, and Dickinson. Just as Thoreau revises the sentimental notions of views, so he revises the equally sentimental view of death. This is a test of greatness. His journey, finally, is not sentimental. When he advises the reader "to read with a large conch-shell at his ear," he doesn't have in mind "The Chambered Nautilus." In learning (to cite Wittgenstein again) that "whereof one cannot speak thereof one must be silent," he has wisely let the sea itself speak and given us a book in which there is no silence.

Three Reviews

Thoreau: A Naturalist's Liberty.
By John Hildebidle. Cambridge, Mass.:
Harvard University Press, 1983.

This quiet, well-mannered book turns on two related arguments, two by virtue of the fact that *natural history* involves the methods of both science and history and, as an inquiry, includes historical material (antiquities, local lore). But since the arguments concern Thoreau's attitudes toward science and history, they can be put as one: that, given Thoreau's ambivalence, he rejected neither as extremely as previous critics have thought nor varied much in his attitudes throughout his lifetime. This argument, to my mind, is dispensable, chiefly because it seldom takes account of the context of previous assessments and Hildebidle himself does not so much disagree with them as modify them—dissent from them, in the sense of the pun. His work is revisionist, and the argumentative framework is functional: to sharpen our interest in the matters at hand and to let him get on with the work of enabling us to see them better. To the extent that natural history depends on seeing, he may be said to be the scholar-as-natural historian, one, incidentally, whose exposition, in its shifting attentions, may have been prompted by his familiarity with this genre. In any case, *seeing* is the focal issue, reminding me of Gary Snyder's "See or go blind!" This, to be sure, is an admonition to undertake a vision quest (in a book concerned with the succession of forest trees, though indebted to Thoreau for other things), but it is a good motto for what, finally, is an insistence of our literature, the need to pay attention to things, to be witness to such firsthand experience.

Hildebidle enables us to see, less so in the chapters on *A Week*, *Walden*, and *Cape Cod*, which do not answer easily to a single view, or, in the case of the latter two, to such binary terms as heaven and hell, elect and fallen; very much so in the central chapters on the method and genre of natural history and on Thoreau's late natural history essays. In the chapter on method he considers Gilbert White's *The Natural History of Selborne* and Charles Darwin's *The Voyage of the Beagle*. In the chapter on genre, where "The Succession of Forest Trees" represents Thoreau's most scientific achievement, he sets out the tradition of natural history writing and redefines the genre. The chapter on late natural history essays—it is called "Schooling the Eye"—treats the following, though never completely or as *writing*: "Dispersion of Seeds," "Notes on Fruits," "Huckleberries," "Autumnal Tints," and "Wild Apples."

Now, in enabling us to see, Hildebidle also enables us to see what he does not. In my view, this concerns the placing of Thoreau's natural history in the context of American literature; that is, of establishing its significance in terms of the most characteristic and important issues. Raising the issue of history, as he does, is one way of doing this, but it is not an especially lively way, even when the proponents of the usable past are offered in testimony. Such allusion to recent work (circa 1915–1930) is decorative, not useful—no use is made of it. This is important, because use could be made of it and of contemporary work, Paul Metcalf's, for example. For one thing it might help to explain what happened to the genre that Thoreau found so congenial and so wonderfully adapted to his own ends. Did it die with the advent of professional science? Isn't there a tradition of nature writing that extends beyond John Burroughs, the last in the Thoreauvian line mentioned by Hildebidle; the tradition in which such diverse practitioners as E. B. White and Annie Dillard, Edward Abbey and Sigurd Olson are enrolled? Thoreau fostered a tradition of nature writing, but this, I think, is not the most important outcome of his work, which may be why Hildebidle doesn't bother with it. But what, then, is the important outcome?

Well, it might *yet* be the outcome now that Hildebidle has described the method and defined the genre for us. Natural history, as Thoreau found it in Gilbert White's letters and in Darwin's journal, was an open form, what Emerson called an "unclosed genre." Emerson himself did not employ it but he recommended it to Thoreau, who more than anyone besides Whitman had been summoned by the project proposed in Emerson's *Nature*. Whitman, too, found an open form and wrote a natural history of the self, and this has been our greatest poetic legacy. But Thoreau, in his way, undertook a similar work, though the burden of nature in it may have put the poets off, disinclined as most poets have increasingly been to be "nature poets." Consider the form: It answers to personal exploration, direct observation, fieldwork. The requisites are knowing at firsthand, with the senses, with all that *physicality* means (what Thoreau meant when he said that before he had "lost any of [his] senses" he had "inhabited [his] body"). When Gilbert White spoke of *parochial history* (local or *parish* history) he noted the importance of men "respecting the objects that *surround* them" (my italics); he knew, whatever the epistemology of subject-and-object, what the essential "stance toward reality" was. The last phrase is Charles Olson's, and I use it because in many ways the poetics of "Projective Verse" is a proposal for fieldwork of this kind.

But consider also: that this genre, according to Hildebidle, is "informal, inclusive, intensely local, experiential, eccentric, nativist, and utilitarian, yet . . . concerned not only with fact but with fundamental spiritual and aesthetic truths." I would emphasize here the inclusivity, the centrality of the observer, his attachment to place (a particular geography), and his "careful attentiveness" to things *and* their relations. The fieldwork involved in writing natural history is a discipline of *hewing to experience*, is literally grounded in nature, in the fact of geography. It involves the disposition, the concern with one's immediate life and references, that Olson, a walker like Thoreau, called "human business"; it is notable for its intimacy, its familiarity. It is always a present activity of discovery, always particularist, more readily serving myth and the allegory of the self than generalization. Hildebidle rightly discusses it in regard to history because, as I see it, the repudiation of history addressed the need to be free of a prescribed destiny (the rectilinearity that Thoreau opposes by going to nature), the need to open a space (in time) for *beginning*, which, as much as anything, is a seeing for oneself, an original relation to the universe. Doesn't Thoreau's walking in nature answer to this? And his way of writing, too, which would follow the syntax of experience? In the journal entry in which he discusses the difficulty he has in "mak[ing] wholes of parts," the journal itself—that is, the writing—becomes "a whole new field," a field composed by "having by chance recorded a few disconnected thoughts and then brought them into juxtaposition." He puts thoughts side by side, as they come, paratactically; and these thoughts "accidentally thrown together" (*conjecture*, as Olson has it) become "a frame," not an overriding concept, "in which more may be developed and exhibited"—endlessly. This is the way his own writing, he says, "may inspire me . . . [to] make wholes of parts." Yes, wholes of parts, which is a good definition of the collage and the ideogram.

Thoreau is one of our eminent *Begründer*, like Melville, a beginner concerned with beginnings, as Olson said. I use Carl Kerényi's word for the mythologist because its root is in *begründen*, to ground and found, and because it applies not only to *Walden* and *Cape Cod*, books of founding and refounding, but to Thoreau's concern with seeds. Hildebidle does not make enough of seeds, the organic-spiritual element in both *Walden* and *Cape Cod*, and he misses what I think may be the image and insistence of greatest importance to Thoreau, the essential of transcendental organicism and nature writing, answering to both nature and self. Louis Sullivan knew this when he advised us to "remember the seed-germ," and we should keep it in mind when reading Thoreau because the entelechy of the seed gives him his own entelechial motive and explains why, in the autumn of his life, he wrote of fruition and ripeness. He puts this motive wonderfully in a sentence as applicable to history as to nature: "We find ourselves in a world that is already planted, but is also being planted." This is to say that we find ourselves, as all his work insists, in a temporal world, where the injunction (of life) is to live forward and when brought to our linear limit to acknowledge the annular miracle of renewal by which time overcomes itself. Hildebidle dismisses the possibility that the large work that Thoreau never completed would have been either a "Calendar" of his locale or a book on Indians. But I believe that the "Natural History of Concord" he merely suggests instead would have necessarily included both for the good reason that in respect to nature and history it would be true to his sense of beginnings and, like the good *paideia* it promised to be, helpful to beginners.

And would it not have been—as *A Week* and *Cape Cod* (and *The Maine Woods*, neglected here) are—a work of cultural or human geography of the kind Carl Sauer has taught us to value? This is one dimension of Thoreau's work that the practice of natural history encouraged. Another, to use a flexible term, is autobiography. Hildebidle makes too little of this. Thoreau turned to natural history because he wished above all to see for himself and for the self. Nature provided him a discipline of self-culture, of growth. Natural history, for him, is *his story* (Olson's pun) or correspondential history (to acknowledge Emerson's profound insistence). An account of a "naturalist's liberty" should not minimize this nor fail to consider it in assessing the changing attitudes expressed in Thoreau's lifework.

Thoreau's Complex Weave: The Writing of
A Week on the Concord and Merrimack Rivers:
With the Text of the First Draft.
By Linck C. Johnson. Charlottesville:
University Press of Virginia, 1986.

Linck Johnson takes the title of this monumental study of *A Week* from Thoreau's allusion to his first book in *Walden*. There Thoreau tells an anecdote of an Indian who, having seen a lawyer's reward in "weav[ing] arguments," sets out to weave baskets, only to find that no one wishes to buy them. Thoreau identifies with the Indian because he, too, "had woven a kind of basket of a delicate texture," and the outcome of his literary endeavor had been equally unrewarding. Anecdotes of this kind—recall the immediately precedent one of the hound, bay horse, and turtledove—*fable* losses, this one due to the failure to gain literary recognition and livelihood. In choosing an Indian to make his case Thoreau refers both to a presence (and loser) in his book and to what may be called his native literary ambition; he also addresses his sense of neglect and difference, even his determination to live in the woods.

The anecdote, placed in the chapter on "Economy," is one of buying and selling in which the Indian discovers that market exchange is not gift exchange (as in archaic societies) and does not acknowledge his gifts. Thoreau treats gift exchange in terms of friendship, the subject of the longest meditation in *A Week;* he considered giving oneself, which one may also do in writing, the exemplary transaction. He was disappointed in both, and in respect to writing the anecdote tells what he had learned in the nearly ten-year trial of authorship from the time of the actual little-recorded excursion in 1839 to the time of the publication of the book, at his expense, in 1849. Johnson's account of the composition of the book—that is, of all the private and public determinants of its final form—is in fact a narrative of literary vocation. It reminds us that, for much of his short life, Thoreau was a literary aspirant who tried "to make it worth men's while to buy [his] baskets." His life, like his book, was remarkably literary. This may be the reason why Horace Greeley, wishing to forward Thoreau's career, suggested that he write an essay on "The Literary Life."

Johnson's title emphasizes the complexity of the weaving rather than its "delicate texture" (its extravagance, after Thoreau's play on *extra-vagance*?). He interpolates *complex*, undoubtedly in recognition of the considerable scholarly task of reconstructing the making of the book. "The design of the basket," he says, "was suggested by two literary forms: the excursion, which provided strong narrative and symbolic elements, and the elegy, the source of important thematic elements"; and, in addition, there were "strands of material on reform, colonial history, and literature." In brief, this is an outline of his study, which treats the journey motif of Thoreau's early and concurrent work, the pastoral elegy ("pastoral of friendship") commemorating his brother's death, and the subsequent materials included as a result of his apprenticeship on the *Dial*, his arrest in 1846, his growing interest in colonial and Indian history, and his pressing difficulties as an author. It treats, it should be said, the way in which these materials enter the book, its composition, chiefly by accretion and elaboration (compare the final version with the fresh, lightly freighted first draft), how from stage to stage it *swelled*, as Thoreau said, becoming, in Johnson's words, "the harvest of his early life and the first great fruit of his literary vocation."

Johnson does for *A Week* what J. Lyndon Shanley did for *Walden* in *The Making of "Walden"* (1957) but on a much larger scale and in closer detail, with a deeper appreciation of its several contexts and acknowledgment of Thoreau's troubled life. His work, which rehearses much (perhaps too much) of what has been written about Thoreau, measures the advance in scholarship since Shanley's book. It is exhaustive, presented with all the editorial care and textual apparatus of the Princeton edition of Thoreau's writing. It is definitive and indispensable.

Even so, and welcome as this study is, I have some reservations. The most important is that in reading the book for us Johnson unravels its strands without giving us in a representative sample an account of the literal activity (the actual work of words) in which the weaving presumably got done. There is a sense, which perhaps his own phrase acknowledges, that he has lived too exclusively in "the limbo of surviving manuscripts." The title of his book claims more than he proves, for *weaving* is questioned by the use of such terms as *mosaic, eclectic, digression*, and *fitted smoothly* (as in jointure), and Emerson's judgment of the structure of the book ("The narrative of the little voyage . . . is a very slender thread for such big beads & ingots as are strung on it") is not repudiated. The fact that a basket is a container (of Thoreau's harvest, "the results of the studies of years," Emerson said) is not considered. Nor is the fact that basketmaking, an aboriginal and native art associated by Thoreau with the "rough-hewn" and "primitive" art of epic times, does not answer (consider "delicate texture" again) to a work more readily placed as "artificial" than "natural." *A Week* is lacking in the "primitive, spontaneous, original, and natural" traits of the greatest poetry according to the Scottish critics endorsed by Thoreau. Much revised, deliberately made, it is a studied and (in much of its materials) a derivative work. By Thoreau's standards it is not a work of genius so much as of talent.

The symbolic action of the book—the journey to source, the recovery of beginnings and the Golden Age—proposes the epic. So does the elegiac burden which goes back to *Gilgamesh*, to the hero's response to the death of his friend. Even the digressions may answer to the didactic, paideumatic function of epic (I am reminded of *The Cantos*); they may also answer to Thoreau's awareness of the need for *size*. *Weaving*, moreover, evokes *rhapsody*, from *rhapsoidia*, songs stitched together, a definition of epic art. The second meaning of *rhapsody*, "miscellaneous collection," does not fairly describe *A Week*, and it is probably not adequately described in conventional epic terms. Yet this auroral book redefines heroic exploit of cultural importance in terms of American history and modern consciousness (the modern is characterized by consciousness, according to Emerson). This, as with *Leaves of Grass*, which Thoreau called "a great primitive poem," may be its original achievement. By finding his literary sources in the East, notably in Greece and India (he goes *widdershins*, as Robert Duncan says of other American literary explorers), Thoreau transformed to his ends (our ends) the westward course exemplified by the actual excursion. These complementary explorations, one rich in American history (the destruction of the Indian and the pristine world was cause for elegy), proposed another way in which "America" was still new, still source, its springs unexhausted, its Grape Islands (like Vinland?) still there, "pieces of unexplored America," to be found round the next bend of the river. With this in mind, *A Week* may be said to be an "epic of inspiration"; that is, the recovery and reenactment in story of the kind of primary perceptual experience that informs myth. In any case it is to be distinguished from the "waltz of inspirations" for which Thoreau admonished Emerson—Emerson, whose *Essays*, published at this time, had added to the anxiety of Thoreau's emergent work.

Johnson considers *A Week* "a flawed masterpiece" and the herald of—indeed, one of—"the seminal works of the American Renaissance." This claim is made in respect to another: "*A Week* [is] an American book in every sense of that resonant phrase." Yet the chapter defending this assessment is the shortest and least convincing, especially when so much of this study shows that the literatures of Europe were "the deepest sources of his . . . inspiration." The *American* quality of American books is surely one of the most difficult things to determine. In a passage cited by Johnson, Thoreau dismisses the inspiration of European art because "it will never make men fit to inhabit this new world." The key word here is *inhabit*. What immediately follows anticipates D. H. Lawrence's essential understanding of our classic literature: "Such [inspiration] is not our beginning life[,] it is the old world a dying in us." Concluding the passage is an injunction to *descendentalism*, one of the legacies of this *Begründer*'s work: "We have got to down into the dirt & grope amid the elements of things for a root-hold [pun] among the nations." *A Week* does not fulfill what Thoreau sets out here. Its work is declarative, and its declarations are not fully demonstrated. The epic fulfillment of Emerson's demand for an original relation to the universe that Thoreau proposed in the metapoetics of *A Week* awaited the completion of another book (a book of inhabiting) begun at this time.

Thoreau's Alternative History: Changing Perspectives on Nature, Culture, and Language.
By Joan Burbick. Philadelphia: University of Pennsylvania Press, 1987.

This cogent book belongs to its time and verifies one of its cardinal points, that insight, like sight, is contextual and temporal. The burden of the book is Burbick's and Thoreau's: the wish to "rescue history from the falsifiers." The falsifiers are the Puritans, who read history providentially as redemptive, and the romantic historians, Thoreau's contemporaries, who read history as progressive, the triumph of civilization over nature. Thoreau's "alternative" history, according to Burbick, is "uncivil" history. Characterizing it this way (surely, it should have been titular), she opposes it to "civilized" history and sharpens our sense of the uses of natural history.

Uncivil is a significant choice, one that the entire book defines and brings to issue in its closing pages. Initially, in *A Week*, Thoreau's work is uncivil because "it forces us to look again at what *is indeed uncivil* about the American past" (my italics). By the time of the last essays, it is uncivil because Thoreau reaches a countervailing *deep* (redemptive) ecological understanding. "No living thing," Burbick says of this realization, "can be taken out of the web of conditions without damaging the redemptive designs of nature's historical continuum." Only nature's economy, Thoreau finds (and Wendell Berry recently concurs in *Home Economics*), promises redemption because the "major legacy of the Puritans" is greed, the spoliation of nature by short-term economies of profit. Redemption is possible only if our culture becomes nature-related in communal, nonproprietary ways such as those Thoreau learned of in his study of the Indians. Thoreau knew that the history of the attempt to redeem nature with culture—civilized history—was a story of violence, of destruction and desecration. Where the romantic historians read future glory in the exploitation of nature, Thoreau read back to a glorious past prior to civilization, and he knew that the time had come (long since, as we say) to redeem culture with nature. For him, "the Fall . . . was the inability to conceive more widely of our place in this [natural] historical reality." Burbick's book is of our time in reminding us of the redemptive possibilities of this ameliorative vista.

Burbick's study might have taken its start from a sentence in *A Week* copied by Loren Eiseley in his *Lost Notebooks*: "Always the laws of light are the same, but the modes and degrees of seeing vary." She attends chiefly to matters of seeing the light, to perception and redemption, in the following works: *A Week,* the *Journal* of 1850 to 1854, *Walden, Cape Cod*, the later *Journal*, and the last essays. An introductory chapter sets out the significant changes in seeing that underwrite the achievement of *A Week*, uncivil history, "a record of the past that . . . dismantles the texts of the romantic or civil historian." Of most importance here is the fact that Thoreau, by entering the landscape as a participant, gives over "the pictorial code" of his earliest work and becomes our pioneer cultural geographer. Like Carl Sauer, he reads the landscape for the record of human (cultural) interaction with it. His "uncivil history . . . includes classes and societies both neglected and suppressed by civil historians" as well as evokes a sense of earth time that challenges the value we place on the short duration of the linear movement we consider historical. In addition, as necessary to a participant, Thoreau rejects the civil historian's authorial omniscience and adopts a first-person mode of description that implicates him in time ("the uncivil historian must . . . rely . . . on the continual apprehension of discrete events that instill a sense of historical continuity"). This mode is fitting to a naturalist but, unlike the naturalist, Thoreau takes as much account of the perceiving subject as of the perceived object. Both of them are of scientific concern to him, even though the former, which often tells his story, is also of autobiographical interest.

It may be said that in studying the relation of subject and object Thoreau makes perception itself and what this implies for correspondential vision the major experiment of his experiment on life. ("So much depends," as William Carlos Williams said.) He is *man seeing* (and sometimes *man hearing*); better, *man in the landscape* (the title of Paul Shepard's study of the aesthetics of nature) *seeing himself see*. In the beginning he followed Emerson in wishing to take symbolic possession of things, and the epiphanic moment when a fact flowered into a truth remained throughout his life a testimony of redemption. At the same time, the bent of his seeing was empirical; he respected particular things and was skeptical of the sovereign-idealist-symbol-making mind. Much of his experiment qualified this sovereignty by showing the extent to which it is conditioned; but when, at the end of his life, he preferred artifacts to fossil bones, it was because they reminded him of "the mind that shaped them." His respect for things calls up George Oppen, who said that "the virtue of the mind / Is that emotion / Which causes / To see"; his respect for mind calls up the closing quatrain on the "wonders of the brain" of Williams' "The Desert Music."

Cartography, Burbick claims, is the major metaphor of *A Week* (even though the title suggests the importance of time), and chronology is the major metaphor of the *Journal*, ordering "perceptual events" and assuring Thoreau, as he said in *A Week*, that "there is something even in the lapse [lap?] of time by which time recovers itself." The major metaphor of *Walden*, Burbick says, is settlement, in keeping with her reading of it as "a fable of the renewal of culture." She believes that "more than the construction of a symbol sequence or a myth of creation that stresses the 'constant theme' of 'spiritual awakening,' *Walden* analyzes the material dimensions of culture and its effects on history, perception, and ultimately, language." This partial truth may amend a partial truth, but it is well to remember that in reimagining the self, the primary witness and resistant force in culture, one necessarily reimagines society and that *Walden* is a powerful cultural critique because the self, Thoreau's and the reader's, validates it.

Here, as elsewhere in Burbick's study, the stringency of argument overlooks and implicitly rejects too much, the most important the seasonal/annular structure of the book, the biographical and intellectual contexts (the exigencies of Thoreau's life and the transcendentalists' recognition of the primacy of self-culture), the profitable reading of *Walden* in terms of sacred and profane space by David Whisnant, and the lifelong concern with phenology that taught Thoreau that nature is round and that empirical law is a warrant of redemption superior to, because more secure than, epiphany. Burbick herself admits that "the myth or symbol reading of *Walden* ends in triumph over any historical or cultural account," that "the mission of enlightenment supersedes the problem of settlement," and that, in the fable of the artist of Kouroo, Thoreau found in art itself a redemptive agency. Though she seems always to work from an adverse position, Burbick has a scholar's integrity.

Burbick accepts the recent critical assessment of *Cape Cod* as a focal work, important because in it Thoreau is most conspicuously aware of the inadequacy of language and the fragile foundation of correspondential vision. Yet she differs with other critics in seeing the book as ironic rather than as a work of "failed vision." The distinction, I think, is not especially important, or only to the extent that it skews her reading. She misses altogether the fact that in "play[ing] with the filters through which we view and hence represent nature," Thoreau found a multiple means, a cumulative way of representing nature that approaches this goal. In a description of the sea that seems to me to fulfill Ponge's idea of *adéquation*, she finds only humor; and Thoreau's use of Greek words is also humorous, though she adds that they are "a reminder of another way of representing the ocean"—yes, and an instance of Thoreau's awareness that all of human experience is needed to represent such primary phenomena. She believes that "the grist of the sea is not to be found in Thoreau's account," when the fact that it is is its notable achievement: *He lets the sea speak.* She takes literally Thoreau's statement that in his account "there is no roar, no beach-birds, no tow-cloth," when the naming denies this, as does so much elsewhere in the book. And of most importance, in view of Burbick's concern with time and redemption, she fails to see that in this book Thoreau uses historical-linear rather than natural-cyclical time to recover the beginning that history has foreclosed.

In the late *Journal*, Burbick is chiefly concerned with Thoreau's study of the psychophysiological functions of the eye and of light, color, and shape, and with his attempt, like the luminist painters, to recover "terrestrial rainbows," the paradisal in nature. In repudiating the "critical opinion that the late *Journal* is largely a compendium of 'scientific' facts," she neglects to mention the extent to which it contains the phenological records upon which Thoreau drew in his last essays. Yet in beginning the chapter on "The Succession of Forest Trees," "Autumnal Tints," "Wild Apples," and "Huckleberries," she acknowledges "the massive observations in his *Journal*" and his need to order them. These essays are the culmination she claims they are, rich in epiphanies and in all that years of observation had taught Thoreau of the laws of redemptive "growth," the ground, as with his faith in seeds, of the now conspicuous prophetic note.

In treating the strategies of these essays and in drawing their ecocultural conclusions, Burbick is especially good, as she is throughout in charting the complexities and paradoxes of perception that Thoreau confronted in his refusal to yield the sacred to either the providential or the scientific view of things. I have already indicated the injudiciousness of hewing too closely to an argument at the expense of wider contexts, and it may be useful to conclude with a few writers and books that Thoreau scholars should take account of: John Barrell's *The Idea of Landscape and the Sense of Place*, a study of John Clare that treats the momentous change at the heart of Burbick's book; Lawrence Buell's *New England Literary Culture*, especially part 3 on the historical imagination, which offers a richer context than Burbick supplies; Carl Sauer's *Land and Life*, the briefest introduction to the cultural geography Thoreau anticipates; Donald Worster's *Nature's Economy*, which provides a history of the mode of participation and closely attends to Thoreau's phenological labors; Gaston Bachelard's *The Poetics of Space*, mentioned by Burbick but not used to the end of understanding how Thoreau's altered stance contributed to the transformation of hostile into intimate space, this, in turn, changing the propensity to conquer nature and supplying the felt content of redemption; and the work of postmodernist poets, like Charles Olson, whose field poetics may offer the closest present analogue to the problems Thoreau faced in entering the field.

Leopold

The Husbandry of the Wild

Forewords are usually last words, commentary on the work done. In respect to what has been accomplished they are placed first in order to open the text, to provide a way in. It seems appropriate, then, in talking about *A Sand County Almanac*, to begin with Aldo Leopold's introductory sentences, to hear how he says what he has to say.

There are some who can live without wild things, and some who cannot. These essays are the delights and dilemmas of one who cannot.

Like winds and sunsets, wild things were taken for granted until progress began to do away with them. Now we face the question whether a still higher "standard of living" is worth its cost in things natural, wild, and free. For us of the minority, the opportunity to see geese is more important than television, and the chance to find a pasque-flower is a right as inalienable as free speech.

These wild things, I admit, had little human value until mechanization assured us of a good breakfast, and until science disclosed the drama of where they came from and how they live. The whole conflict boils down to a question of degree.

37

We of the minority see a law of diminishing returns in progress; our opponents do not.

These sentences exemplify one of Leopold's best styles, an easy, open, straight-on, vernacular, spoken style. Every declaration is measured and firm but not contentious; ingratiating, rather, as prefactory statements should be, even though from first to last what is set out, characteristically, is polarized, a matter of opposition and conflict. This is a personal style, not the objective style of scientific work, for example, Leopold's *Game Management*, which begins with a definition against which his achievement in *A Sand County Almanac* may be measured: "Game management is the art of making land produce sustained annual crops of wild game for recreational use." Leopold's personal style belongs to what, in his large archive (how did one who sat so long at a desk have time for fieldwork?), are called "philosophic and literary writings." This is a separate category in keeping with two critical distinctions, *leisure* (as against *work*) and *country* (as against *land*), both, in turn, related by a sense of adventure and "defiance of the contemporary."

Almost all of Leopold's philosophic and literary writings required revision. The easy style didn't come easy; its artfulness was earned by attending to style as attentively as he attended to all serious matters. Leopold was always a writer, but this doesn't mean, as we sometimes say, that he was a natural writer. He had to learn to write, and in doing so traveled a long way from the occasional humorous scribbling of such early publications as the *Pine Cone* and the forceful and certain field dispatches of the enthuiastic forester. It does not detract from his achievement, then, to note in the first sentence ("There are some who can live without wild things, and some who cannot"), as elsewhere, that he mingles with his own voice the voice of E. B. White. The voices, say, of Thoreau and Muir, great writers whom he acknowledges, were not contemporary; there were profound historical reasons that prohibited their direct appropriation, one of them the diminishment of the singular that much besides ecology fostered, the awareness, as with White, that all a writer who speaks *in propria persona* can serve up is one man's meat. White, incidentally, brought out his essays under that name in 1942, essays written during his retreat to a saltwater farm in Maine. About this time Leopold proposed a Christmas book of essays that did not include many "shack essays," as those in the almanac section were called, or take its title from the round of things he did on the sand county farm he purchased in 1935.

Especially resonant of White in this opener are the way of speaking and what is said. There is, for example, the political terminology, the insistence on freedom and inalienable rights that belonged to a time of domestic and global strife—the Great Depression and World War II. An unobtrusive terminology ("cost," "progress," "'standard of living'") introduces an important economic perspective. A scientific perspective also enters, with the word *science*, unquestioned here, a discloser of evolutionary and ecological knowledge and not, as Leopold knew, an agent of economic forces, the "mechanization" he refers to, the "diminishing returns" he recognizes. Leopold, himself a scientist, pits *ecos*/ecology against *econ*/economy, and by way of the former, which he hoped would teach us to love the land and have community with it, rallies to his side the power of *eros*. He answers a question that seems to me to be implicit in some of the questions ("*How do you grow a lover?*"; "*How do you grow a poet?*") asked by Robert Kroetsch in *Seed Catalogue: How do you grow a lover of the land?*

Leopold pits a subversive science—ecological understanding is both subversive and moral, subversive because moral, which is why Paul Goodman considered it the fitting science for writers—against the dismal science of getting and spending, knowing that subversives like himself are a minority, belong to the margins, as Wendell Berry again reminds us. Hence, with little chance of victory, he settles for amelioration ("a question of degree") and writes in the spirit of accommodation. More than anything, this connects him with White—as in this instance it also connects him with Lincoln at Gettysburg. This is evoked by "now we face the question whether" and "whole conflict." The ecological crisis—*crisis* in a medical sense, the pathology evident to anyone willing to see it and especially to someone trained to see it and, in addition, the owner of a worn-out farm—the ecological crisis, as he knew from the asperity of his work on the Wisconsin Conservation Commission, might very well find an analogue in civil war. At the outset of the *Almanac* Leopold makes this connection and reads in terms of *the* Civil War the present irreconcilable (irreconciled) conflict of man and land.

White's accommodation is spelled out in the title of his book: It grants that one man's meat is another man's poison, that my satisfactions need not be yours. You are not deprived of television (just beginning to transform our lives when Leopold cited it) because I hanker after geese. But is this live-and-let-live resolution of the conflict the case in the crucial opening sentence? *There are some who can live without wild things, and some who cannot.* This may be read as saying that it is possible to live without wild things, that one may choose to live a meager life of this kind even though living with wild things is richer. The antithesis of the sentence is also compromised by the fact that its restricted meaning plays against our knowledge that, ultimately, we cannot live without wild things—without the wild, to which, we inevitably recall Thoreau saying, we owe the preservation of the world.

To introduce *wild* in the first sentence and insist on it in the first sentences of the subsequent paragraphs confirms Leopold's genius. The minority for whom he speaks now includes Thoreau ("Life consists with wildness") and Muir (whose remark, "In God's wildness lies the hope of the world," echoes Thoreau) and many others, chiefly the "radical amateurs," as Stephen Fox calls them, who comprise the militant moral tradition of conservation or, in Donald Worster's phrase, "the party of conscience." White's accommodation is characteristic, Leopold's is not. Like Thoreau in "Walking," an essay in significance to be paired with "Civil Disobedience," Leopold wishes to make an extreme statement. "I wish to speak a word for Nature," Thoreau says, "for absolute freedom and wildness . . . to regard man as an inhabitant, or part and parcel of Nature." Such concern for the wild allows no compromise.

The accommodation of the foreword is rhetorical, the good sense of a writer who, having lost immediate battles, wants to be heard, even, as he suggested, in the *Reader's Digest*, the magazine equivalent of any number of popular forums—garden clubs and PTAs, for example—that he addressed. The difficulty of placing his book and an editor's skeptical reception of his "philosophical reflections"—nature writing was welcome but not challenging ecological thought, which one publisher's reader found "fatuous"—all this, as well as the counsel of a former student, may have prompted Leopold to discard an earlier foreword notable for the polemical force of its autobiographical witness.

This foreword, in the revision of 31 July 1947, is a major document, and new editions of *A Sand County Almanac*, the first edition wisely enlarged to include some complementary essays from *Round River*, should add it. Nothing of Leopold's that I have read is so summary, filled as it is with salient thoughts that he says were "the end-result of a life-journey." There is something conclusive here, and in the reiterated *during my lifetime*, that evokes a journey's end and asks us to consider his book as testamentary. These thoughts—"These essays," he now begins, "deal with the ethics and esthetics of land"—these thoughts are final. This may explain his willingness to express once more his "discontent with the ecological *status quo*"—that is, with the economic uses of science and the impotence of the conservation movement—and it may explain the unusual presence of the personal, even the need to confess his sin.

Leopold's enthusiasm for hunting (he had hunted from boyhood in Iowa, coming to nature study in this way, and the shack was purchased for a base-camp), this enthusiasm, and the very enterprise of game management, have always disturbed me. I share Muir's view of both, that hunting is "murder business" and that protective measures such as game management arise because "the pleasure of killing is in danger of being lost from there being little or nothing left to kill." Leopold's defense of hunting as an ethical discipline as against the wantonness of sport doesn't convince me. So I was happy to find that Leopold, after twenty years, admits that the predator control he fostered was "ecological murder." He participated, he says, in "the extinguishment of the grizzly bear," in his mind the wilderness itself; he was "accessory to the extermination of the lobo wolf" and rationalized it "by calling it deer management." Having done this he contributed to the "erasing [of] the wilderness" practiced in the name of range conservation, for once a wilderness area has been proclaimed and the predators killed to increase the game, logic (of a bureaucratic kind) requires roads to enable the hunters to "harvest" the game, and access destroys the wilderness.

I mention this folly because he does in the narrative of his career and because the education of Aldo Leopold may be said to begin here, in his official capacity as a forest ranger and chief of operations in the Forest Service in Arizona and New Mexico. Leopold makes the point of noting that he is a "research ecologist" and that in appraising his work we should remember that his predecessors, Thoreau, Muir, Burroughs, Hudson, and Seton, "wrote before ecology had a name, before the science of animal behavior had been born, and before the survival of faunas and floras had become a desperate problem." Few writers, he says, "have dealt with the drama of wild things since our principal instruments of understanding them have come into being." He is one of them, a scientist by training, and, of course, a professional, an expert, in the service of government and university—the University of Wisconsin, which had fitted Muir for his joyous exploration of nature and had created a professorship of wildlife management for Leopold.

Leopold's education, at least in this summation, was disenchanting largely because of its institutional character. The crucial lesson belongs to the 1920s, when he worked for the Forest Products Laboratory in Madison and found "the industrial *motif* of this otherwise admirable institution . . . little to [his] liking." At this time, he would have us believe, he took the trips to the Sierra Madre Mountains that taught him that "land is an organism" and that hitherto he "had seen only sick land"—trips he actually took a decade later. As a result of his *work* at the laboratory, he claims that he wrote, among other philosophic essays, "The Land Ethic," a composite work incorporating earlier attempts to set out an ecological ethic that was actually written in 1947 and 1948; and as a result of his *leisure* in the mountains, he wrote "Song of the Gavilan" and "Guacamaja," sketches in *A Sand County Almanac* that he placed with his trip to the unspoiled delta of the Colorado, thereby associating healthy land (wilderness) with his youth. The reasons for these departures from chronology are profoundly autobiographical and tactical. He asks us to see these writings in relation that we may better realize the complexity and unity of his thought, its grounding in experience—how the man who appreciated *country* ("the personality of the land, the collective harmony of its soil, life, and weather") troubled over *land* ("the place where corn, gullies, and mortgages grow"), how *leisure* entailed habits of *work*.

The shack journals that he kept at the farm, for example, do not contain thoughts so much as records of work done and things seen. There are few initial compositions of the kind that allow you to read the journals of Thoreau and Muir, simply records, neat, schematic, and indexed, the data keeping of a scientist, such brief daily entries as the Forest Service requires. Yet, even as the journals make us wonder how such data were transformed into essays, they tell us how much there is to see, how rich the field of attentions—that this record is one of familiarization, the requisite participation that enables one to inhabit a place. Leopold methodically employed science to this end, in order, in Heidegger's term, to *dwell*. This is why he says of the last episode of his narrative, the purchase of the farm, that his "education in land ecology was deflected."

Deflected at first seems curious, but the import of Leopold's story turns on it. We may understand its use by recalling his initial dismay at the destruction of the land and the doubts he early had about "man in the role of conqueror." The ethics and aesthetics of land have become his concern because, as he says in the juxtaposed sentence, "During my lifetime, more land has been destroyed or damaged than ever before in recorded history." Science, he finds, has encouraged rather than halted this destruction (of land bureaus, agricultural colleges, and extension services, he notes that "no ethical obligation toward land is taught in these institutions"), and his own scientific education, making him aware of what is invisible to others, has penalized him by isolating him, forcing him to live alone in "a world of wounds." "An ecologist," he says, "must either harden his shell and make believe that the consequences of science are none of his business, or he must be the doctor who sees the marks of death in a community that believes itself well, and does not want to be told otherwise." Leopold's education, accordingly, involved the concurrent growth of perception and conscience, a crisis, moreover, of scientific conscience, and prompted him, like the good doctor in Ibsen's play, to become an enemy of the people.

Ethics and *aesthetics* enter his vocabulary where hitherto agronomic terms had been prominent. *Aesthetics* identifies his thought with the preservationist concern for something more important than profit and marks his subscription to the tradition of nature writing in which we find Thoreau and Muir—the "arcadian" tradition as against the "imperial" tradition, to borrow Donald Worster's way of distinguishing the opposing strands of ecological thought. The beauty Leopold saw in the natural world exercised aesthetic judgment, the subjective certainty of right and wrong, and demanded ethical action. For him, beauty in nature was not a genteel satisfaction, never aestheticized or ideal; it was a summons, a reminder of obligation. So having bought the farm, a weekend place fifty miles from Madison, a place of leisure not of work, he fulfilled a wish more clamorous than the desire to hunt: the wish to own land, not to have it as a possession or resource but to have it as a responsibility, to become a participant in its life, a citizen "in a community of which soils and waters, plants and animals are fellow members, each dependent on others, and each entitled to his [and her] place in the sun." The democracy of this community probably owes something to the Wisconsin Idea, which arose in opposition to the ruthless pioneering exploitation of which the abandoned farm was a testimony. Still, the point of Leopold's practice of the "land ethic" is that individuals, citizens, a last resort in bureau-ridden society, must enact it, and, equally important, that restoration must become their work. This goal is wonderfully put by what was actually done at the farm: "the husbandry of wild things on our own land." Such husbandry, as Wendell Berry to some extent exemplifies it on his farm, has "feminine" connotations of nurture and care; it is not the work of man the conqueror, and it stands against the unsettling of America. The husbandry of wild things is a valuable radical idea and should not be confused with the gentrification more frequently hoped for by weekenders who have purchased abandoned farms. This idea provides the unity that seemed questionable in Leopold's book. "These essays," he says, "are one man's striving to live by and with, rather than on [or off] the American land." This idea is their meat, answering to the dismay Muir expressed when he said that "most people are *on* the world, not in it—have no conscious sympathy or relationship to anything about them." Because of this idea, *A Sand County Almanac* is Leopold's most important and deservedly prized work.

A Sand County Almanac did not immediately find a shape for this conviction. The small volume that Leopold proposed in 1941 did not have the three-part structure of the book that was accepted in 1948 and published posthumously in the following year. Some shack essays, as we saw, were included, but there was no almanac, and there were none of the didactic essays that comprise the last section. The book lacked its present framework of significance; its argument was not yet structural.

Most of the essays belonged to what is now part 2 ("Sketches Here and There") and the volume took its title from one or another of them: *Marshland Elegy and Other Essays* or *Thinking Like a Mountain and Other Essays*. These are fitting titles because the essays celebrate the several biota Leopold had known, some historically, of a frontier time, others primordial, of the Pleistocene, in almost every case to end in threnody, with a sense of loss, even of doom, equalled, I think, only by Faulkner in "The Bear," the central ecological fable of *Go Down, Moses*, published in 1942. *Once lost, forever lost* is what these essays tell us—that, as Leopold knew, "the creation of a new wilderness in the full sense is impossible."

What was possible, the rearguard action he had taken, was not sufficiently represented in this version of the book, although "Great Possessions," the working title of *A Sand County Almanac*, suggests it. In this shack essay he says of his farm, "I am the sole owner of all the acres I can walk over," and in this Thoreauvian spirit adds, "not only boundaries . . . disappear, but the thought of being bounded." Place has given him cosmos. There is no indoors in *A Sand County Almanac*: He is outside, *in* the world, at home in intimate space, dwelling with all that is "in a house," as Muir said of similar experience, "of one room." When I think of Leopold two images of him always come to mind, neither of the horseman, hunter, or canoeist, nor for that matter of the scholarly professor. The first image is of the early riser sitting outdoors on a rough-hewn bench heating coffee over the fire, with every sense taking in the morning world; the second is of the watcher who, having cleared a swath, sits near the shack awaiting the sight of deer—the deer that for him, as for George Oppen whose words I cite, cry faith in *this in which*.

The idea of an almanac, or at least the need to concentrate on it, was suggested by an editor. It may have been congenial because some early installments had been directed to farmers and published in a booklet, *Wild Life Conservation on the Farm*, in 1941. At this time, Leopold made an unusual entry in the shack journal: "What we hear of conservation is mostly what transpires in the parlor of land-use. This is a factual account of what happens in the kitchen. The particular kitchen of which I speak is one of the sand counties of Wisconsin." He had used the parlor-kitchen figure to a different end in *Game Management*. Now it accords with the remarks on land use at the conclusion of "Cheat Takes Over," also completed in 1941: "I found the hopeless attitude [of ranchers] almost universal. There is, as yet, no sense of pride in the husbandry of wild plants and animals. . . . We tilt windmills in behalf of conservation in convention halls and editorial offices, but on the back forty we disclaim even owning a lance."

The reviews of the published book were neither as attentive nor as stringent as the reader's report of Alfred Etter, a professor at Washington University. This report, coming two months after Leopold's death, was not significantly acted on except for the change of title. "Sauk County" became "Sand County": A little-known place yielded to a familiar biota. But *almanac* did not, as Etter suggested, yield to *seasons*, a more agreeable disposition of the material because he felt in several instances "the obligation of a calendar [to be] unfortunate." This is just: The materials are disproportionately distributed and sometimes lack calendrical necessity. Had Leopold lived to revise the manuscript, he might, Etter thought, have replaced the "weak links" and managed a tour de force. But in its present form he found the almanac diffuse and its essays "considerably less potent than those of the second and third Parts." He meant by this that they lacked "keen intellect," and what he called their "vague impression" was associated with the most frequent comment on the writing in this part—that it was "a little too sweet." Etter believed that this detracted from "the Professor's personality"—

diminished the force of the man who was known professionally for his forthright integrity, a man, we might add, in many ways representative of an ideal type of his time. Thus, to reiterate, as Etter does, "The total effect of the Professor's personality [and presumably of the book as well] would be increased by the elimination of flowery or delicate words which inevitably find their way into writings on these subjects." Reviewers were not troubled by this; several were nature writers and were not as sensitive as Etter to the ways in which sentimentality may compromise scientific ecology.

What Etter saw is of little consequence in light of what he didn't see: the three-part dialectical play of the book. Leopold himself explains this in the foreword as a movement from an account of seeking "refuge from too much modernity" and trying to reclaim "what we are losing elsewhere," to an account of previous experiences that taught him "the company is out of step" (a way of speaking he sometimes used to characterize himself), to an exposition of the ideas that would enable the company to "get back in step"—where *back*, surely, is a crucial word. Each part, he might have pointed out, has its own compositional unity and function and presents a different aspect of the author. Beginning in the present, the book treats simple, undemanding rural pleasures, the weekend activities of the husbandman of wild things. Then it recovers the past when, as adventurer, Leopold had known wild biota—recovers this in present recollection and therefore with a sense of loss. The conclusion, again in the present, belongs to the professor for whose different demanding discourse Leopold (the artist) has set the stage. The three parts might also be designated *Thoreau, Muir,* and *Leopold,* for the participatory seasonal record, if not the family activity, recalls *Walden,* the double ply of adventure and conservation recalls any number of Muir's books (written in recollection), and Leopold, their successor, brings both forward in the uncompromising upshot of the conclusion, where his divergence from the managerial conservation of Gifford Pinchot, in which he had been trained, also shows the extent of his education.

The dialectic of this structure serves the deepest instructional purpose of the book. "See or go blind," Gary Snyder's injunction in *Myths & Texts,* names it—see things and their relations. Luna Leopold, in the preface to *Round River,* speaks of his father's "lifetime of developing perception," and this is what is artfully set out in such a way as to foster ours. And not only perception but the action it entails. Consciousness, as the French know in having one word for both, awakens conscience. To see and refuse to act is to go blind, is not to follow the way perception opens. The professor and the husbandman are active men. Like Thoreau and Muir before him and Snyder after him, Leopold speaks for an unacknowledged constituency, for the wild, the silent world (Ponge's phrase). Like them, he is a figure, the exemplar of his own thought, and this gives it authenticity.

The almanac need not be complete nor detailed in order to be useful. We do not need to know what to observe but only to observe, to be the hunter in "The Deer Swath," the last shack essay, written in 1948 and published in *Round River*—the hunter who has learned that "the world teems with creatures, processes, and events," that every ground, whether city street, vacant lot, or illimitable woods, is hunting ground. An almanac reminds us to keep our eyes open to the seasonal, annual, and annular aspect of things; it fosters the idea of cycles, the recurrences that are the wonder and delight of the seasons, the "cycles of beginnings and ceasings" Leopold notes at the outset, that representation of reality, the round river, "the never-ending circuit of life." Much of the data in the shack journals pertain to phenology, the science, according to Webster's dictionary, of the relations between climate and periodic biological phenomena, such as the migrations and breeding of birds, the fruiting of plants, and so on. *Phenology* is a contraction of *phenomenology*, the observation of just those phenomena, as in Thoreau's "Kalendar," that enable us to anticipate nature. But the rootword is also worth remembering because perceptual experience roots us in the world.

In a study of the rhetoric of *A Sand County Almanac*, Peter Fritzell says that the almanac is composed of "perceptual situations." These situations might also be called "events," a term from Whitehead's philosophy of organism in keeping with Leopold's awareness of process. Susan Flader, the preeminent student of Leopold, speaks of "the person and the place," a phrase evoking the postmodern poetics of the poet-in-the-field, and nothing covers the poetics of the almanac so well as William Carlos Williams' dictum "No ideas but in things." Thoreau begins the year with the thawing clay of the railroad cut, with the melting ice of the pond and the return of geese, and Leopold marks March with the last. But perhaps in eagerness to begin, to set things in motion, he attends a January thaw, tracking a skunk in the snow much in the way Thoreau tracked a fox. There are several morals to be drawn from this simple act of going outdoors to look (his motion of beginning, simple because winter has abstracted the landscape): that little is as good as big because what matters is relation; that participating in nature, economic as he reports it in the case of mouse, hawk, rabbit, and owl, is by virtue of this very act of mind more than economic; that the "pathetic fallacy" of taking the perspective of each creature is not in fact sentimental unless granting biotic equality to all things is sentimental; that observation and meditation are inextricable because, as Heisenberg teaches, observation alters what is observed, and because, as Emerson says, "man is an analogist, and studies relations in all objects."

The analogies Leopold draws work both ways, but most often the "animal analogues" serve, as in Amerindian medicine, as instructive "analogies to our own problems." The mouse, for example, who has everything "neatly organized" to satisfy its needs, finds that "the thawing sun has mocked the basic premises of the microtine economic system." For the mouse the thaw is a catastrophe of the kind that destroys civilization—a catastrophe as much of natural happening (nature is violent, and the communal life of organisms is prompted by climatic change) as of tunnel vision and reluctance to change. The mouse may be said to illustrate an evolutionary lesson out of Veblen.

Leopold is speculatively present but not omniscient. He would accept Emerson's definition of the poet as the integrator of all the parts if it did not seem willful, if it acknowledged the mystery of harmony ("the great orchestra") and represented the ego as necessary only to seeing (hearing) the integration. That he heard the great orchestra is not literary fancy and distinguishes him, as it did Thoreau, from those who only see the world. The form Leopold used to compose his observations is itself instructive of this: an ideogram of six fragments presenting a complex event called "thaw," a multiphasic occurrence that bespeaks community because whatever exists in the same space belongs there and plays its functional part, however unwillingly, whether for good or ill, with everything else. An ideogram does not impose form so much as assume that the reality it represents is united in ways beyond our understanding; it asks us to look for relationships. It is the mode, in this instance, of someone who has learned humility.

The almanac may be diffuse, but in taking us over the ground, much as Thoreau and Muir do, Leopold allows us to share his experience. We come to know the place and learn some of its ecological lessons. One of the most important concerns evolutionary and historical time. The latter is truly *time*, the furious linear assault of progress that Lévi-Strauss says, in *Tristes tropiques*, betrayed the paradisal promise of America. In one of the most cunning essays, Leopold tells time in terms of sawing down a shattered oak. He reads back from the present, as we must do in order to know our places; reads cultural or human geography in Carl Sauer's way to show us how man in the landscape disturbs its ecological stability, diminishes its power of self-renewal, and visibly alters it. The immigrant road that passes the shack made the Westward Movement possible. It is the archetypal road, the great destroyer of wilderness, precursor of the railroad whose iron, Hart Crane said, "always . . . dealt cleavage." Thus, to read back is to realize that settlement was also an unsettling of a climax culture, that the economic waste of wildlife, forest, and marsh was prodigal, that only eighty years stand between the sawyer at the shack and Muir, who in 1865 wished to establish nearby a sanctuary for wildflowers and even then exemplified the "mercy for things natural, wild, and free" that Leopold believes we must now acquire.

There are many glimpses of paradisal (wild) America in part 2, "Sketches Here and There." Most notable are those of the Delta of the Colorado, explored by Leopold and his brother before its abundant wildlife was supplanted by cantaloupes, the Sierra Madre Mountains, a haven of singing river and birds, and the mountain world of the Southwest, the place of "heroic" manhood where he was "on top" and "every living thing sang, chirped, and burgeoned." Here, in the mountains, the initials he finds carved in the aspen tell of romance (as much an aspect of ecology as the peenting of the woodcock in part 1)—tell of "the glory of [his] mountain spring." For at this time he married Estella Bergere. Nothing perhaps marks his difference in temperament from Thoreau and Muir so much as this—as, say, the loving flourish of the dedication of the *Almanac* "to my Estella," where *my* does more than distinguish wife from daughter.

The exuberance of the writing belongs to youthful adventure and is measured by an elegiac counterpoint. It is also measured by the landscape of the enclosing frame, the marshland, initially of Wisconsin, long since drained, and finally of Clandeboye in Manitoba, now threatened with extinction. "The marshlands that once sprawled over the prairie from Illinois to the Athabasca," Leopold concludes, "are now shrinking northward." And when they are gone we will no longer coexist with the Pleistocene, live "in the wider reaches of evolutionary time," and hear, as he also did in the green lagoons of the Colorado, the bugling of the cranes, "the wildest [because oldest] of living fowl." The fate of marsh and bird, of course, is as good an example of land use and conservation as any.

"A roadless marsh is seemingly as worthless to the alphabetical conservationist," he remarks, "as an undrained one to the empire-builders."

The section on Wisconsin links parts 1 and 2 and among other things provides an earth history of the sand counties and a political history of the governmental efforts to remedy their poverty. The failure to improve the counties contrasts with Leopold's self-elected work of restoration in part 1—his effort "to rebuild," as he says in the foreword, "what we are losing elsewhere" in the way our land use contributes to the downward wash to the sea of atoms once locked in stone and subsequently almost endlessly recycled in food chains. We extinguish biota as well as species—the passenger pigeon is an example of the latter—and we cannot even keep a small portion of a river wild.

As an ecologist Leopold follows Whitman's advice to study out the land, its idioms and its men. "Illinois Bus Ride" is the best and briefest instance—and of the mordant-ironic style he reserves for the economic-minded and ecologically mindless: farmers, agriculture and conservation experts, sportsmen and other nature consumers. This is indeed the style of "keen intellect" and registers dismay. Recollection evokes it because Leopold is moved by what Bachelard calls reverie toward childhood, the very reverie of childhood that suggests to him that "growing up" is "growing down." He tells us in "Red Legs Kicking" that "my earliest impressions of wildlife and its pursuit retain a vivid sharpness of form, color, and atmosphere that half a century of professional wildlife experience has failed to obliterate or to improve upon." This—and much of the writing—confirms Edith Cobb's view of the ecological imagination of childhood, of the perceptual wealth that vouchsafes genius. This ecological imagination, in his account, is complemented by an equally vivid sense of the ethical restraint imposed by the act of killing. And later, when he shoots a wolf and watches the "fierce green fire dying in her eyes," he learns an ethical lesson of even greater ecological importance. He learns, as Buber had in answering the gaze of animals, that animals have being (are *Thou* not *It*) and have every right to biotic equality. Leopold acquires the foundation of his thought; for thinking like a wolf is as requisite as thinking like a mountain.

To think like a mountain is to think ecologically, in terms of relationships and land health, in ways, that is, that do not promote "dustbowls, and rivers washing the future to the sea." Reminded of *The Grapes of Wrath* (1939), we recall the natural and social consequences of what Steinbeck called "the system." Shortly after, in the phrase "peace in our time," we are asked to remember the price of appeasement and are not allowed to settle for that. Leopold shows us how he changed his ways—conversion is the archetypal pattern of his book—and he writes in order to change our ways, to build "receptivity into the still unlovely [unloving] human mind." His book itself may be said to be ecological because it is generous and generative, written in the spirit of gift exchange, the social analogue of the cyclical transfer of energy; a fertile book, having "the ability of the soil to receive, store, and release energy." Nearly forty years after its publication, because we have so little heeded it, its value may be said to have increased. Leopold says that "the outstanding scientific discovery of the twentieth century is . . . the complexity of the land organism" and, as much as anyone, he made us appreciate its life. In doing so he spoke of impending doom. He knew, as he says in the discarded foreword, that "our foothold is precarious, not because it may slip, but because we may kill the land before we learn to use it with love and respect." *Kill the land*, as he had once killed predators! Destroy the very ground under our feet!

The ethical bearing of Leopold's work is notable but what is not mentioned is his resistance to his own entropic vision. Jeremiad might have served him, but he chose other literary forms and addressed us as citizens, taking advantage perhaps of our predilection to think well of ourselves. Neither *A Sand County Almanac* nor *Round River* is addressed to fellow experts but to men and women of good will, the kind of people who, in another time, began the conservation movement by forming the Sierra Club. In "A Man's Leisure Time," the prefatory essay of *Round River*, Leopold expatiates on hobbies (among them, his and his wife's hobby of archery, which connects this essay to leisure at the farm), expatiates on a notion I found suspect until I recalled that the conservation movement, so well described by Stephen Fox, had begun as a hobby and—this is Leopold's strategy—must again become one, farther down the line than vigilant protest, now in the leisure-time practice of the husbandry of wild things. It may be quixotic to think, as he did, that the battle will be won on the back forty, but some of us here apparently agree. In any case, like some of his predecessors, he "created cultural value by being aware of it, and by creating a pattern of growth." A cultural value because the problem involved *culture*, not only an errant agriculture but "how to bring about a striving for harmony with the land among a people many of whom have forgotten there is any such thing as land, among whom education and culture have become almost synonymous with landlessness."

When Leopold sent off the earliest version of the book he told the editor that he didn't want to write "mere natural history" and that "field skill and ability to write [such as his] seldom occur in the same person." In saying this, he repudiated "amateur natural history . . . of the dickey-bird variety," the result of "ladies and gentlemen wander[ing] afield not so much to learn how the world is put together as to gather subject matter for tea-time conversation." To be sure, this is not what Thoreau did at Walden Pond, though in a sentimental age it was an outcome of the transcendentalists' correspondential vision of self and world that authorized a symbolical appropriation of nature in the interest of self. Natural history in Thoreau is also a mode of autobiography. Thoreau went to the woods to find *himself* in relation to nature, to the end of self-culture, soul making. More than a century later, Leopold went to the farm as a trained scientist in order to recover a relationship to the land and further its health. The spiritual legacy of Thoreau and Muir belongs to his social idealism; he does not share their Idealist philosophy and was better able to look at nature without looking at himself. He shares this stance toward reality with many contemporary poets and thinkers and finds his place with them because he believed that "the detection of harmony is the domain of poets" and because he gave some of them the legacy of *inhabiting*, of living in place. He stands with them also because the reference of his work is Western Civilization itself, its world alienation and landlessness, the necessity it is under to transform ego-thought into eco-thought. "To change ideas about what land is for," he wrote just prior to undertaking *A Sand County Almanac*, "is to change ideas about what anything is for." In doing this he did what Muir thought almost impossible: He obtained a hearing in behalf of nature from a standpoint other than that of human use. Moreover, he proposed a correlative action, not only the preservation of the wilderness but the husbandry of the wild, the *wildering*, John Stilgoe's resonant term for the irrepressible return of the wild, that any of us might foster on abandoned land. In Leopold's work the attitude toward what was once fearful—the presence and encroachment of the wilderness—has changed; his is not a howling but a singing wilderness and a measure of health. Its ecological importance is recognized and it is encouraged. The wild returns as the predators do, in the interest of climax, of a complex, diverse, stable biota. Such wildering, I find, goes with *worlding*, another resonant term, this one Richard Pevear's, because the husbandry of the wild is a discipline of familiarization that enables us to live in the world.

I honor Leopold for these reasons. In studying him, I have come to recognize one of the few professors whose leisure-work (I join his polar words)—whose leisure-work, in the words of another great professor, has exemplary validity.

Aldo Leopold's Counter-Friction

Once you learn to read the land, I have no fear of
what you will do to it, or with it.
—Leopold, to his students

The centenary of Aldo Leopold's birth has given "the most significant conservationist of the last seventy years" (Stephen Fox, on the dust-
jacket of Curt Meine's *Aldo Leopold: His Life and Work*) more than usual
notice and added substantially to the scholarship concerning his life and thought.
Meine's book is the first biography, which is to say a fuller account of the
life and, accordingly, a somewhat less-focused, issue-oriented study than Susan
Flader's *Thinking Like a Mountain: Aldo Leopold and the Evolution of an Ecological Attitude toward Deer, Wolves and Forests* (1974), the first major study
and the first to make use of the extensive Leopold Archive, and still the most
incisive and best written. Meine's book, some 650 closely packed and heavily
documented pages, is more than twice the size of all the commemorative publications, chiefly the *Companion to A Sand County Almanac*, edited by J. Baird
Callicott, and *Aldo Leopold: The Man and His Legacy*, edited by Thomas Tan-
ner. The first collection brings together some of the best early essays on Leopold
as well as newer work; the second gathers some of the proceedings of a week-

long celebration at Iowa State University (which recently announced a recommendation to phase out "environmental studies because of waning interest"). Inevitably, given the handful of Leopold scholars, the collections overlap. Worthy of mention also is the handsome "Special Commemorative Edition" of *A Sand County Almanac* (Oxford University Press), special, I think, because Robert Finch supplies an excellent introduction guided by his concern, as a nature writer, with the poetic understanding of nature and by his literary sense of how Leopold *figures* in his book. All of this work, much of it academic, acknowledges the environmental crisis, which more than ever before has awakened interest in nature writing (or, better, ecological writing)—writing, according to Barry Lopez, that will "not only one day produce a major and lasting body of American literature, but . . . provide the foundation for a reorganization of American political thought."

Meine has done large and valuable work, and the wealth of detail in his biography may be said to compensate for its defects. Leopold, in his sometimes folksy way and from pride in outdoor cooking, would have noted both the plentiful raisins and lumpy pudding. For style, in every sense but especially in respect to focus and felicity, is lacking. As with many recent biographies, data not portraiture is primary, and the reader who wants the "life" must do most of the "graphing." Meine has done more than anyone to fully document Leopold's family background, childhood, education (at Burlington High School, Lawrenceville Preparatory School, and Yale), early career as a forester in New Mexico and Arizona, and courtship of and marriage to Estella Bergere (of a wealthy, long-established New Mexican family). Much of this is recovered in Leopold's letters, and some of it is told on a daily basis. He sees the importance of Leopold's birth in Burlington, Iowa, in 1887, for Burlington was a portal to the West, to the frontier whose closing Frederick Jackson Turner would soon announce, and he is aware of the fact that Leopold's life intersects history, that at birth he was given the issues of economic and industrial expansion and wasteful land use that confronted him (and that he confronted) for the rest of his life. He knows the history of conservation, which he uses, as had both Susan Flader and Stephen Fox (his *John Muir and His Legacy: The American Conservation Movement* is Meine's model), to provide the context in which Leopold's life and the transformation of his thought from Pinchot's narrow economic managerial to all-encompassing ecological views took place. But his grasp of psychological matters is not comparable. He has none of the skills of a psychohistorian (trained, say, by Erik Erikson) and fails to open the foundational material, to probe what most needs probing, how Leopold in his deepest being was "called" to the vocation (the true calling) of naturalist.

The boy who, at Lawrenceville, was known as "the naturalist," which is to say by some standards seemed odd, needs explaining, and crucial episodes, such as his probation at Yale, which highlights his relation to his parents, and the failure of his first reconnaissance in the Blue Range, need further investigation. Leopold's courtship (much of it epistolary) might have been searched more deeply, and this is also the case with his family life, which, as often in his relation to students, seems to have been remarkably considerate. Meine is aware of Leopold's personality but his assessments belong to throwaway sentences: "It took a large task to balance out Leopold's own high opinion of himself." His literary assessments are equally brief and more often superficial: "His prose always carried a smooth rhythm." Meine is not a literary critic who appreciates the significance of literary and imaginative activity—all the more important when writing of a man who was so much a writer—or the significance of reading, for example, the "nickel volume of Whitman" that Leopold told Estella that, in their usual fashion, they must read together. What were the books they read together? We need a catalog of them, and all the others. And then there are the clues provided by obsessive words, perhaps the most important for the naturalist the word "adventure," frequently associated with wilderness and given summary point in this early comment: "If I were trying to please myself alone I would be in Canada and Siberia & South America seeing the world." The mythos here belongs to Darwin and Muir, both of whom had read Alexander von Humboldt, and it measures a life, as in the much later comment, "I am glad I shall never be young without wild country to be young in."

In wishing to preserve and restore the open country of his youth—that is, a permanent human possibility—Leopold transformed the received opinion of his intellectual inheritance, so that even adventure, which initially belonged to his days on horseback in the West, finally found a place on some worn-out acres of sand county land and the predator control he had once fostered gave way to eco-restoration. The work of the life was nothing if not reeducation, which, for a practical idealist, entailed the advocacy (much of it of a public relations kind) that enlisted his pen. It was an education of such drama that, as Leopold knew, the story of conversion best told it. (This story is now available in the discarded 1947 preface to *A Sand County Almanac*, published in the *Companion*.) Meine tells it, too, stage by stage, issue by issue, sometimes so close to events that the text reads like a journal in which are noted, say, the trouble Leopold was having with trigeminal neuralgia and with the annual committee work on deer population or, it may be, what he was teaching in class or doing at the "shack." For the most part this many-plied exposition is distracting, but in the accounts of the restoration at the "shack" and of the composition of *A Sand County Almanac*, themselves the fullest we have, it provides a rich context of impinging private and public events.

So I appreciate this veritable archive in lieu of the Archive and consider it indispensable. To follow Leopold's development here is one way of entering his thought and realizing, as he and some others did so early, that the largest claim to our concern is the fate of the earth. He knew that science, errant in both its alliance with industrialism and atomic defense, was "false, ignoble, and self-destructive." From the beginning his thought was ethical and always involved responsibility. Even when he granted the Christian view that the earth exists for the benefit of humanity, as he did in an early paper, he called for responsibility by defining humanity's special nobility in ethical terms and by speaking of a "society decently respectful of its own and all other life, capable of inhabiting the earth without defiling it." Moreover, he believed that "conservation was something that happened between an individual and his [or her] environment"—a belief he derived from his own experience and fully enacted in the restoration of an abandoned farm. It is here that he both delivers his essential message and offers us the decisive example of ethical practice. Meine, to his credit, sees this clearly. And now, having done the work, he should edit a volume of some of the important essays Leopold wrote in order to redress the education that he said was not education because it "omits to picture man's infinitely delicate symbiosis with land."

The *Companion* is a book about a book, but only three essays treat the literary artifact, and one of these is as much concerned with Leopold's "doctrine" (John Tallmadge's word) as most of the others. The editor, J. Baird Callicott, a philosopher of environment, has made the book markedly his, not only in the preponderant attention to Leopold's aesthetic and ethical ideas but, as the dust jacket has it, by being the "principal contributor." He includes two essays of his own as well as a preface and an introduction. In the latter he surveys the contents of the volume, enters his disagreements, especially with Roderick Nash, and awards his praise ("Fritzell's essay is a marvel of subtlety and sophistication and in my opinion the most insightful study of *A Sand County Almanac*, as a whole, ever made"). Such claims are never measured, neither here nor in the assertion that Leopold's book is "wonderfully unified and tightly organized," and, granted that the "upshot" of the *Almanac* deserves urgent attention, isn't it the part already best known to Leopold's students and associates? As Albert Hochbaum, one of Leopold's closest students, discovered, it was not the "Professor" but the writer of the "shack" and adventure essays who was new to them, the man whose personal education in land use and exemplary practice of wildlife management and restoration clarified what he meant by the land ethic.

Callicott has organized the *Companion* somewhat in the fashion of the *Almanac*, adding to its three parts a fourth on "The Impact." Of the three essays introducing Leopold-the-author in part 1, the most valuable are Susan Flader's abridgement of her classic essay, "The Person and the Place," and Roderick Nash's essay on Leopold's intellectual heritage. A useful biographical profile by Curt Meine is now superseded by his biography—and in another part, his study of the composition of "The Land Ethic," though fuller, is adequately covered in his book.

Flader, among the best writers in the *Companion*, provides the necessary earth and socioeconomic history of Wisconsin's sand counties. She tells of the settlement by pioneers such as Daniel Muir and the hardship of farming there as recalled by his son John; and she reminds us of the frontier thesis of Frederick Jackson Turner, who returned to Madison in the year Leopold arrived and lived nearby on the same street and was equally present in his thought. Finally, in the context of the multiplication of governmental agencies in response to the conservation ferment of the 1930s, she sets off Leopold's purchase of a sand farm and his family's dedication to the husbandry of the wild.

Roderick Nash, whose *Wilderness and the American Mind* has become a standard work, considers the antecedents of ideas of ecological community and the rights of nature, ideas that inform Leopold's land ethic; and what he may be said to take away from Leopold in amending Callicott's view (Leopold's "originality," Nash says, "must not be distorted"), he amply repays in supporting testimony. He knows that the guiding principle of intellectual history is that nothing comes from nothing, and so we are asked to remember Thoreau, George Perkins Marsh (who "proposed 'geographical regeneration,' a great healing of the planet beginning with the control of technology"), Muir, Darwin, Lecky, Edward Payson Evans, J. Howard Moore, Liberty Hyde Bailey, and Schweitzer. In sketching the development of Leopold's ethical ideas, he shows their reliance on Charles Elton, who advanced the idea of the biotic community, and on P. D. Ouspensky, whose *Tertium Organum* supplied the terminology of *phenomenon-numenon* that Leopold found useful in speaking of the organismic, holistic character of land. (Callicott, in his essay "The Land Aesthetic," overlooks this source, first documented by Flader.) Of most importance, Nash challenges us, where Leopold most challenged us, by reminding us that his ideas have not been widely received because they run counter to "basic American priorities and behavior," priorities and behavior, as both Wallace Stegner and Edwin Pister later testify, that are still too much with us. "The land ethic," Stegner says in an essay reprinted from *Wilderness*, "is not a widespread public conviction. If it were, the Reagan administration would not have been given a second term."

As for the book itself, Dennis Ribbens, in an essay published some years ago, provides the primary findings of archival research. He recovers from correspondence Leopold's thoughts about nature books and nature writing and his wish to write "ecological essays" (inevitable, as we will see, for someone who had learned to read the land). Ribbens also documents the stages of the making of the *Almanac*, which was appreciably altered by the stringent criticism of Albert Hochbaum, who at one time was to illustrate it. And he tells how Leopold wrote it, not, he insists, from the data of the "Shack Journals" (although the familiarization they record was surely ground), but apparently without preparatory notes, in the early morning, in the quiet of his office.

That Leopold altered the kind of nature book we expect is also pointed out by John Tallmadge in what, to my mind, is the best literary study of the *Almanac*. Tallmadge places the book in terms of White's *The Natural History of Selborne*, Darwin's *Voyage of the Beagle*, Thoreau's *Walden*, and Muir's *My First Summer in the Sierras* and finds that Leopold shares more with Thoreau than the others because he, too, practices "social criticism based on the standard of nature." Leopold assimilated the literary strategies of his predecessors but refused his editors' counsel to write only a "Gilbert White book." His book is continental in scope rather than local and universal rather than parochial in its truths, and it artfully combines the generic elements of early nature writing and confessional autobiography with a program for social transformation. Its end is advocacy, its intent "subversive," and its style is concordant.

Leopold's prose, Tallmadge says, is smooth and transparent *and* dense in implication. He likens it to "hand-scrubbed wood" and notes its "epigrammatic conciseness" and "techniques of compression." Of these, two are notable: *concentration* and *engagement*, the first making every detail advance the plot (the sketches are stories—Finch calls them fables), the second, by way of synecdoche, allusion, irony, understatement, and rhetorical questions, engaging us in filling out the shorthand of the text. These rhetorical means rather than a "poetic vocabulary," Tallmadge adds, "give [the] prose its memorable succinctness."

Meine tells us that Leopold studied the Bible and was fond of Psalms, Proverbs, and the prophets (he published in the *Journal of Forestry* an article on "The Forestry of the Prophets"), and Tallmadge, who calls Leopold an "American Jeremiah," considers his style "parabolic." The sketches, he says, are parables, and this more than anything else accounts for the "perennial freshness" of the book and its power to change "our angle of vision," both our understanding and our commitment.

Attention to style is important because Leopold presences himself in his verbal behavior. His style, according to Tallmadge, is "peculiarly attractive," giving us a warm and engaging man of conviction and an outsider in an unpopular cause, whose wit entertains and challenges us. Leopold challenges us, of course, because his nature writing is ecological and represents an unusual stance toward nature. Two casual but connected observations about him are of profound philosophic significance:

> Landscape as such hardly seems to interest him.
> What goes on *in* the land is what fascinates [him].

> He read human life in the context of nature and not the other way round.

The first observation tells us that Leopold, as Callicott shows so well in an essay on the land aesthetic, is not an observer of scenic views but a participant in process; the second, that by standing within, not outside and above nature, he has replaced ego- with eco-thought. Nothing is more radical and subversive of the Western tradition of philosophic idealism, as Whitehead remarked in *Process and Reality* when he said that in Kant's philosophy the world emerges from the subject, where in his own philosophy of organism the subject emerges from the world. This is the conversion experience the *Almanac* records, an education and praxis that addresses us and may be too little remembered in some of the subsequent philosophical essays on doctrine.

Peter Fritzell's essay, devoted to literary analysis, belongs just as much to the two sections treating Leopold's doctrine because its primary concern is "conflicts of ecological conscience." The conflicts turn on man as conqueror and man as member (citizen) of the biotic community, on dualistic versus holistic conceptions of relationship to nature, and on a reading of evolution that accords man-the-conqueror a natural place in nature. Fritzell, as Callicott notes, deconstructs Leopold's fundamental ideas. For him, the *Almanac* is a "composition of opposites," its coordinates "converging from two radically divergent directions," making it "a fabric of ironies, ambiguities, and paradoxes." The book, he says, may argue overtly for the land community and the land ethic, but covertly it presents (like Fritzell's heavily interrogative prose) a "pattern of questions, doubts, and contrary impulses." By reading it backward, from part 3 to part 1, he erodes, with skepticism, what had seemed to be the sure lessons of its doctrine.

This essay, as well as Callicott's on the land ethic, is troublesome because there is too much conceptual finesse, too little awareness of the way practice itself resolves these issues. (Callicott, who, in one essay, nicely describes an excursion to a bog, seems dissociated from the thinker of his other essay.) It also seems to me that the argument from evolution has been clarified by Loren Eiseley, who recognized that the "second nature" (culture) produced by the human brain and hand in the course of evolution is both part of and a threat to primary nature and that, *knowing this*, we must choose to act wisely in respect to the primary. This is what Pister, a fishery biologist, and Stegner emphatically tell us and what Holmes Rolston III, in "Duties to Ecosystems," with admirable speculative richness and good sense, insists on.

Rolston considers the relational complexity of organism and ecosystem, the "tightness" of the one and the necessary "looseness" of the other, and the fact that an ecosystem is a "satisfactory matrix, the projective source of all it contains" and the "survival unit, without which organisms cannot survive." The imperative of his essay is that "an ecologically informed society must love lions-in-jungles, organisms-in-ecosystems, or else fail in vision and courage." He supports Leopold in maintaining that the ecosystem is prior and that humans owe something to it. For "the system creates life, selects for adaptive fit, constructs increasingly richer life in quantity and quality, supports myriads of species, escalates individuality, autonomy, and even subjectivity, within the limits of decentralized community."

Ecosystem, for literary critical purposes, may be thought of as context(s), and with the salutary "looseness" of the one in mind, I regret the narrowness and "tightness" of the other, as found in the *Companion*. The environmental crisis, acknowledged by Callicott (a crisis "rooted in our whole way of doing things"), is insufficiently addressed. Leopold's attack on the industrial economy (resumed, for example, in the work of Wendell Berry, who writes in *Sabbaths*, "I go from the woods into the cleared field: / A place no human made, a place unmade / By human greed, and to be made again") is hardly noticed. Nor is the support his work has in philosophers of relationship, like William James, Whitehead, and Buber, or in the thought of other cultures, or in the work of many contemporary poets and deep ecologists. The land ethic, with its clear demand for better land use, is not an academic issue, as readers of Wes Jackson know. Nothing is more exigent, and Leopold, having himself learned this, knew that the land ethic, as Stegner says, is "a task."

Aldo Leopold: The Man and His Legacy is "loosely" made, at once less constrained and more diverse than the *Companion*—and more companionable. Only the first section is academic, devoted as it is to essays focusing on the land ethic by several contributors to the *Companion* (the single newcomer is Craig W. Allin). The second section is testimonial, and the third is essentially reminiscential, concerned with recollections by members of the Leopold family (a family of remarkable distinction in science), with the family philosophy, as Sharon Kaufman educes it, and an account of the research and restoration work of the Leopold Memorial Reserve. Like Meine's book, it is well illustrated.

The overlapping essays in the first section are by Nash, Callicott, and Meine, although there are modifications in each. Callicott takes happier account of Nash's work and recognizes the Amerindian land ethic, and Meine, in treating Leopold's concern with the farmer as conservationist, gathers material from his biography but, in doing so, points up Leopold's insistence on individual obligation. Allin supports this in tracing Leopold's thought in respect to the wilderness system he did so much to promote, and Flader answers those philosophers, who, as Zennists say, "haggle in the weeds."

Flader brilliantly shows how the land ethic developed from Leopold's deepening understanding of erosion and land health. She recognizes, with greater perception than Meine, that "the esthetic appreciation for wildlife that was so integral to his youth . . . and so vital to his mature philosophic reflection was seemingly suppressed at mid-career, when he was chiefly concerned with wildlife management." Later on, fostered by ecological understanding, an aesthetic appreciation (his "personal motivation") enabled him to move beyond a manager's determination on control to the larger work of conserving and restoring the ecosystem. When he learned to appreciate the integrity of the ecosystem and that human beings had their being within it, Leopold, according to Flader, had ground of his own for an ethic and no longer felt the need for "definitive philosophical answers."

The distinction of this collection is its unequivocal endorsement of Leopold's claims for obligation and activism. All the testimony to Leopold's influence—both Raymond Dasmann's and Bruce Babbitt's, in the context of the global ecological crisis, and Dale McCullough's and Huey D. Johnson's, in respect to deer ecology and the empowerment of resource professionals—and all the evocation of the "world scene" and the "real world" call for active engagement. Johnson, a resource manager, remembers the inspiration of Leopold's ideas and "the example of his activism—to carry out action in addition to thought." Like Stegner, he knows that the conservation/land-use policies of the Reagan administration are "a throwback to the first 100 years of the nation's history when exploitation was the practice of the day." He believes that had Leopold lived he would have acted to reverse such policies and that the most fitting way to commemorate him would be to launch a crusade to that end—"to manage resources for permanence, or what Leopold called a more enduring civilization."

Lopez

Making the Turn

REREADING BARRY LOPEZ

We are back (yes, *back*) at Wolf Lake—have been for ten days, long laboring days of settling in and setting things to rights. Spring is advanced this year; there is mowing and brushing to do and the gardens to be got ready (they wait on the Deere, which for the second time refuses to run at the beginning of the season). We have already dragged away huge piles of branches, the crowns of trees cut last fall. We have stacked some of the wood, leaving the larger logs to be split and stacked later. Making wood involves so much labor I am inclined to garner every last twig, but we already have enough wood for three years. So I was not reluctant to give a truckload to the young man who had come to help—willing, in this instance, to sacrifice economy to beauty, though in a proper *ecos* they are not separate but correlative.

I write this not so much for the record—such chores are customary—but in order to make a start here, in the little cabin in which I am now free to spend my mornings. It is salutary to divide the day between the work of the mind and

67

the work of the body—the *vita contemplativa* and the *vita activa*, the latter, as I practice it, *menial*, according to Hannah Arendt—and it is necessary. The work of the body, outdoor work, is *out*: To do such work is a primary way of being-in-the-world, of finding oneself in the cosmos, in touch with things, physically "at home." The work of the mind, indoor work, is *in*, doubly interior: To do such work is too often a way of withdrawing from the world, of living with its images. I use the spatial distinctions (*in/out*) that accord with the dualisms of *mind/body, subject/object, self/world*, but these are the dualisms I wish to overcome: when *out*, by a participatory activity of mind, and when *in*, by a meditative activity that seeks in words to hew to experience.

This may account for my interest in "nature writing." Not most of it, which doesn't challenge dualism so much as exploit it by giving the mind sovereign play, sometimes in sentiment and sentimental spirituality, and most often by a show of literary sensibility. Nature writers—I'm thinking of many of the contemporary writers represented in the *Antaeus* collection edited by Daniel Halpern and in *Words from the Land: Encounters with Natural History Writing*, edited by Stephen Trimble—are "fine" writers. As Trimble says, those he has selected "see themselves as writers first." They are personal essayists, often of distinction, who find some of their material in nature, and many of them, as in the Charles Addams cartoon I've posted here, sit for their own portrait when they go there. Seldom are they naturalists like Thoreau, Muir, and Leopold, who articulated a profound, lifelong engagement with nature, more often wrote to live than to make a living, and preferred advocacy to pacification. Taken together, the *Antaeus* collection and *Words from the Land* give us a canon and establish nature writing as fashionable, a genre ready-to-hand for writers' workshops.

I have spent an hour this morning looking for a few pages I had written several years ago on this entry in John Muir's journal: "Not like taking the veil—no solemn abjuration of the world. I only went out for a walk, and finally concluded to stay out till sundown, for going out, I found, was really going in." I cannot recall my exegesis now (the absence is palpable and disturbs me) but only that it provided the ground of my concern with *out/in*, about which I have been making notes, knowing that this insistence has proposed itself for writing. I have not lost the quotation: I know it by heart and have it here, tacked on the wall. And I probably have the exegesis (for some reason I do not think I can now engage Muir's sentences as I did then in the readiness of the occasion) and will find it in the cluttered study in Iowa City. When I do I will fill this morning's gap by appending it.

The thought thought me because I was thinking about Barry Lopez, whose *Crossing Open Ground* I had just read by way of making the transition to what is now best defined as subrural. (*Sub* for *suburban* and *beneath*. The narrow sand road to our place has recently been named and we have been given a house number.) This collection of fourteen essays written over the last ten years is coherent and substantial, a wise selection from many journalistic pieces, and it seemed to me to be an entrance (because *entranced?*), a place to begin. The title, for which Lopez offers no explanation, imposes itself by virtue of three resonant words: *crossing*, which calls up Whitman's great poem on the intrinsic value of experience, one that the landscape permits us to share with the author, in this instance the experience of open ground and the ongoing process; *open*, which plays on the full range of the unbounded and modifies *ground*, a substantive of fundamental importance, by giving it sky and thus defining a spacious landscape. All told, I think of Olson's "In Cold Hell, in Thicket," where the resolution on change involves crossing:

> he will cross
>
> > (there is always a field,
> > for the strong there is always
> > an alternative)

I also think of Olson because nature writing, as Lopez exemplifies it, belongs to the project proposed by the new poetics—by an *open* poetics (*field* poetics, *composition*) and ethnopoetics. Both writers situate us in the field, *world* us.

And both are concerned with landscape(s) and practice the cultural geography so notably represented in the work of Carl Sauer, whom both acknowledge. Sauer notes that Friedrich Ratzel said that "the geographer is naturalist," Yes, and the naturalist and the poet are geographers. Olson gives us Gloucester; Lopez, in *Arctic Dreams*, gives us the Arctic, and more often than not the essays in *Crossing Open Ground* present landscapes. For both, incidentally, birds are eminent examples of being-in-the-world. They figure in the opening and closing essays of Lopez's book and may be said to provide its measure by enclosing it in the wisdom he attributes to them.

A central essay in *Crossing Open Ground* treats landscape in relation to narrative (a focal issue also of *Arctic Dreams*) and seems to me to serve better as an introduction to Lopez's stories—*Desert Notes, River Notes, Winter Count*— than to his essays, though all he writes is characterized by intimacy, the indispensable element, he believes, of the storyteller's art. This quality, in his case unguarded but discreet, derives, he says, "from the listener's trust and a storyteller's certain knowledge of his subject and regard for his audience"; and it "deepens if the storyteller tempers his authority with humility" and the landscape ("the physical setting") is shared.

This meditation on the art he aspires to practice turns on an experience of listening to hunting stories in a village in the Brooks Range in Alaska. The original title, "Story at Anaktuvuk Pass," situates the essay in a landscape, which is carefully described, and the essay itself demonstrates the concordance of visual and verbal landscapes with which Lopez is concerned. Lopez employs some elements of the new journalism and as a storyteller assimilates the fantastic realism of recent Spanish American writers, but his primary model is an oral, "primitive" art. An early book, *Giving Birth to Thunder, Sleeping with His Daughter*, is a collection of retellings of stories about Coyote, and when he gets to the heart of the matter of landscape and narrative, his example is the Navajo. He says of his experience of stories that "the landscape seemed alive because of the stories" and that they "renewed in me a sense of the purpose of my life." This reminds me of Leslie Silko, whose *Ceremony* enacts these very things in the way myth (what is said: story) is made to work against the realistic prose of contemporary fiction and whose essay "Landscape, History, and the Pueblo Imagination" is essential commentary on her art and Lopez's essay.

Aldo Leopold, who claims that in learning how to read the land we will learn (at last) how to live with it, would have appreciated Lopez's ability to study out the land, its idioms and its men (Whitman's phrase). To see relationships is the fundamental lesson. One of the personal essays, "Children in the Woods," is about just such ecological initiation and the way it "nurtures the heart." "Landscape and Narrative" also insists on this ("One learns a landscape . . . by perceiving the relations in it"), and many of the essays recount brief journeys in and out of landscapes during which perceiving relationships is the necessary work, the most intense activity. Perhaps the title of the collection is intended to suggest the movement of this journey-work, for nothing here tells of inhabitation, and what is lacking (to be found in *Desert Notes* and *River Notes* and the extensive regional journeys of *Arctic Dreams*) are, in Silko's words for the Hopi way, "interaction [participation] and interrelationship." The landscapes here are seen, not lived in, and, though Lopez is better able to see them because he enters the field with humility, he is still too much an observer, a reporter not yet wholly within them. *Landscape*, as Silko notes, is a visual term, speaking for the power of the eye (and *I*) to compose the scene (seen): "a portion of the territory the eye can comprehend in a single view." Landscape art—and sometimes the similar work of nature writers—is a Romantic art founded on philosophical idealism; yet *landscape*, used in an areal sense by Sauer and Olson, remains a serviceable word, much in the way *ground* does in the title of Lopez's book.

"I think of two landscapes—one outside the self, the other within." This is the way in which Lopez poses the problem of *out/in*. Presumably these landscapes correspond. In the efficacious storytelling of "aboriginal peoples," they are brought together, or, better, as with the Navajo, the "sacred order" of the exterior landscape, "the perceived natural order of the universe," grounds the interior order, that is, every aspect of the "indigenous philosophy." This wholeness (holiness, health) is the gauge of what is wanting as a result of the very Western mind that predicates *out/in*, the MIND, which I capitalize because Ed Dorn, in *Recollections of Gran Apachería*, sees it as "the highest mutation of force," the power that overcame the Apaches' holistic, mythic way of thinking ("I am Thinking Earth").

Dorn says that the Apaches' leading ideas came "directly from the landform." This puts ideas in their place, much in the way that Williams' "no ideas but in things" does. Lopez, too, thinks that this is the proper order. When he speaks of the *authority* of the landscape, he has this priority in mind, and an ethical measure comparable to Leopold's *integrity* of the land. He believes that the "relationships in the interior landscape," arranged as they are "according to the thread of one's moral, intellectual, and spiritual development," answer to the exterior landscape. "The interior landscape," he insists, "responds to the character and subtlety of an exterior landscape; the shape of the individual mind is affected by land as it is by genes." I agree that we are "deeply influenced" in this way but that rather than "draw[ing] on relationships in the exterior landscape and project[ing] them onto the interior landscape," we too often project—impose—our ideas on the world.

It is just because for us these landscapes do not correspond and we do not project the order of the exterior onto the interior landscape that we need storytellers to do this healing work for us, to do what Lopez wishes to do in nonfictional as well as fictional forms: "reorder a state of psychological confusion through contact with the pervasive truth of those relationships we call 'the land.'" This healing work is ultimately religious: "If you can really see the land . . . lose your sense of wishing it to be what you want it to be . . . strip yourself of the desire to order and to name and see the land entirely for itself, you see in the relationship of all its elements the face of God." I cite from an interview with Jim Aton, where Lopez recalls Laurens van der Post's phrase, "the pattern we call God," and goes on to say that the landscape has authority "because its order is, at least in some places, still innate." By *still innate* I think he means *still undisturbed*. In some of the far places to which he goes God still authorizes the landscape—it is still, as he says, "creation"—because we have not yet done the devil's work.

The critical question is the extent to which language may be made to answer to such complex representation of reality, and there is the moral question of the truth or honesty of *our* relationships that the functionalists, for example, put in terms of function and form and of the necessity of building from the ground up. Lopez says directly that "lying is the opposite of story" and adds that for the writer "truth reveals itself . . . not in dogma but in the paradox, irony, and contradictions that distinguish compelling narratives." What must be resisted are "reductionism in science, fundamentalism in religion, fascism in politics."

Lopez also considers national literature in terms of storytelling, as a literature that respects the land (the "source") and our relation to it. This is why he thinks that nature writing, so conspicuous now, "will one day produce a major and lasting body of American literature . . . [and] provide the foundation for a reorganization of American political thought."

Reorder, repair, restore, rediscover, reclaim, rethink. I haven't clustered all the words with this prefix (*re:back*), just a few that come to mind, enough to suggest the work of literature to which Lopez *recalls* us. "To repair a spirit in disarray"—such art, as with other contemporary writers, especially the poets, *recov-*

ers the shaman's work, the primary work of *poesis*. "Landscape," Silko says, "has similarities with dreams."

Even in the frantic effort to control the blaze, I thought of Thoreau, whose notoriety in Concord came of having set fire to the woods. Given wind enough and time, I would have. Maybe the interval in writing—easily explained in terms of *maintenance* (from Old French, *maintenir*, to which I add *now* from *maintenant*)—is better explained by the sour-burnt-plastic smell that fills this cabin. The wreck is only a few yards away, up against the white oak that stopped the truck's forward motion and that didn't burn, no more than the oaks of the oak openings of the prairie. So much for moving a truck to make room for a bulldozer; so much for two inches of rotten neoprene tubing. Nothing unusual, the insurance adjuster said. What's unusual is the speed with which the volunteer firemen from Cass Lake got here—eight miles in ten minutes. And the efficiency of volunteers, our butcher, and others whom we recognized among them.

When I read "The Stone Horse" in *Antaeus*, I found it artful, maybe because it seemed so in that context, and I was annoyed by such exact yet literary sentences as "The dark mouths of gold, talc, and tin mines yawned from the bony flanks of desert ranges" and "Wood smoke hung like a lens in the trees." Reading the essay now I am happier with the moral bearing of its deliberate art and appreciate its moral exemplarity, the reason, perhaps, that Lopez opens the collection with it.

The incident recalled is simple—and paradigmatic, as we now say. Having been given directions by an archaeologist with the Bureau of Land Management (the expert), Lopez enters the desert to inspect an artifact, a stone horse, an intaglio made by a Quechan three hundred years ago. The immediate context is the wholesale vandalizing of aboriginal sites, the destruction of evidence of human occupancy now believed to go back more than two hundred thousand years. Lopez tells of post–World War II occupancy and the more recent story of vandalizing (as also told in Tony Hillerman's *A Thief of Time*) that "devour[s] history."

He is, of course, a privileged observer, granted permission to see the intaglio because, as the essay shows, he is a pilgrim. Journey, for him, is pilgrimage, as in other essays, and involves withdrawal from and return to "civilization." (The fullest example is the next essay, "A Reflection on White Geese.") The occasion is meditative, never rushed, ritualized in the telling by the careful prose and the reenactment of formal art. His search for the primitive—the very search itself—is sacred, for landscape is sacred space to be entered reverently in expectation of realizations intense enough to be called epiphanic.

He approaches the stone horse at dawn, observes it during sunrise, in process, animated as it were, not in the frozen moment of an aerial photograph. He is not above the object, recording it, mapping it; he is present with the horse, as its maker was, seeing it from various perspectives and in various lights and summoning as a necessary part of the experience of wonder all that the essay tells of geography, cultural history, and personal recollection. The stone horse, to cite Kerouac, is the jewel-center of the associations awakened by the occasion.

Lopez, a learned writer, is an intellectual historian as well as nature writer. Culture as much as nature concerns him. He does not leave out of account the fact that on the way to Tule Lake to see the geese he listens to Bach; in another essay he speaks of his pleasure in bibliography. In "A Stone Horse" he tries to earn respect for the plundered landscape by reminding us of the Dordogne and by suggesting its value as archive. For the history it holds is "a kind of medicine": It nullifies our belief in the sovereignty of the self and of the present. By permitting "the great breadth of human expression to reverberate," history of this kind clarifies and encourages, and reproves the vandals whose scorn and disrespect "create the awful atmosphere"—it is felt as menace—"in which totalitarianism thrives."

"With a slight bow I paid my respects to the horse, its maker, and the history of us all."

"The Stone Horse" belongs with "Searching for Ancestors" and "The Passing Wisdom of Birds," for these essays also treat the "original wisdom" to be found in "tribal America." The ancestors for whom Lopez searches are people like the Anasazi, who were "intimate with the landscape, a successful people": They "responded resourcefully and decisively to the earth and the weather that together made their land"; the land was their "arbiter," and they lived with it with "utter honesty." Thinking of them (and the Peabody Coal Company now ravishing their land), he proposes what is surely his—and our—work: *"to find some place between the extremes of nature and civilization where it is possible to live without regret"* (my italics). The diversity and impenetrability of ways of life, witnessed in this instance by archaeological search for the Anasazi, humble him, a requisite condition for what he experiences on their land, under the open sky: "The slow inhalation of light that is the fall of dusk is now complete. The stars are very bright. I lie [here] recalling the land as if the Anasazi were something that had once bloomed in it." (Flowering, the moral-aesthetic measure of contact with the environment in *In the American Grain*; a sentiment of being, deeply nostalgic, matched by the recollection of dusk in *A Walker in the City*.)

"The Passing Wisdom of Birds," the concluding essay, mentions Leopold and, like the essays at the end of *A Sand County Almanac*, makes the strongest, most direct statement of Lopez's case. Where Leopold uses the killing of Odysseus's handmaidens to inform our sense of ethical evolution, Lopez uses Cortez's destruction of Tenochtitlán (as Williams had) to mark an enormity we must now repair. In Leopold we look forward to a "land ethic," and in Lopez we find it by going back to what Dennis and Barbara Tedlock, in the title of their book on Native American lore, call *Teachings from the American Earth*.

Cortez's destruction of the city he had described as "the most beautiful city in the world" was completed in the most gratuitous act, the burning of the aviaries. Lopez finds this act so grotesque and unmitigated that even the recognition of the "dark side" of human culture fails to account for it. For him it images more than the "destructive madness . . . of imperial conquest"; it images "a long-term failure of Western Civilization to recognize the intrinsic worth of the American landscape, and its potential value to human societies that have since come to be at odds with the natural world." The measure of Cortez's enormity is that it "flies widely in the face of a desire to find a *dignified* and honorable relationship with nature" (I italicize *dignified*, a moral term repeated elsewhere). And the measure of our need is that we long to "find our way back to a more equitable set of relationships with all we have subjugated," a way that involves "rethinking [thinking back] our relationships with the natural world (i.e., in figuring out how to get ourselves back *into* it)," a way that aboriginal peoples may teach us.

Lopez's proposals for our difficult reeducation are exemplified to a large extent in his own attitudes and practice. Like Eiseley and Leopold he respects science but knows its limitations, appreciates fieldwork and the "indispensable element of personal experience." Like Wendell Berry, he knows that the necessary transformation in attitudes is private and comes of individual effort and that each of us must "cultivate . . . a sense of mystery." To this end, he would preserve the still undisturbed landscapes and the learning of aboriginal peoples (the diverse ecosystems and nature-related cultures from which we have much to learn), give greater support to field biology and more attention to our libraries and the education in natural sciences and natural history of the next generation.

I am struck by his hopefulness. We are, it seems, still Nature's Nation. In his rethinking, this nineteenth-century characterization of America is given new currency:

> The philosophy of nature we set aside eight thousand years ago in the Fertile Crescent we can . . . locate again and greatly refine in North America. The New World is a landscape still overwhelming in the vigor of its animals and plants, resonant with mystery. It encourages, still, an enlightened response toward indigenous cultures that differ from our own.

Perhaps he placed "Grown Men" between "Searching for Ancestors" and "The Passing Wisdom of Birds" because it speaks for his faith and hope. This personal essay pays tribute to three men ("grown," that is, mature men), the "grandfathers," tutelary figures whose behavior furthered Lopez's moral and spiritual education. One of them, he says, "introduced me to a perception of America's indigenous people more complex than anything I was later to read about them." All of them had "integrity" and "implacable conviction" and when faced with trouble "act[ed] to help . . . rather than to assign blame."

This—as well as a sense of complexity—may explain why Lopez is never strident. In "Yukon-Charley," where he argues most fully in behalf of wilderness, he simply notes that "the Reagan administration regards such arguments from science [the gene pool] and ethics [animal rights] as frivolous." Measuring riches in the way Leopold does, he considers a limited economic understanding of wilderness "impoverished." In "A Reflection on White Geese," he comments on the Reagan administration in parentheses as if to suggest how out of place it is in the rich experience reported there. His appeal to a sense of beauty grants us the freedom to choose to foster the richer way: "We grasp what is beautiful in a flight of snow geese . . . as easily as we grasp the beauty in a cello suite; and [because we do,] intuit . . . that if we allow these things to be destroyed or degraded for economic or frivolous reasons we will become deeply and strangely impoverished."

I am reminded again of Leopold in reading "A Reflection on White Geese" because the crane, whose bugling is as old as the Pleistocene, awakened his sense of beauty and mystery and filled him with bitter regret for the economic expedience that drained its wetlands. Wildlife management is very much an issue in Lopez's essay. That we seem to be able to preserve the geese only by allowing them to be hunted is as paradoxical for him as it was for Leopold and Muir.

Lopez does not neglect crucial political issues of this environmental/ecological kind. He does so quietly (without rancor) and perhaps with more point because they are part of the personal experience that sets them off, questions them, and makes us realize the reversible equation of public issues and private woes. So in "Yukon-Charley," where Lopez's claims for the wilderness are verified in the experience of canoeing the Charley River, he challenges federal policy by defending resident subsistent hunters, like the Moores, who belong in the Yukon-Charley Rivers National Preserve because "they have a manifestly spiritual relationship with the landscape." On the one hand, legislation is often too simple and, on the other hand, the issues are often complicated. In "Borders," the rewarding experience of a day spent searching for the unmarked boundary between Alaska and Canada raises the question of the arbitrary and the abstract and provides a measure of the frantic-oppressive emotion Lopez feels when, on return, he is confronted by legislation he has not had time enough to examine but nevertheless must decide on.

And morally. "A Presentation of Whales," the longest essay, considers the complications and cross-purposes of scientists, police, bureaucrats, press corps, and curious and concerned onlookers when whales, stranded on a beach in Oregon, create an opportunity for scientific research, a media event, and a health hazard. Lopez studies human beings—attitudes and angles of vision—as well as (other large) animals, and this essay, like one on cowboys who work the rodeos and another on people rafting the Colorado River in the Grand Canyon, is a presentation of humans, of "the worst and the best human behavior." Scientific research, questioned here, is more thoroughly taken up in "The Lives of Seals," a by-product of *Arctic Dreams*. The gathering of ecological data involves killing seals (the perspective is that of the Eskimos, who, in visiting the Tule Lake refuge, had been appalled by the wasteful hunting that jeopardized their lives), data that will be used "to guide oil and mineral development." Lopez's sentiments are clear enough: He would like this immemorial hunting and fishing land to remain inviolate. But he also respects knowledge, the scientific inquiry that seems always to be used to alter old ways and stable ecosystems. So he does not settle the matter "as if there were no seals" but uncomfortably stands "in the middle of the question" in the way he stands between the scientists and a crew that abhors the killing. As a writer accompanying marine biologists, his work, figured in gathering shells for the crew and represented by the essay itself, is to create the atmosphere of tolerance in which profoundly difficult questions of the propriety of human acts may at least be considered. His work, suggested in "A Presentation of Whales," is not to settle fundamental questions but to add the witness of a point of view too often omitted: "No novelist, no historian, no moral philosopher, no scholar of Melville, no painter, no theologian had been on that beach."

This determination on truth, I recall Warner Berthoff saying, is the hallmark of American literature.

I think that Lopez's distinctive work is in the three slim volumes of *Desert Notes: Reflections in the Eye of a Raven* (1976), *River Notes: The Dance of Herons* (1979), and *Winter Count* (1981). Slim volumes, like volumes of poems, and in their imaginative range, care for language, and formal shape, poetic. To read them requires the concentrated attention we give to poetry, though we also attend because they treat (and are) a discipline of being upon which our lives depend. As with all literary work that claims our attention, they engage us in *ta 'wil*, the exegesis of the soul. These books involve sacred space: not just the landscape of desert, river, or plains but the deep interior landscapes of self and imagination, landscapes at times undifferentiated, surreal. These landscapes are places of quest, of vision quest and shamanic flight. Lopez's desert is not Edward Abbey's or Gary Nabhan's; it has other dimensions and is as much out of space and time as it is out of mind, a place of mystery, disorientation, and self-transformation, where one goes crazy and comes to oneself, though a certain craziness—despair of the world—is needed to go there in the first place. Fancy hardly covers what is found there.

Notes, in the title, belongs to the humility that comes of uncertainty and incompleteness—to a book that questions itself. Telling of entrance to initiation ("the way inside"), *Desert Notes* is no farther along at its close than at its beginning. It is framed by a concern with spatial and spiritual directions which have as their measure the totality of the cosmic medicine wheel ("where everything is coming from") of the stories "Perimeter" and "Coyote and Rattlesnake." Native American lore, with the desert, grounds the book, belongs to the landscape Lopez has come in search of ("everything I'd come here to find out was hidden inside"); and at the end, in "Directions," where he "hear[s] a map . . . well spoken" from a man named Leon, he acknowledges the need for help from someone (a grandfather?) who has been tested by primary experience and has learned sufficiency.

Desert Notes is a guidebook without a map—maps, we are told, are "too thin." It is a spoken guide, its mode often oral, often dialogic, intimately addressed to the reader. "I would like to show you what lies before us," the narrator says at the outset, and, as with Prufrock, we go with him and, as with Whitman, we assume what he assumes, the ultimate seriousness of the quest. For in coming to the desert he is making, as Thomas Merton says of the Desert Fathers, "a clean break with a conventional, accepted social context." He does this not only for reasons of psychic health but in order to save a civilization he has been told is approaching its end. "We are here . . . to change things," he says. "It is why I came to the desert."

The representative anecdote of the book, "Coyote and Rattlesnake," fables this cultural role. In this story the desert figures as the last outpost of nature facing an advancing civilization that is destroying the habitat and the old ways. This is adumbrated in "The School," where a woman tells of white occupancy as temporary as the mining that occasioned it. (See Lopez's update, "California Desert, a Worldly Wilderness," *National Geographic Magazine*, January 1987.) "The Shisa," Coyote realizes, "will take even the desert," and so, instructed by Otter to purify and prepare himself, he goes to see Akasitah "about a new way of life." Coyote has a vision such as Black Elk had ("They had broken the circle and made it straight like a stick"), but Akasitah assures him that the Shisa, whom he himself had set free, will now—is there a better word?—self-destruct. This story is not in Lopez's or any other collection of stories about Coyote I've read. I suspect that he created it just as Silko, in *Ceremony*, created the more ferocious story of white Europeans and witchery, a story of world-alienation, one of the great eco-fables of our time. (Unerringly, Jerome Rothenberg includes it in the revised edition of *Shaking the Pumpkin*.)

Lopez acknowledges his debt to Native Americans in "Twilight," where juxtaposing two prose modes, he tells the sometimes sordid history of a Navajo rug that had become an article of exchange and that now is used by the narrator for its original sacred purpose. Spreading the rug on the desert floor, he is both in and on the world of the rug; their landscapes have become one. *Raven*, in the subtitle, also indicates the extent to which Lopez assimilates the Native American vision. Prominent in the mythology of the tribes of the Northwest and subarctic, Raven belongs in the desert because of the spiritual power attributed to him. Raven, purged of the qualities of crow, is not unlike a benign Coyote—and the story Lopez tells has some of the anecdotal character of Coyote stories. For him, Coyote and Raven are interchangeable, and in *Giving Birth to Thunder* he sometimes substitutes Coyote for Raven, a liberty, incidentally, not granted anthropologists. Even so, he understands their scruple, has relied on their work and mastered the scholarship, and given good reasons for wanting the tales more accessible in every way. The seriousness of his concern is unquestionable; he dedicates the collection "To the Native Peoples of North America." See also "The American Indian Mind," edited by him for *Quest*, September–October 1978, another effort at better understanding.

In reading "The Blue Mound People," I thought of *The Narrative of Arthur Gordon Pym*—the prototype of fantastic realism? The Blue Mound People are "entirely out of the order of things"; sophisticated methods of archaeological inquiry cannot *explain* them. Notable for their "unusual [close] relationship with the desert," they remain a "mystery." Imaginary or not, they are the ancestors the narrator searches for.

The cover photograph of the paperback edition is by Lopez: a sharply defined desert landscape empty except for an empty rocking chair. The chair is anomalous if not surreal. It is not mordantly ironic in the fashion, say, of Michael Meyers' drawings in *Recollections of Gran Apachería*. It invites us to sit and wait, for as much as anything learning to wait is our business. First we must abandon civilization and give over the ego, as the narrator does in stepping out of his moving van. Then we must strip ourselves. (The discipline is universal, but the instance that comes to mind is Ike's initiation in "The Bear.") There is also the need to purify ourselves in the hot spring (told in a story less portentous than the narrator's first-person admonitions in "Desert Notes," which, stylistically, signals a break with convention). Finally, there is a correlative story of nakedness, of the repossession of the body and the anima. In this story of a white woman who comes into intimate relationship with the land, the play of mind and light enacts a cosmic eros that is salutary as against the perhaps more explicitly sexual *and* miniaturized instance of the ant (a male) with the seed.

To wait, and to be alert. As the old man says in "Conversation," you stay in one place and "you wait for yourself." You also wait "until you see for yourself." This passivity belongs to egolessness, but it is a wise passivity, as in Thoreau, alert. As for alertness, Ortega says it well in *Meditations on Hunting*: We are alert when, like the animals, we live "from within [the] environment." Hunting is the initial discipline of alertness in the "absolute *outside* of the countryside." But meditation, as in Ortega's book, is the hunt of the hunt, a discipline of alertness in the "absolute *inside* of ideas."

To answer Thoreau: Lopez hears the fishes when they cry. More than a century later, only now in the West, he responds once more to the manifest destiny of spoliation, the destruction of nature and Native Americans that Thoreau elegized in *A Week on the Concord and Merrimack Rivers*.

(The *re* cluster, I see, is matched by the *de* cluster. *Destroy*, and its cognates, is obsessive. We are a culture, Lopez says, that "devours the earth." Forward motion or *progress*, too often destructive, calls up the necessity of return.)

Lopez has acquired the "Indian wisdom" Thoreau claimed for himself. By participant activity, by "direct intercourse and sympathy" and with the "finer organization" of his senses, he has come to know his immediate world. (He lives in Finn Rock, Oregon, a logging village on the McKenzie River.) *River Notes*, even more than *Desert Notes*, proves that Lopez is one of the aspirants to nature study who, Thoreau said, "will smell, taste, see, hear, feel better than other men." He has especially learned to listen. "I have trained myself to listen to the river," the narrator says, the river, with all of its extensions, its watershed, an *ecos*; and in the river's notes he has heard Gaia weeping: "The running . . . of rivers is the weeping of the earth for what is lost." We are told this at the beginning of the book, at the ocean, before he undertakes the spiritual journey, the return "up river . . . [to] begin again." But even when he finds the "springs of celebration," he knows that the tears of ravens are the source of the river: "It is from *them* that the river actually flows, for at night they break down and weep; the universal anguish of creatures, their waiting in desolation, the wrenching anger of betrayals—this seizes them and passes out of them and in that weeping the river takes its shape." This is as true of him as of these tutelary birds (the Native Americans also weep), and as true of the book as of the river that runs through it. Hence the sadness of this unique book and its inimitable tone, its burden (as with all of Lopez's work) being to bring the desolate human spirit in "the last days" into concord with the desolated but still vital spirit of the world and so make good a double loss.

We go to nature, we say, to heal ourselves (*natura sanat*), but this now requires that we heal nature, learn to practice healing ways. This spiritual need joins *Desert Notes* and *River Notes*, makes them companion books. The first, in order of time and experience, involves the waiting, the vigil that has exhausted the distraught narrator at the beginning of *River Notes*; the second involves doing, the activity, ultimately, of dancing, the joining-with of at-one-ment. At the beginning, where the heron is wonderfully evoked, the narrator says that "I believe we will dance together someday [when he acquires the understanding and discipline the book records]. . . . I cannot believe it is so far between knowing what must be done and doing it." Though the raven is still present, the narrator addresses the heron as *thou* and "expect[s] the wisdom of the desert out of you." Now the vision quest, proposed in "The Search for the Heron," has become explicitly ecological, that is, of *ecos* and itself ecological in being instrumental in restoring *ecos*. The narrator may be said to have an eco-imagination, one that is profoundly imaginal (of the psyche, as treated by James Hillman) and profoundly resonant (awakening Bachelardian reverie). "The images are irrefutable, requiring only patience to perceive," the narrator says; and the story of what he perceives is myth, if myth, as Olson claims, reenacts our primary perceptions of self-and-world.

The unity of outer and inner landscapes accounts for the visionary power of the book. These landscapes interpenetrate or, in a book so fluvial, may be said to flow together. The stories, modulated by first- and third-person narration, are essentially oral and performative. Their slow dance—I think of the sarabande of Crane's "Repose of Rivers"—is as much a sacred gesture as the dance of the herons in which the narrator finally participates. In the overwhelming fable of eco-loss and recovery that closes the book, the narrator's sacred (selfless, gratuitous) gestures are acknowledged by the animals in the "old way" of Native American stories. Blue Heron says:

> We were the first people here. We gave away all the ways of living. Now no one remembers how to live anymore, so the river is drying up. Before we could ask for rain there had to be someone to do something completely selfless, with no hope of success. You went after that fish, and then at the end you were trying to dance. A person cannot be afraid of being foolish. For everything, every gesture, is sacred.

Because he has done these things, the narrator enters the ever-present reality of Native American myth. He had been told by Hanner, in the story of how the river (in a way comparable to drought) taught the salmon and the bear, that everyone lives by "agreements and courtesies." These "obligations" remain unchanged. "Time has nothing to do with it," Hanner explains. "When you feel the river shuddering against your legs, you are feeling the presence of all these agreements."

The true feeling of worlding is aesthetic and moral: The harmony of nature is the result of (ecological) agreements. The terms of Hanner's eco-fable are moral, and just as significant is the fact that Hanner tells it as a medicine man had told it to him. This confirms the storyteller's shamanic role (when Hanner's voice changes, the narrator's hair rises and he feels threatened by "something in the dark": He has entered what Eiseley calls the night country) and it confirms that the healing, which always tried to restore harmony with nature, is now the essential ecological work. *No one remembers how to live anymore.* Lopez tells stories in order to teach us to see in the old ways (see Snyder's *The Old Ways*) and to behave accordingly: He would restore our ecological sense. And he tells stories because in them, to the extent that he may be identified with the narrator, he, too, must learn these hard lessons from those whose experience gives them moral authority.

Hanner's story, an apologue that supports his account of the disappearance of a utopian community, stands against the "rubbish" of popular history. So, too, the narrator's stories stand against, and are measured by, "The Rapids," which renders a reporter's search for what he thinks the public considers "human interest" wholly in the direct (often deadly) speech of his respondents. The narrator himself gathers stories, some of which remind me of Anderson's *Winesburg, Ohio*: "The Log Jam," for example, not only for the story of Rebecca Grayson but because all of its stories, of a logging village, comprise a community of suffering. And, as often as not, Lopez's "grotesques" are afflicted in the spirit. There is the man who "pondered gentleness" and made the stone fish in "The Salmon"; and there are Rebecca Grayson and the nameless woman of "Dawn," whose burdens of erotic loss (appropriately so in an eco-imagination) are spiritual rather than simply sexual. These anima figures are unacknowledged or hidden presences whose recourse to the river recalls Chopin's *The Awakening*, even though they do not enact the Ophelia-death treated so well by Bachelard in *Water and Dreams*. The polarized world of "Dawn" as well as the use of two voices anticipate Susan Griffin's *Woman and Nature*; repetitive phrasing recalls Stein. The unseeing fishermen have a counterpart in the absent fisherman in Snyder's "The Elwah River," a poem of the grieved anima.

These analogues are not important except to show that Lopez draws on literate as well as preliterate sources and shares the deep concerns of our time. In fact, the book closest to his own is Snyder's *Myths and Texts*, which belongs to the same logging country, employs modernist and archaic techniques toward shamanic ends, and treats the initial stages of the arduous journey back to love that is at the heart of all eco-fables.

(Toward shamanic ends. "The initiation / of another kind of nation"—Olson, in the last volume of *The Maximus Poems*.)

The narrator performs gratuitous acts (of atonement, for childhood guilt, among other things) and dances with the herons because he has been enabled by another dance, which, in turn, seems to be the reward of careful attention (without "arrogance or presumption") to the natural relationships of the little-traveled upriver country. He studies this part of the river in the hope of "a larger vision," meaning by this both ecological understanding of the watershed and something truly visionary, befitting a return to source. A single sentence makes the transition and explains how the one occasions the other: "In this way [Way?] I came to a bend in the river . . . from which I could see a house." He has undertaken an archetypal journey, a quest of the kind that distinguishes our literature. *The springs of celebration*: How often we have sought them in childhood and a world elsewhere; how seldom in the heart of darkness. Yet, isn't the significant aspect in this instance the extent to which the narrator has made ecological study serve this end? the extent to which he has gone *out* in order to come *in*? With him, it may be said, the discipline of ecology heals the psyche and the healed psyche serves the unhealed world.

So the journey doesn't end in the deep interior space (the landscapes fuse) of the homecoming of "Upriver." Here he finds the anima and dances with her (the book is dedicated to Lopez's wife). This is told, appropriately, in the clairvoyant manner of dream or fairy tale, and it is recognized as such, as a mysterious occurrence whose moral meaning is nevertheless clear. *He dances and tells stories*: With these sacred gestures he celebrates the springs. He has been called as artist to restore the springs, and the springs themselves, as in Duncan's dream of Olson, are the source of myths. And he knows that he must do this in the realization that art, like rivers, is born of anguish and that the hope vouchsafed in dreams must, on return, encounter the terrors of the fallen world. Thoreau knew this, too, when on the return from source in *A Week* he left summer behind and entered the autumn of adult work.

(I should have mentioned "The Forest Path to the Spring," the patently autobiographical story of how Malcolm Lowry learned from his wife to appreciate the feminine in the nature of the world. This fable of gratitude to the anima is surely cognate.)

The spiritual counsel of *River Notes* and *Desert Notes* belongs to the religious manuals of other times. There are chapters of explicit instruction: "The Bend," in which the ego yields its search for correspondences and becomes part of nature; "The Shallows," in which the narrator takes us by the hand and teaches us how to read things; "The Falls," in which a man, to be distinguished from the narrator, remains true to the vision quest of his youth, follows the old (rough) ways and disciplines of nature. Stories of egoism, presumption, ambition, violation, trespass, and irreverence are foils for the virtues of guilelessness, compassion, forgiveness, and humility. And it may be, in a book so much indebted to the archaic, that it brings this to our attention in order to provide, as Charles Bernstein says of the archaic, a "chastening lesson . . . of our own ignorance and the value in acknowledging it."

When the river begins to dry up, the realtors move in. "Men with an intolerable air of condolence have appeared, as though drawn by the smell of death, dressed comfortably, speaking a manipulated tongue, terminally evil. They have inquired into the purchase of our homes." What would an eco-fable be without realtors and developers?

Even so, the beaver return (as on the river here) and a pair of osprey build their nest (as here). They live, the narrator says in one of the few ironies he allows himself, "as well as [may] be expected in that country."

Winter Count lacks an introduction, a feature of the previous books, probably because the narrator is no longer desperately troubled by the need for self-transformation and the stories he tells do not have the resolution of quest. The narrator now teaches at a university, and his familiarity with a wide range of books and with high culture defines him. Where the narrative fabric of *River Notes* is fittingly woven of references to raven, salmon, and heron, it is now (as with good academics) fittingly woven of bibliographical references.

A winter count, as a note informs us and the titular story exemplifies, is a personal history, a sequence of memorable events and determinative encounters. (*His story*, to cite Olson's special view of history, the record of an individual life tracking itself?) The narrator's stories are just such personal history and match those of the Plains Indians, recounted in "Buffalo" and "Winter Count 1973," in telling of foreboding, loss, and "fundamental anguish." His predicament is not as extreme as theirs—what it portends for our "tribe" may be—but it is comparable. For his allegiance is double, to both civilization and nature (Europe and America)—to define the issue as American writers in the nineteenth century did. He finds himself *between*, compelled by nature and native cultures (*nature*, *native*, and *nation* have the same root) but unable to dismiss the claims of civilization represented by European Culture. Story after story treats this dilemma, the condition in which Lopez also finds himself. This accounts for the resonance of his statement in *Crossing Open Ground*: "One of the great dreams of man [and woman] must be to find some place between the extremes of nature and civilization where it is possible to live without regret."

Restoration seems to be a way of mediating the extremes. The above statement, from "Searching for Ancestors," concludes a paragraph commenting on the zeal with which we now search out, record, and preserve the archaic past—"We worry over what is lost." And *Winter Count*, the title declaring a historical motive, names the work of the narrator and, more explicitly, of the exemplar in the initial story, "Restoration." Edward Seraut, a European book-restorer, practices his art with surgical aestheticism. He is not especially concerned with what the books in René de Crenir's library tell of de Crenir's intellectual life, although his recognition of this use prompts the narrator's investigation. Since the narrator is familiar with many of these old books on exploration, travel, and the natural history of North America, it is clear that de Crenir, a Frenchman who lived on the family cattle land in North Dakota, is an "ancestor."

His intermediate situation and intellectual interests survive in the narrator. The first is evoked when the narrator says in the course of an elegant dinner at the local hotel, "I was now deeply affected by the atmosphere of ideas and history that emanated from Seraut, and periodically stunned by the sight of young, ferine men cruising in slow-moving pickups on the other side of the window, or distracted by the . . . ranchers' voices and the din of country-and-western music in an adjoining bar." (See Snyder's "I Went into the Maverick Bar" and Williams' "The Desert Music.") The second plays off the first because it involves the almost insuperable difficulty of coming to know what is alien to one's ideas—the difficulty, that is, of altering perspective and perception. De Crenir had understood this ("a cultural and philosophic bias had prevented nineteenth-century European naturalists from comprehending much of the plant and animal life they saw in North America"). He had even understood that "les bêtes sont les propriétaires," that, as the narrator explains, "in North America the indigenous philosophy [Native American lore] grew out of the lives of animals." This insight, so singular then, disturbs the narrator, who wonders, "Whom might he have spoken with about it?" It is a question of present moment for him (and the author of *Of Wolves and Men*) because the issue now is animal rights.

In this story multiple perspectives and inclusivity of perception accommodate the very dilemma they present. For this reason, the concluding paragraph has the power of revelation. Far and near, out and in, past and present—everything, however anomalous, is sharply seen synchronistically, as belonging together.

> Out of the window we could see several miles across the rolling brown hills. In a draw below the house there suddenly appeared six antelope, frozen so still they seemed to shimmer in the dry grass. I saw sunlight glinting on the surface of their huge eyes, their hearts beating against soft, cream-white throats, their slender legs. Surprised by the house, or by us in the window, they were as suddenly gone. At the end of the room, beyond a blue velvet rope strung between polished brass stanchions, a line of tourists passed. They stared at us and

then looked away nervously into the shelves of books. A girl in yellow shorts was eating ice cream. In a shaft of window light I could see the wheat paste dried to granules under Seraut's fingernails and the excessive neatness of my own notes, the black ink like a skittering of shore birds over the white sheets.

("Only the copied text," Walter Benjamin says in a lesson on reading, " . . . commands the soul of him who is occupied with it.")

The copied text in this instance is preceded by an example of accommodation. Seraut, in talking of Montaigne's misgivings, "spoke in a genial way, as though misgivings were a part of everything."

This may be the wisdom of Europe, steeped in history and evil, as we have been taught to believe by Henry James and other American writers. "The Tapestry" is a Jamesian story of a passionate pilgrim ("I was awed by European culture") whose European legacy involves knowledge of the evil in the world and presentiment of catastrophic end. This is the vision bequeathed him by the fifteenth-century Flemish tapestry that his Spanish grandfather had purchased—the end of a vision quest that takes place in a museum, in the Prado, where the tapestry is stored. The tapestry, of course, represents the grandfather with whom the narrator is said to be in temperamental accord. Thus the "innocent brooding" that characterizes the arrested world of the tapestry belongs as well to grandfather and grandson, brooding, however, that allows the grandfather but not the American grandson to accept uncertainty without being tyrannized by it. In telling of a search for the past, the culture (Culture) of Europe, this story also tells of rejection, especially of a tradition so heavy (so institutionalized and protected by museums, curators, and documents) it makes for stasis and hopelessness. At the end, in a gesture that recalls Columbus, who belonged to but opened the world of the tapestry, the narrator sails for home.

Europe is not the way back. (Remember what Olson said of Pound and the "Western box.") But neither is America, except in a diminishing number of places where sometimes are to be found people farther back. (And remember Lopez's injunction to take better care of "the repositories of our own long-term cultural wisdom.")

Yet the narrator sails for open ground. "Winter Herons" puts the dilemma in terms of East and West, New York City and Montana—in terms of *Les Syl-*

phides and the dance of cranes, and of a ballet dancer whom the narrator tries to initiate in the ways of the "north" but finally fails to win. ("She stood at the river's edge with her arms folded across her bare chest looking down the river with a chin line hard enough for that country. She had tied a flicker's feathers in her hair.") His solace, perhaps, is the recollection of a snowy evening when, having been left by a friend, he sees a flock of great blue herons descend into the canyon of the city street.

(Is this Lopez's addition to the myths of swan maiden? Had he read Snyder's study of a Haida myth, published in 1974?)

In this book of stories Lopez is more than usually concerned with actual and spiritual fathers and with a correlative reverie toward childhood. (Bachelard supplies the calculus: The well-being recovered in such imaginative work often belongs to the recovery of our cultural "childhood" in the natural world.) A notable instance is "The Orrery." Set in the desert country Lopez had known as a child, it tells of returning to find a man whose "grip seemed sure, as though whatever it was he was doing was as good as one might hope to do." With artful artlessness and liberating discipline this solitary man joins self-sufficient practical arts (baking bread, gardening, even the art of native medicine) with high culture (he plays Bach and Satie on a clavichord). He belongs with the woman in "The Woman Who Had Shells," for she, too, joins the worlds the narrator finds himself between. The narrator says of this conspicuous anima figure, who enables him to imagine that "it was possible to let go of a fundamental anguish," what may also be said of the man: that "we carry such people with us in an imaginary way, proof against some undefined but irrefutable darkness in the world." To this desert father, whose eighteenth-century orrery is the model of the celestial world he has set out in stones on the desert floor, the narrator owes an experience of cosmicity that restores the well-being of childhood. (No prayer rugs here, no sand paintings.) And to him, he owes good counsel. "With enough care," he is told, "almost anything would keep. It was only a matter of choosing what to take care of." And this, in conclusion: "If one is patient, if you are careful, . . . there is probably nothing that cannot be retrieved." (*Retrieved*.)

"The Lover of Words" glosses this fantastic story. In this instance another solitary man, a Mexican gardener in Los Angeles, an autodidact whose self-making is in the chrysalis stage, is destroyed by self-awareness and loss of innocence. The acute account of his anguish and self-destruction is Andersonian and may be read as a critique of individualism, the norm of most of the stories. For Lopez is very much an American writer in seeking to solve within the self the social, cultural, and moral problems that must also be confronted outside the self, concertedly, in community. The gardener's dilemma is also the writer's: It is not enough to appreciate "how words healed" (even now as I write them), the refuge to be found in them.

The character closest to the narrator is Roger Callahan, the anthropologist in the titular story, "Winter Count 1973: Geese, They Flew Over the Storm." Callahan teaches at Nebraska State College and has spent his life studying the Native Americans of the high plains north of the Platte River. Is he intended to call up Loren Eiseley, a Nebraskan who worked this country—and, incidentally, was as skeptical of science as Callahan and expressed the kind of weariness he feels at a professional meeting? ("The Woman Who Had Shells" also calls up Eiseley, his essay "The Star Thrower," where a gratuitous act suggests the dance in Lopez's "Drought." And shells are important for the association with Venus established by the woman who gathers them but no longer keeps them, this goddess-figure to whom the narrator gives the single small shell he had chipped from the ice of an Arctic beach. Consider, then, the significance of Lopez's gathering shells in "The Lives of Seals.")

To anyone who has been to professional meetings the story of Roger Callahan is doubly pointed in not being as parodic as it seems. Such meetings are sometimes extreme situations, as this one is for Callahan, who has not attended for years and feels himself to be marginal if not a Native American clown, wholly outside. It is also extreme for the narrator, a younger man, for whom Callahan's crisis raises the question of whether entering the profession and seeking advancement denies the necessary spirit and so precludes entering another culture. What Kenneth Burke calls the scene/act ratio makes the issue vividly clear: The meeting, in a hotel, is suffocatingly enclosed, an interior world shut off from the weather, the storm that enters the room when Callahan, finally, decisively, opens the window. There is no better resolution of the dilemma of *out* and *in*, which is why the subtitle records it as a winter count. The world is permitted to enter; its wet air fills the lungs; and "in the deepest distance" Callahan hears "the barking-dog sounds of geese, running like horses before a prairie thunderstorm." (In Callahan's winter count this is associated with childhood, with having gone with his father to see the flight of whooping cranes, an experience "crucial in the unfolding of his own life." It is to be associated with the presence of birds in other stories; for example, "the pounding of wings overhead" in "The Woman Who Had Shells.")

"He remembered a friend's poem about a snowy owl dead behind glass in a museum, no more to soar, to hunch and spread his wings and tail and fall silent as moonlight."

Callahan remembers Lafcadio Hearn because he entered another culture and became an informant. The insignia of Callahan's membership is a medicine bundle; the winter counts that punctuate his memory like found material in a poem ("1891 Medicine bundles, police tore them open") have become a living part of his personal history and enable him to defend the dead from professional inquisition. His own paper on winter counts is a defense of personal, even divergent, histories; it exemplifies his belief that history is story, to be told, "unpacked," "unfolded." No longer concerned with theory and proving himself right, he urges the professionals to tell "the story as it was given to you" and to tolerate "the individual view, the poetic view, which is as close to the truth as the consensus."

"His own count would be personal, more personal, as though he were the only one." This story is Lopez's apologia—and serves as well for a generation of writers, who, as Creeley said of Whitman, believe that "the authenticity of the personal" is warrant enough. Lopez claims no expertise. He is only a "writer." Even his reporting is storytelling, always personal, and confirms his belief, expressed by Callahan as the deepest Native American wisdom, that "everything is held together with stories. . . . That is all that is holding us together, stories and compassion."

> "I will tell you something about stories,
>   [he said]
>   They aren't just entertainment.
>   Don't be fooled.
>   They are all we have, you see,
>   all we have to fight off
>   illness and death."
>   —Leslie Silko, *Ceremony*

Remembering (Hannah Arendt). Re-memberment.

1847 White buffalo, Dusk Killed it. This winter count, remembered by Calla-han, confirms the mysterious event told (recounted) in "Buffalo." Method is the issue here, for the disappearance of the great herds of buffalo upon which the Native Americans depended is not in question, but rather the truth of its visionary correlative, the story of white buffalo who ascended a mountain. The Native Americans acknowledge the event but at the time and for most of the nineteenth century are unable to fathom its meaning. White people, at a meet-ing in 1911, remain skeptical of its factual truth and do not recognize its poetic truth—they do not "understand the purpose of such a story." The narrator, whose research begins when he finds factual evidence of buffalo at that unusual height in the *Journal of Mammology* (see vol. 36, p. 470), follows the advice of a Native American to seek another truth. This, of the poetic kind, is, as the Arapaho have come to believe, that the buffalo, reported to have sung a death song, "tried to show them how to climb out through the sky," or, as the nar-rator rephrases it, how "to get away from what was coming."

This puts the deep rationale of Lopez's storytelling, which is made urgent by the ever-presence of myth, shown here by the *fact* that the narrator, who has gone into these mountains, awakes (in a double sense) to find his legs broken.

The concluding story, "The Location of the River," is also about method and may be read as a prolegomenon to *Of Wolves and Men* and *Arctic Dreams*. Like the story of the buffalo, this story involves an unusual event—the disap-pearance of the upper Niobrara River for a period of several months. This is not disputed by Benjamin Foster, a historian who had spent much of his life with Native Americans. Still, it is a phenomenon he tries to verify, first with "tradi-tional methods" (scientific) that fail, then with "less conventional" (Native American) that succeed. After a long vigil, he reads the disappearance of the river in the shapes of the clouds. Nevertheless, as the narrator comments, "This must have been slightly disquieting for Foster living in two worlds as he did . . . thinking what he did not know, could and could not prove."

Methodological doubt comes of being between, and the narrator shares it. To some extent he identifies with Foster, whose biography preoccupies him. Yet he believes that the river never disappeared—that Foster, "troubled by the destruc-tion of native cultures," went mad. On the evidence of Foster's essay, "Studying the Indian," this seems to have been the outcome of having been told that he

"learn[ed] everything wrong." An illustration depicts a fragment of this manuscript with "I got everything wrong," inscribed in Foster's hand, situated between land and cloud-filled sky. It is a cautionary motto for historians, among
them the narrator, who, in turn, finds the flooding Niobrara at night but loses
it in the morning.

Of Wolves and Men belongs to an occasion: Lopez signed a copy for us when
we happened into Prairie Lights Books during his visit to Iowa City. He did this
in a fashion wholly his own, having first established, in conversation, a personal
relationship. He recognized us as attentive listeners at his lecture and reading,
and this facilitated gift exchange. It might be said that this is the way he does
business. The dedication of *Winter Count* is "For Friends, Their Uncommon
Grace"; that of *Crossing Open Ground* acknowledges the men and women with
whom he traveled and worked; and that of *Of Wolves and Men* is "For Wolves,"
in their behalf, an "effort at understanding," and in gratitude for their "company."

The only wolf that I have seen is Lobo, the stuffed animal in a glass cage at the
entrance of Morrell's Trading Post in Bemidji. He is as much a part of the
folklore here as the statues of Paul Bunyan and the Blue Ox in the amusement
park across the street. What I know of wolves I have learned mostly from Farley
Mowat and Lopez and witnessed, at second hand as it were, in the behavior of
two of our dogs, Flash, a female Siberian Husky, and Mukwa (Black Bear), a
male German shepherd–black Labrador, both, incidentally, acquired from Native
Americans, here on Wolf Lake. (Having initially to fend for themselves, they
remain good hunters, whose presence now outside my cabin reminds me of the
skunk they killed on this morning's walk.) My appreciation of the crushing
pressure of a wolf's jaws derives from a recent experience of the 750 pounds
per inch exerted by a German shepherd, an enactment (almost) of the myth of
Fenris and Tyr.

Of Wolves and Men follows *Desert Notes* and the collection of stories about
Coyote. It is Lopez's first "big" book, a work of travel and research (landscape
and library) like *Arctic Dreams*. It brought him recognition and the John Burroughs Medal for natural history writing. It did this, I think, because it exemplifies his belief that "a viable natural philosophy, one that places us again within
the elements of our natural history," may be found in the study of wild animals.
Such study, he says, may draw us back "into an older, more intimate and less

rational association with the local landscape"—it is one of the ways of familiar-ization—and it may prompt us to question the "objectivity" and "troublesome lack of heart" of "Western Science."

An epigraph from John Rodman's "The Dolphin Papers" leads us to discover there another instance of the anti-Cartesianism of recent thought, especially the antitheriophobia that characterizes Lopez's work; and Lopez's work gains power by its concurrence with and contribution to a main current of revisionist think-ing. The epigraph from Rodman, noting the aversion to "a Heraclitan world," names the patron philosopher of many avant-garde poets and philosophers, and with other epigraphs from Henry Beston and Montaigne announces the moral concern that as much as anything is the moving force of Lopez's work.

More than most writers of natural history—or more conspicuously—Lopez is a moralist who has taken to heart Montaigne's remarks on presumption and Bes-ton's belief that animals are not to be "measured by man." He does not so much admonish us as figure his own thought. His moral stance (and stand) is attractive because it does not overlook the claims of (and moralistically deny) what it opposes.

A notable instance is the conclusion of the section on wolf killing in nineteenth-century America, an enormity he likens to a pogrom, even to the Holocaust. Here he recalls the old wolfers he had interviewed and says, "You could not blame these men, at least I could not, for what they had done, as though it had all happened in a vacuum." He does not blame them because *we*, as much as they, had been moved by a complex of motives and actions called Manifest Destiny: "We killed hundreds of thousands of wolves. Sometimes with cause, sometimes with none." This obliges us to do what he has done, "go back and look at the stories we made up when we had no reason to kill"; that is, look to ourselves, to our imaginings, to our psychological projections, to what moves us when we literally have no reason. His natural history has the distinction of including (I borrow an Emersonian title) both the natural history of intellect and the history of intellect, its errors and follies, in its encounter with nature. To recover a more natural, more hospitable and humble relation between self and world is the overriding intent of his work.

(I associate Lopez with Terrence Des Pres. He, too, is a moralist, his *The Survivor: An Anatomy of Life in the Death Camps* one of the essential moral investigations of this generation of writers. *Of Wolves and Men* also treats survival, not only the survival of wolves but of endangered Native Americans whose lifeways involved them. "By 1900," Lopez notes, "there wasn't much point in being either a wolf or an Indian in the United States"—the Indian who might have asked the Great Spirit, "Help me to fit, to be valuable in the world, like the wolf.")

I am not pleased on this rereading as I was initially because I am not as much aware of Lopez's presence (his entry into my life) as I am of youthful earnestness and nostalgia for the primitive. I also notice the popular character of the book and its pedestrian style. Lopez achieves the clarity but not the elegance he seeks, the latter compromised by colloquialism ("you may think I'm pulling your leg"), patronizing identification ("the English philosopher Alfred North Whitehead"), and expositional signal ("I would like to close this chapter . . ."). The data he has collected are simply set out in workmanlike fashion. (The book, he told an interviewer, was written "in longhand," in twenty days, "at the rate of about five thousand words per day.") Where possible he employs anecdotes and stories; accounts of his own experience are few—he tells what he learned by raising two red-wolf pups, and he tells more about his work in the Pierpont Morgan Library than in the field. He admits that he is not "an authority on wolves," and how to incorporate his experience with that of the experts is a fundamental problem better solved in *Arctic Dreams* and *Crossing Open Ground*.

My present reading of Richard Nelson's *Make Prayers to the Raven* undoubtedly contributes to the above criticism. Lopez brought this book to my attention ("a non-Cartesian field guide, grounded in historical research, on lengthy interviews, and the author's own experience") and narrated the TV documentary based on it. Nelson's use of Koyukon oral material and his own journal, set out as "found" material in a collagist way, distinguishes this scientific study, already distinguished by its respect for the ecological wisdom of indigenous natural history. Nelson's journal entries are especially fine, sensitive, and well written—expressive of much that scientific discourse does not admit.

The four-part structure of *Of Wolves and Men* makes the argument of the book. The scientific findings of part 1—Adolf Murie published the first ecological study only as recently as 1944—give us an essentially unbiased but limited view of wolves (their sociality requires the plural) and acquaints us with these remarkable animals, one of the "other nations," Beston says, "caught with ourselves in the net of life and time." It provides objective knowledge, the kind of knowledge we respect, and invites our partisanship by giving us the truths that make us privy, as it were, to the inside narrative.

Part 2 both implements and corrects the (modern) scientific view by juxtaposing to it the ancient "vision" of the Eskimo and other hunting peoples whose life-ways "correspond" with those of wolves. Lopez begins this section of the book by noting the distrust of science already evident in part 1 in his comments on the methodological risk of typicality and unconscious biases of perception ("The male hunter—male leader image of the wolf pack is misleading . . . perpetuated by males, who dominate this field of study"). He would open the closed (assumption-bound) ways of field biologists by introducing them to the open ways and inti-mate knowledge (and oral culture) of hunters. He proposes a participatory mode of scientific study based on the practice of the Nunamiut as well as the kind of widening of concern represented by his own work. "What I am saying is this," he editorializes in a passage I cite also for its style: "We do not know very much at all about animals. . . . to approach them solely in terms of the Western imagination is, really, to deny the animal. It behooves us to visit with a people with whom we share a planet and an interest in wolves but who themselves come from a different time-space and who, as far as we know, are very much closer to the wolf than we will ever be."

Lopez asks biologists to enter the field in the way poets have, responsively, at-tentive to the particulars of each occasion, in intimate relation to the landscape of experience. He would have them hunt for facts in the way peoples whose lives depend upon it hunt for animals. This means that he would have them (and all of us) recognize a metaphysics in which animals and humans do not live in separate realms but have life in common. He talks at the boundaries of the mod-ern and the archaic, and the title of his book, in its double meaning, suggests their collision. For *Of Wolves and Men*, which in its totality is about the many ways men throughout history have viewed wolves, is at heart about the similar ways of wolves and men—those people who live in the same landscape and depend on the same ecology as wolves and, accordingly, have learned from them. Lopez's fundamental assumption is that the social organization of these hunting animals and hunting people is alike. We may question this and still acknowl-edge that he celebrates the primitive because he values social interdependence, the virtues of hard survival, intimacy with the immediate world, and a way of life made sacred, ultimately, by what he calls "the conversation of death."

Parts 1 and 2 set off the enormities described in parts 3 and 4. "The Beast of Waste and Desolation" in the title of part 3 is not the wolf but man himself, who exterminated the wolves of America. Lopez's sense of moral outrage is both explicit and expressed by the data that saturate the exposition, and he thinks we should "answer to ourselves for all this":

> As I have tried to make clear, the motive for wiping out wolves (as opposed to controlling them) proceeded from misunderstanding, from illusions of what constituted sport, from strident attachment to private property, from ignorance and irrational hatred. But the scope, the casual irresponsibility, and the cruelty of wolf killing is something else. I do not think it comes from some base, atavistic urge. . . . I think it is that we simply do not understand our place in the universe and have not the courage to admit it.

In part 4, Lopez searches in history for the imaginary wolf. He focuses on the demonology of the Middle Ages and extends the study of human ferocity. There may be too much about such things as werewolves and the Inquisition, but this serves as a foil for what is of most interest here, Lopez's "alternative gospel." In this gospel, the "new wolf" he claims we are now ready to look for is the wolf-mother, the benevolent wolf, as in the legend of Romulus and Remus, who "nurtures." Lopez does not spell out this essentially feminist insight nor connect it with his own fictive search for the anima. But this good news is the soul of the book. *Of Wolves and Women*, then, for *animal*, in an etymological sense that goes to the root of things, depends on *anima*.

I first read *Arctic Dreams* during the winter of a sabbatical we spent here at the lower edge of the boreal forest, where the frozen expanse of the lake and the subzero weather and the diminished things (the abstraction of that season) provided enough similitude for valuing an earned account of the Arctic world. It was, as much of my reading had become, the pleasure of the evening and the snug warmth of a down comforter, and it soon became the subject of long breakfast conversations before the fire.

Now, even in a summer of extreme heat and drought, I respond to it with as much enthusiasm and with a critical (more exacting and exact) sense of its remarkable achievement. It is one of the best books about landscape I know—of a different kind, say, than Ronald Blythe's *Characters and Their Landscapes*, which comes to mind because it is informed by a similar unassuming disposition (gentleness, as Jim Summerville says of Lopez in a recent letter) and is written with equal clarity and elegance. Here is (a) man *in* the landscape (Paul Shepard's title), who, as Shepard's subtitle has it, appreciates the "Esthetics of Nature" and exemplifies a practice favorable to it. Favorable to it, and in favor of it, because *aesthetics* in his understanding, as in Aldo Leopold's, refers to the beauty and harmony of the world realized by us in an ecological awareness of its interrelationships and interdependencies and in recognition of its ultimate mysterious reality. *Aesthetics*, which hitherto involved the visual appreciation of nature (or Nature), the spectatorial viewing of its scenery, is now a cover-word for depth of ecological understanding, for "living as if nature mattered," to cite the subtitle of *Deep Ecology*, by Bill Devall and George Sessions, which appeared before the publication of *Arctic Dreams* and, accordingly, does not list Lopez in its bibliography. From the writers listed there—among them, Leopold, Berry, and Snyder—we have been learning what it means to have a living world and *to world*, to live within its complex web. To live as the animals, plants, and native people of the Arctic have done in order to survive. For the Arctic, the vast panorama of challenging landscapes in Lopez's account, dramatizes urgent global problems and conflicts of ideas. The simplest formulation—too melodramatic perhaps, insisting too much on good versus evil—puts *ecos*, in its wide and deep understanding, against *econ*, the narrow determination on utility and development with which it is often confused.

Arctic Dreams treats the desire to live with(in) the *ecos* and give over its exploitation, the desire, in a word, to resanctify life. It is the work of a master, where *Of Wolves and Men* is the work of an apprentice, work of the order of a doctoral dissertation. *Of Wolves and Men* is also indebted to the Arctic and—this holds for most "serious" writers—comes from the same generative center. In the chapter entitled "Migrations" in *Arctic Dreams*, Lopez tells of having observed wolves on Ilingnorak Ridge and of having thought much about hunting. He says that eventually he came to experience this primary human activity and understand it better as a "dialogue" with the land. This is to say, as Buber's word for what occurs *between* tells us, that he recognized that the Eskimo hunters had an I-Thou relationship with the landscape, a relationship of utmost eco-moral significance, and that this primitive subsistence lifeway challenged the I-It relationship, the objectification and depersonalization, that characterizes modern Western culture. For Lopez, as for Richard Nelson, the native hunters of the North possess a deep ecological understanding. Ecology is their preeminent science as well as theology—a *paideia* transmitted by story.

The recovery of the primitive is central for Lopez because it involves the being-in-the-world to which he aspires, the worlding that puts an end to world alienation. He would like to be "fully *incorporated* into the landscape"—I italicize to stress the bodily as well as communal nature of having "the land around you like clothing." The sacrality and sociality of hunting move him, the moral discipline imposed by the first ("most men understood how to behave") as well as the shared endeavor of the second ("in no hunting society could a man hunt successfully alone"). He admires the ability to closely attend the always shifting patterns of *what is*—"a frame of mind that redefines patience, endurance, and expectation"—and the fear that acknowledges ignorance of "perfect harmony" and contributes to *nuannaarpog*, the "quality . . . of taking extravagant pleasure in being alive." In sum, he values the "*struggle* . . . to live with dignity and understanding, with perspicacity or grace." The Eskimo hunters, he says, "know something about surviving" and, he adds, "they are a good people to know . . . facing as we do our various Armageddons."

Survival. This is the ecological measure of success, and learning to live in harsh environments, as both the animals and humans he describes have done, teaches us to respect an adaptiveness of incomprehensible complexity and defines a kind of heroism (of sufficiency) we seldom consider. There are many accounts of heroism in *Arctic Dreams* (discovery and exploration necessarily involve this), but none seems so much to the point as the brief story of an Eskimo. We appreciate the story of Comock's competence (the pragmatism of *what is*) just as we recognize the often arrogant ignorance of explorers because Lopez has already given us a scientifically grounded sense of Arctic landscapes (eco-scapes), a strategy like that of *Of Wolves and Men*, where knowledge precedes lore. Faced with starvation, Comock and his family undertook a journey over sea ice to an island, and on the way, when the ice opened beneath their camp, they lost most of their possessions. With what remained, Comock "reconstructed his entire material culture, almost from scratch, by improvising and, where necessary, inventing." For Lopez, this is not the story of an Eskimo Robinson Crusoe but a parable of "people who lived resolutely in the heart of every moment they found themselves in, disastrous and sublime." *And who survived*: "He survived. His family survived. His dogs survived and multiplied."

In reading *Make Prayers to the Raven*, I noted by way of summary that to live in the world you have to get your living there. This is why a market economy jeopardizes the subsistence lifeway of Eskimos and why most of us are beyond the possibility of recovering a primitive (primary) way of being. Lopez admits this in the epilogue, where he tells of participating in a walrus hunt and of "brood[ing] about hunting" and the paradox of life sustained by death ("the horror inherent in all life"). He understands how a sacral sense of life allows one to live with this contradiction and how "making your life a worthy expression of a leaning into the light" may help one do this. Even so, the butchery and blood on the snow trouble him. He himself is not a hunter, and he does not know how to bridge the "gap [in lifeways] between civilized man [estranged from the land] and the society of the hunter." He can do only what he does in this book—use imagination to transform desire—and, in the end, he can only (literally) bow to the landscape, to whose smaller mysteries of living things it has become his habit to pay respect. Like the man who dances with the herons, his is a "gesture of reverence." I borrow Richard Nelson's term, used by him in speaking of the Koyukon Indians: "Because spiritual power is everywhere in nature, gestures of reverence are nearly constant as people interact with their environment, as they carry out the necessary activities of subsistence and survival." *Arctic Dreams* is such a dance, the action Lopez takes because he knows what the dancer in the story knew, "that without such an act of self-assertion no act of humility had meaning."

Perhaps it is inevitable that hunting, as with Ortega, becomes a metaphor that enables Lopez to speak of the requisite alertness of another kind of experience, that represented by the arduous tracking of (and in) the landscapes of this book. "By hunting," Lopez says, "I simply mean being out on the land." This also means—and not so simply, for the discipline is demanding—having a "state of mind" or stance (to use Olson's word) that allows us to be receptive to and engage in conversation with the land.

Conversation with the land. Lopez acquired this phrase from Maurice Haycock, a Canadian landscape painter associated with the Group of Seven. Haycock used the phrase to describe his work of painting the subtleties of the land and air of Cornwallis Island—subtleties that Lopez also attends throughout his book and especially in the chapter "Ice and Light." A painter in the Arctic (not Rockwell Kent, whose stance was heroic and whose "imagination worked against [the land]"), Haycock, found by Lopez among the scientists of a research station, is one of the grandfathers. He is one of "the estimable rather than famous people," someone whose previous work as a geologist increases rather than cancels his appreciation of the aesthetics of nature. His singular presence among scientists, who for the most part are on Cornwallis Island as the advance guard of development, points up what is lacking in our "swift and efficient possession of places"; and the fact that Lopez treats him in relation to the Luminist painters, who, like the Group of Seven, were not especially indebted to European tradition, suggests the extent to which "leaning into the light" may be learned in encounters with American landscapes. ("The European culture from which the ancestors of many of us came has yet to make this turn ["of unknown meaning before coming home"]. . . . It has yet to understand the wisdom, preserved in North America, that lies in the richness [not riches] and sanctity of a wild landscape.") Haycock, then, is the kind of hero Lopez wishes to become, the kind of hero proposed by his own conversation with the land. At the end of the book, where he speaks of landscapes as "crucibles of mystery," he says that they "are not solely arenas for human invention": "To have no elevated conversation with the land, no sense of reciprocity with it . . . shows a certain lack of courage, too strong a preference for human devising." The hero stands with the land; his "especial province," as Olson said of the Sumerian kings, "is the guardianship of the earth."

I have often thought of Olson when reading *Arctic Dreams* because he is a preeminent poet of landscape (he, too, admired the Luminists and leans into the light in *Maximus* III) and because the stance he defines in "Projective Verse" is essentially the stance Lopez has adopted. Olson pushes harder than Lopez, is didactic and dogmatic and sometimes bellicose—and more explicit in his attack on Western culture (the tradition of philosophical idealism), the threat of which he especially felt after World War II in the Old World's attempt to retain hegemony. But his project, the work now of two generations of poets, is also Lopez's, not derived directly from Olson but from sources and concerns common to both. And, for all of his disclaimer, Lopez is a poet because of his care for language and his subscription to the shamanic role (the communal, healing art) set out in ethnopoetics.

Olson's fundamental demand, like Lopez's, is personal: that we yield the ego (the agent of heroism) in obedience to something larger than self, that we give over the "will to power" that moves us to possess things instead of living openly and responsively (and responsibly) with them. Olson presents this radically new (and archaic) stance in the figure of Maximus, who comes home to the landscape of Gloucester, his native place, by carefully and closely attending the particular things that compose it and by the equally necessary searching out of its past, the history of its geology, discovery, and settlement. Lopez does comparable work in *Arctic Dreams*, where the use of personal experience to frame each chapter is the significant literary advance on *Of Wolves and Men* and the propriety of its management a measure of his achievement. He speaks not of himself but of a narrator who is "a refinement of something that's inside of me that I found useful technically"—useful, clearly, in moderating the "enormous act of ego" always involved in writing. Yet, even though he claims that the narrator is "the number two guy . . . [and] never intrude[s] on the reader's ability to enter the environment," Lopez himself is present and his way of entering the environment is a notable and instructive aspect of the book. He enacts the way to perceive about which he also writes—has *humilitas*, "an humilitas sufficient," as Olson says, "to make him of use."

Lopez travels the vast spaces of the Arctic by ship, airplane, truck, and snow machine, but he relates to the landscape, as nature writers always have, by walking. (Is there any other way to approach a plover's nest to see the eggs glowing "with a soft, pure light, like the window light in a Vermeer painting"?) He is, as Olson said of himself, a walker (from "the last walking period of man") for whom walking is a mode of attention and meditation, a participant activity in which outer and inner come together. "The Country of the Mind" may be the most abstract chapter, as he claims, but it is also the most personal, half of it devoted to a walk on Pingok Island. This "circumambulation," to borrow again from Olson, is a winter's walk, like Thoreau's excursion, and serves as the representative anecdote of Lopez's proceeding. And it has instructions for ours.

"The Country of the Mind"—the chapter title itself is a metaphor for the metaphoric relationship of the terms contained in it, and much of the chapter is devoted to fundamental categories, that is, to how we imagine time and space. The issue for Lopez is not metaphor itself but the way in which we use it to privilege the mind and give it sovereignty over things. Yet metaphor in our literary tradition is, as Stephen Owen argues in *Traditional Chinese Poetry and Poetics*, a "substitution trope" in which one term displaces another, that is, in which the world is displaced by mind; we have not been prepared by "Western theories of literature" (derived from Plato) to read poems, as the Chinese have, as "omens of the world." Metaphor, for us, seems inescapable: "Man is an analogist," Emerson says in the chapter entitled "Language" in *Nature*, and cannot "be understood without these objects, nor these objects without [him]." Lopez acknowledges the incredible power of the mind by employing *imagina-*

tion, the arch-Romantic word, in the subtitle and by describing the imaginings (and their often disastrous consequences) of the many explorers who, it may be said, tested themselves in this Romantic way against the ice. Closer to his own experience—cautionary—is what he says of the artist's exploration: "Relationships with the land that are intensely metaphorical, like [Rockwell] Kent's, are a lofty achievement of the human mind . . . a sophisticated response, like the creation of maps. . . . The mind can imagine beauty and conjure intimacy. It can find solace where literal analysis finds only trees and rocks and grass."

That this projective power may be anthropomorphic does not trouble him. Anthropomorphism, a "very old human tradition," is not *sophisticated*; it respects mystery, has none of the arrogation conveyed by *intensely* and *lofty*, and does not mislead us in the way mistaking the map for the territory does. For the risk, he knows, is in "finding our final authority in the metaphor rather than in the land," in imposing "mental maps" (and two-dimensional grids) on a landscape that others, the Eskimos, experience in three dimensions and know as a "country of the mind": "the landscape evident to the senses, as it is retained in human memory and arises in the oral tradition . . . as a repository of mythological and 'real-time' history." Where "mental maps" are abstract, the "country of the mind" is particular, belonging to the local culture, depicting its reality in the way its language does. For this understanding of language and culture, Lopez, like Olson, turns to Benjamin Whorf but reads him differently. He claims that, for Whorf, language is created by man and imposed on the landscape, instead, as Lopez would have it, of evolving from a conversation with the land.

Whatever the truth (I don't have my Whorf here), the point, as with metaphor, is clear: Imposition must yield to "gentle interrogations" and conversation; to I-Thou. The Eskimos with whom Lopez talks about their land claims wonder at the men who make land-use surveys, "the men who owned the maps"—wonder at their indifference to the corroborative details of Eskimo history. This disregard of what native people know is what *Arctic Dreams* redresses at a time when what they know about "a good way of life is disintegrating" and "the sophisticated, ironic voice of civilization insists that their insights are only trivial."

Lopez's narrative art is a practice of *humilitas*. He speaks, in an interview, of cultivating "a sense of yourself as the one who doesn't know"—and he presents himself as an inquirer, never as an expert. He usually thinks of *expert* in respect to scientists and always associates the word with authority. (His own authority is moral, the result of the "shaman-light" of his storytelling, and his expertise is that of an artist who is not as deferential as he was in *Of Wolves and Men* to the scientists whose findings he now uses to compose a more inclusive ecology of the Arctic world.) The authority, he says, "will always be with the subject," in this instance, the largest subject, the landscape itself.

Lopez's conversation with the land begins with three progressively larger essays. In these prefatorial installments Lopez situates himself (and us) and establishes the themes of this well-orchestrated book. I think of chapter 1 ("Arktikós") as prefatory because, with the preface and the prologue, it does the initial work of familiarization. It gets us beyond Greek myth and the notions of early European culture and alters as well our temperate-zone perspective. By following the sun's course through the tropical, temperate, and boreal zones we learn about three major ecosystems, how each adapts to the solar radiation on which all life depends; and we come to appreciate the light that for Lopez is the primary phenomenon, a wonderful fact that flowers into a wonderful truth. (The essentials of the phrase are Thoreau's for the attending that eventuates in wonder.) This solar journey brings us to "the final landscape," a realm of two seasons, of limited flora and fauna, of little diversity and stability.

Because it is "inherently vulnerable," the Arctic (also a last frontier) serves admirably the purposes of eco-fable. The significance of the central episode of the prologue—the destruction of the ecosystem and the native people in the nineteenth century by the whalers at Pond's Bay—is now footnoted in regard to the "stress" brought about by industrial and other developments: "Arctic animals are apparently unable to tolerate both the inherent stress to which, in an evolutionary sense, they are accustomed and new stresses of man-made origin—oil blowouts, pollution from mine tailings, noise from Arctic shipping, and the unnatural patterns of sea-ice disruption associated with icebreakers." Since the stability and well-being of the *ecos* is the standard, economic development is an "intrusion" and the Eskimos, who think of us as "the people who change nature," become the guardians of the *ecos*. They have the wisdom of restraint—*restraint*, one of the most important moral qualities that Lopez thinks we can acquire in a search for the primitive.

In the first half of the book, Lopez treats animals in the spirit of his own counsel: "To try to understand the animal apart from its background . . . is to risk the collapse of both." Musk-oxen, polar bear, and narwhal—he considers each of these large animals in terms of a different place, a different *ecos*, and all of them, like the Eskimos who hunt them, are truly wonderful examples of adaptation and survival, both animals and people threatened now by economic development. Each chapter is a smaller but equally rich *Of Wolves and Men* and fulfills the literary task, proposed by Neruda, of taking animals off the shelf and bringing them to life. And bringing us "off the edge [of the land], into the ice and sea," where "Migrations," the culminating chapter in this sequence, puts us into the air with the birds as well as into the sea with the fish and marine animals. Brilliantly, in surging prose, Lopez gives us an entire *ecos* in motion over geologic time, an intricate dance to the rhythms of life in all the spaces of the Arctic world, searching always for new niches. (Darwin's "tangled bank," though in this adventurous book the Darwin of *The Voyage of the Beagle* more often comes to mind.)

"Migrations" also gathers earlier thought into a meditation on hunting that establishes the norm of primitive lifeways and makes the transition to the other imaginations and desires (the Western human presence) treated in the rest of the book. Here, as Lopez says, "I deal with ice, with icebergs and the behavior of sea ice; with the behavior of light—arctic sunlight, cathedral architecture, landscape painting, and so on. . . . I deal with how mind imagines place, and time and space . . . [and] with history—who went up there, why they went, and what they were looking for. I . . . show historically what conceptions of time and space have done to *our culture*" (my italics).

Neither his summary nor my previous use does justice to these remarkably rich and learned chapters. Much of what is canvassed here is the historical analogue of present exploitation—set off, it should be noted, by the fullest descriptions of the sublimity of Arctic ice and light, the fearful beauty of "the floor of creation." I have stressed economic developments, but Lopez doesn't; in his narrative they are a subtext. His accounts of traveling with scientists does not belabor this aspect of their work, and only briefly, and in this instance in the manner of the new journalism, does he report on industrial development.

What he writes of two excursions, one by truck and one by air, to the oil fields at Prudhoe Bay follows immediately on an extensive treatment of early polar exploration in which he points out that our ideas do not necessarily fit the land and that the land cannot be possessed, only manipulated by technology. So the road to Prudhoe Bay and the pipeline it parallels are manicured, the roadside planted to blue grass—the road that Leopold knew divided and conquered the wilderness and Benton MacKaye said was the spearhead of the metropolitan invasion of the indigenous environment.

At Prudhoe Bay the road (the way to wealth) ends, Lopez says, in a "landscape more austere than any I had ever seen in the Arctic." It has been made so by "muscular equipment" and "muscular engineering," the former "sitting idle like . . . [clenched] fists in [the] oil-stained yards" near a wretched bungalow camp of desperate workers, the latter part of the immaculate and luxurious controlled environment of the well-secured base of operations. He thinks of Cape Canaveral, and the revulsion expressed by leaden prose and what he says of lack of dignity ("Without dignity . . . people are powerless . . . you can direct any scheme you wish against them") remind me of concentration camps, though he is reminded of state prisons and "factory life in America, [the] ugly way the country has arranged itself." He notes the colonial sensibility and economic vocabulary of the supervisors, and he is disturbed most by the misogyny of an all-male society, by men who think of women and treat them in the brutal way they treat the land. (They are not likely to see, as he does, an "image of vulnerability" in the genitalia of a female polar bear.) To their "what else is it good for?" his book answers, and he writes it as much to save them (us) as the native people and land their (our) technology "mangles."

Not Prudhoe Bay but what follows—the exalted sense of beauty he experiences at Axel Heiberg Island—is the Northern Passage and homecoming he seeks. This prompts him to say:

> In approaching the land with an attitude of obligation, willing to observe courtesies difficult to articulate—perhaps only a gesture of the hands—one establishes a regard from which dignity can emerge. From that dignified relationship with the land, it is possible to imagine an extension of dignified relationships throughout one's life. Each relationship is formed of the same integrity, which makes the mind say: the things in the land fit together perfectly, even though they are always changing. I wish the order of my life to be arranged in the same way I find the light, the slight movement of the wind, the voice of a bird, the heading of a seed pod I see before me. This impeccable and indisputable integrity I want in myself.
>
> One of the oldest dreams of mankind is to find a dignity that might include all living things. And one of the greatest of human longings must be to bring

such dignity to one's own dreams, for each to find his or her own life exemplary in some way. . . . A way to do this is to pay attention to what occurs in a land not touched by human schemes, where an original order prevails.

The moral exploration of this original order ("the pattern that we call God," to recall Laurens van der Post's phrase) and the love of light ("the *relationship* between God and man was light," he says in discussing cathedral architecture)—these seem to me to warrant thinking of Lopez as a legatee of the transcendentalists. To subscribe to the original order of nature is to accept, as they did, the organic mandate and to think of relationship as light—Emerson spoke of "ray[s] of relation"—is to grant ecology the depth that allows for "numinous events" and, as Lopez says of the Arctic ecosystem, "a forgiving benediction of light." The question that he asks now and answers in revisionist terms in *Arctic Dreams* was once asked and answered by the transcendentalists: "What does the nature of the heroic become, once the landscape is threatened?"

Beston

Coming Home to the World

ANOTHER JOURNAL FOR HENRY BESTON

I imagine them always sitting opposite each other at the ends of the large table in the farm kitchen, each of them writing, as professional writers of their time were said to do, the daily portion of well-made sentences. I do not know how they financed the sometimes fashionable and always comfortable life at Chimney Farm (near Nobleboro, Maine), sent their daughters to private schools, and often spent the cruel winter elsewhere in the sun. But they were gentry, and, again, they were professional writers and wrote a lot, maybe as many as forty books between them. I gauge their success in this tough trade from the fact that the small college library near our woods has twenty books by Elizabeth Coatsworth Beston and six books by Henry Beston. These disproportionately large holdings are to be explained perhaps by their usefulness in courses in children's literature. Two of the books for which Henry Beston is known are exceptions, *The Outermost House*, acquired, in time, as a minor classic (the library has yet to fill out its collection of Thoreau), and *The St. Lawrence*, probably acquired with other volumes in the popular series on "The Rivers of America," edited by Stephen Vincent Benét and Carl Carmer, their roster of writers notable for the number of established authors and the paucity of bona fide naturalists.

Even Henry Beston thought of himself as only a "writer-naturalist." This is exactly right because his career as a writer turned on the realization, noted in the inscription in *The Outermost House*, that "La Nature, voilà mon pays." This dedication, in French, is also exactly right, of the essence, because Ste. Catherine-sous-Rivière, known in boyhood, was "the first place," he said, "in which I encountered and knew and loved the earth"—*earth*, which more often than not replaces *Nature* in his lexicon.

"The Rivers of America," incidentally, was a project initiated by Constance Lindsay Skinner to keep good writers at gainful work during the Depression and to foster the "American celebration." These books often compensate for the photodocumentaries of that time, those visual indictments of a failed society. The practiced prose, as skilled as the photographers' image making, nostalgically, elegiacally revisits the Nature of the "old America," "Nature's Nation." Nature writing is put to the uses of civil history and not, as with Thoreau in his river(s) book, uncivil history. This is the conservative company to which Henry Beston belongs.

His generation of writers—and his social class—experienced the status revolution of the late nineteenth and early twentieth centuries and wrote about Nature (it was still *Nature*) just as Eliot and Pound wrote about Civilization and Culture, from the perspective of dispossession, in regard to what they felt had been lost in the swift course of modern history: an America that for them had been home, had been stable and solid. Henry Beston's houses belong to this landscape. The change they center and celebrate is of the natural and cyclical, not the social and linear (historical) kind. Beston thinks of his outermost house on the beach as a *house*, not a cottage or a shack; and the old farmhouse in Maine belongs more to a permanent rural eighteenth than to the accelerating urban twentieth century ("the age . . . humming like a dynamo," he says in *American Memory*, a reminiscential anthology published in 1937). *Northern Farm* may be said to work out the implications of its initial refrain: "Home. Going home." And *American Memory* and *The St. Lawrence* may be said to allow him to identify his dispossession with that of the earliest dispossessed, the Indians, and, imaginatively, to recover a sense of the oldest America, "the old, dark, Red Indian land." The past, he believed, was a "first and intenser world," and now we live in a fallen world, nothing quite as good as it was before the Industrial Revolution.

Having been dispossessed of "America" so many times, it is no wonder that the Republic, as Edmund Wilson said, has had to be saved again and again. This has been an essential task of our literature and now, more urgently, of nature writing.

Emerson: "In the woods, we return to reason and faith."

Like many New England writers before him, Henry Beston belonged to the comfortable classes and had the best (if not the very best: Irish descent, Catholic religion) credentials. Born in 1888 in Quincy, Massachusetts, with the boon, as he said, of "a New England boyhood of sea and shore," he attended Adams Academy and Harvard University (B.A., 1909; M.A., 1911) and began to publish in the *Atlantic Monthly* in 1916, when his first book, *A Volunteer Poilu*, was also issued by Houghton Mifflin. (No little magazines or small presses for him.) At Harvard, T. S. Eliot was a contemporary, and Van Wyck Brooks (who included Beston in his *A New England Reader*) preceded him there by a few years. In some ways Beston's best work, admitting both the ancient springs and the American place, is an amalgam of elements of their work, with more concern than either for the immediate world he inhabited and to be distinguished from theirs by his profound subscription to Nature. He is, of course, the outstanding nature writer of that impressive literary generation, a generation whose war experience he shared by having seen active duty with the American Field Service in France. He speaks of "the long, murderous years," and the restlessness that frequently followed them may account for his probation as a "mere journalist," his characterization of the considerable work he had done (six books, numerous articles in national magazines, the editing of *Living Age*) before he found his vocation and message in the vision quest of *The Outermost House*.

Like another journalist and editor, the writer-naturalist had, as Emerson said of Whitman, a "long foreground." Like Thoreau, with whom he had difficulty in acknowledging filiation, he experienced the moratorium Erik Erikson attributes to an identity crisis. Henry Beston Sheahan wrote under three names, Henry Sheahan, Henry B. Beston, and Henry Beston, the last adopted in 1924; and like Thoreau, who also renamed himself, he tried a solitary life *in* Nature: He went to the ocean in 1926, and not to a pond, for the ocean, after all, was his childhood place, in order to undergo the crisis of his life, his "moulting season," as Thoreau would have it. *The Outermost House*, ostensibly so little concerned with self and notable for the absence of ego, was for the writer—and remains for the close reader, thereby partially explaining the "persistent life" in print remarked by Winfield Townley Scott—a book of radical self-transformation and rebirth: It tells of initiation and emergence. Beston does not insist on this; by not allowing fact to become symbol, he subdues this, and only the striking, because anomalous, image of the swimmer, called as it were from his own depths, announces the advent.

Robert Finch, in the introduction to the most recent edition, finds *The Outermost House* "a young man's book . . . full of a sense of discovery and self-discovery," and for him, as for Winfield Townley Scott (and for me), it recalls *Walden* more than *Cape Cod*. Scott, whose "A Journal for Henry Beston" is the only study to consider all of Beston's significant work, speaks of the book as "an escape to freedom," as an "anti-domestic" book especially compelling to men. It may be both of these things, and yet the man who wrote it was in his late thirties and had staked more than vocation—though perhaps he wisely saw it as a condition of fruitful vocation—on writing it. Finch reports Elizabeth Coatsworth's (apocryphal?) ultimatum: "No book, no marriage." But in the foreword to *Especially Maine: The Natural World of Henry Beston from Cape Cod to the St. Lawrence*, Elizabeth Coatsworth simply notes that "after *The Outermost House* was published . . . Henry and I were married." In any case, as the title of her indispensable reader attests, her life with Henry, especially in Maine, mattered most to her. She gives the largest part of the reader to *Northern Farm*, the "*companion* piece" to *The Outermost House*, as Scott says (the italics are mine), "the domestic orchestration of [its] themes"; and while she acknowledges his "classic" book and the honors it brought him, her brief, introductory selection from it omits the penultimate passage describing the naked young man emerging, again and again, as he braves the waves and Beston's explanation of the pleasure witnessing this gives him. Did a young man actually emerge from the sea, and if he did, did she find his emergence questionable? Did she see this as someone with a fin de siècle sensibility might see it? Or read it as a breach of taste and privacy? Before he was married, Beston wrote to Scott about the primacy of sex: "Aphrodite rising from the woods to take an intelligence test! Sex, of course, and nothing but." Nothing but: The slip of the pen admits as much.

A passage of such resonance invites several readings, all of them probably of considerable truth. But it is enough to take Beston at his word: "All my life it has given me pleasure to see beautiful human beings." It is enough to recall his pleasure in physical work and approval of the shirtless men in the hayfields, mentioned in telling Dr. Luther Neff that he had "always liked physical man held up against Nature, and busy at the work of man and Nature," and to remember that when he writes about "living by the body," he is generalizing his appreciation of Lawrence, the young farmhand who, according to Elizabeth, "had become a part of Henry." It is not so much that Nature is eroticized as that it has become an erotic realm of permissible freedom. Like the lyric poem, in Stephen Owen's account of it in *Mi-Lou: Poetry and the Labyrinth of Desire*, going to Nature may be said to break the shield-line and permit us to stray; and later, when domesticated, it may permit us to live happily because we have attained that level of being.

(I prefer to remember the Beston, probably shirtless, who wrote that there was no farm work he enjoyed more than haying on a "blazing day" rather than the "spiffy dresser" who noticed clothes and cut off and saved the buttons of the rotted navy jumper he found on the beach.)

Beston extols the physical, especially the freedom of the body out-of-doors, as the natural cure for the unprecedented alienation (and "thin blood") produced by modern civilization, and all of his work proposes, he said, not a "return to nature" but a "return to a poetic relation to nature." This, he believed, an "earth life," especially a life connected to the past and the oldest mysteries, restores. Nature, for him, vouchsafes the body, and the "animal faith" we need returns when we again become "creature[s] of earth." The physical, then, is essential, an aspect of what Heidegger calls "dwelling," for it not only removes the palaver from one's style, as Thoreau said, but opens the way to being. (We have to be in the world to have our being there.) "He who possesses rhythm possesses the universe," Charles Olson believed, and for the profoundest reason, that "all nature," as Beston concluded in *The St. Lawrence*, "be motion in its secret essence." (This is a corollary of the concluding truth of *The Outermost House*: "The creation is still going on. . . . *Creation is here and now.*") Beston's style inscribes this truth and is one measure of his superiority as a nature writer. Another, noted by Donald Federman, is the realization, necessary to his stance and style, that nature predicates itself, that "nature's rhythms are not given significance by the mind; rather the mind is given significance when it . . .

accord[s] with the pulse of nature's rhythms." Before Leopold asked us to be ethical in regard to nature, Beston reminded us that "grim arrangements" notwithstanding, nature's economy (ecology) "has an ethic of its own." In a famous passage in *The Outermost House*, he said that "the animal shall not be measured by man . . . [that] animals are not brethren . . . [but] other nations," meaning, I think, that we should keep the respectful distance he does in his participation in nature.

Haying calls up Tolstoy, but Beston is not much concerned with social relations (so congenial in Nobleboro), just natural relations, and with aesthetic-moral matters that, for me, echo Horatio Greenough of an earlier New England generation and D. H. Lawrence so prominent in Beston's own. When Greenough tells of "gaz[ing] with joy on the naked Apollo" and glorifies "the human frame, the most beautiful organization of earth," we must indeed change our lives, for the correlative moral injunction (a touchstone of the organic mandate of our literature) is: "That which the human being was made to bear, the human being was not made to bear the want of." With Lawrence, the spokesperson of a generation that was overwhelmed by the rediscovery of sex, the mandate is simply more explicit. Beston, to be sure, shares more than this with Lawrence—anti-intellectualism and hostility to modern industrial civilization, earth and even blood, if not their cult—and joins him most, as he does Greenough, in finding in Nature the ground of an instinctual critique of civilization. The highminded and genteel ways in which Beston mounts his critique belong to his generation and largely explain the ready reception of his work (Pessoa: "No age transmits its sensibility to the next"); but the critique itself, still of great importance to us, is sufficient reason for his popularity.

This means, among other things, that Beston should figure for us as a writer of several books, not just *The Outermost House*. There is no better introduction to Beston's "natural world" than Elizabeth Beston's *Especially Maine* (naming the center of his New England region). Not only does it gather much that is choice from his best work (*The Outermost House, Herbs and the Earth, Northern Farm*, and *The St. Lawrence*), it makes available letters, poems, journal entries, photographs, and tokens of other books, the introduction to *White Pine and Blue Water: A State of Maine Reader*, and some commentary from *American Memory* (recently adapted as prose poems by Rosmarie Waldrop). This book, of course, has special authority and is valuable for its biographical details and, even more, for what Elizabeth Beston selects from these books, thereby reconstituting them to portray her husband. All told, her editing adds another book to Henry's lifework. They had collaborated before on children's books and once by writing companion books (*Northern Farm* and *Country Neighborhood*), but this memorial is the great collaboration.

Her selections warrant study, for her Henry, set pieces of nature writing aside, is more often than not an eloquent propounder of moralities on the many causes of and the single cure for alienation. True enough: He doesn't have many themes or sound many notes, and when he is high-minded he thinks in the melodramatic way endorsed by the more combative Van Wyck Brooks. What he says—the eloquence, too—may now seem parochial, having both the advantages and the disadvantages of a marginal life. He, too, is alienated, not *by* but *from* cities and has his being outside of modern life. Deeply troubled as he was by World War II (he wrote a condemnation of the atom bomb for the *Catholic Worker*), his vision is not tragic because it opposes rather than includes the dark. Still, for someone like me who is presently living at the margins, every detail of what he reports is significant and his sense of elemental nature and "the ritual of the burning year" is, as Aldo Leopold said of what he found on his worn-out acres, a "great possession."

Beston starts with the sun, as Lawrence said we should. He sums up the "full circle" of his solitary year on the Great Beach with the declarative certainty of accomplishment: "I had seen the ritual of the sun; I had shared the elemental world." In his work the solar round is the most important figure as it is surely the most important aspect of the natural process. "The adventure of the sun," he says early in *The Outermost House* (glossing the title by speaking there of "outer nature"), "is the great natural drama by which we live." *In which he lived*, he might have said. For he had the "joy in it and the awe of it" (he experienced the sublime) and, pagan at heart (from the Latin *paganus*, country-dweller), ever afterward gladly followed the footsteps of "the journeying god." He did this, it should be noted, week by week, more closely and ceremonially and communally, in *Northern Farm* (1948), and this later experience of the "noble [Nobleboro] ritual of the burning year," summary of a long-established life, is the perspective, provided by the 1949 preface to *The Outermost House*, in which he asks us to read it.

Where *The Outermost House* follows the pattern of withdrawal from and return to civilization, *Northern Farm* merely evokes it, making withdrawal from the city and the suburbs an action happily completed by return to the farm, the *sedes*, the seat of a good and settled life. In Beston's beginning, it might be said, was his end. All of his work is a homecoming. And Eliot's words in "East Coker," especially those in part 5, where he takes account of "the years of *l'entre deux guerres*," are very much to the point:

> There is only the fight to recover what has been lost
> And found and lost again and again: and now, under conditions
> That seem unpropitious . . .

In rereading *The Outermost House* in 1949, Beston said that he saw in it "the meditative perception of the relation of 'Nature' (and I include the whole cosmic picture in this term) to the human spirit." Again the perspective is from the end and makes known his distinction: He is a poet of cosmos who, like Whitman (already in his work in the image of the swimmer, the "me myself"), finds cosmic space not hostile but intimate, and who, like Muir, is exhilarated by the elemental life. *Elemental life*: an open unprotected life, restoring the "birthright of physical sensation"; life in *the* elements—earth (soils, sands), air (wind, clouds, rain, snow), fire (sun, stars), and water (waves). These, and their motions, are what he is chiefly concerned to attend and describe. He is a good but not the closest observer of fauna and flora (herbs excepted). He says that "one may stand at the breakers' edge and study a whole world in one's hand," but he doesn't study this world as attentively and thoroughly as Rachel Carson in *The Edge of the Sea*. Even so, Beston arrives at the same ecstatic conclusion: that life unremittingly seeks favoring niches and is ever-creating—"Urge and urge and urge," Whitman enacts its wave-erotic rhythm, "Always the procreant urge of the world." A naturalist of life's urgencies, with Beston, as Whitman said of himself, "You . . . shall possess the good of the earth and sun."

Participating in this elemental cosmic world allowed Beston to enter the precincts of *mystery* and *poetry* (cognate words, obsessive with him, used allusively, terministically) and to be in Nature, with yet distanced from the "other nations." Houses (and earth) were essential to this and to his sense of cosmicity (well-being) because the security they provided allowed him to adventure in the spaces of the sea and the sky. In his work, the *domestic* and the *antidomestic* (Scott's terms, critically popular in the 1950s, refined later by William Spengemann's study of the poetics of domesticity and adventure)—these terms go together, are polarities. *The Outermost House*: The title, like *Walden*, is a constitutive metaphor. But because of its ambivalence it is also, as Bachelard teaches us, a primary poetic image inviting the deepest reverie. The house, associated with shelter and security, stood on the "wild, houseless outer shore," as he describes this place of "Nature in the elemental mood" in "The Wardens of Cape Cod," an article he wrote in 1923; it faced the "most *masculine* of seas" (my italics). Yet because it is outermost it may also be taken to be the very fearful cosmos that it literally domesticates. At the same time, by calling the outermost house the "Fo'castle," Beston unsettles it, puts it to sea. (And what of "the dialectics of outside and inside" that involves ontological questions of alienation, being and nonbeing? Bachelard asks, "Is he who opens a door and he who closes it the same being?")

The title of the French edition also invites reverie, perhaps of another kind: *Une Maison au bout du monde* (A house at the end of the world). "These sands," Beston says at the outset, "might be the end or the beginning of a world." This adumbrates the fact that he had come to an end—and to the edge of the sea—that he might begin again, and by *worlding*.

"The shore," Rachel Carson says, is "a testing ground in which the precise and perfect adaptation to environment is an indispensable condition of survival."

"The Fo'castle stood like a house built out into the surf on a mound of sand." Beston is speaking of the most perilous experience, the great winter storm that vibrated the bricks of the chimney and caused the dune beneath the house to tremble. The ocean now "besieged [his] door." (I cite an early metaphor that became literally true.) And now, it might be said, he first inhabited his house, felt its security ("It was singularly peaceful in the little house"), yet in the "fury unbelievable" found himself in the cosmos, in "a house," as Han Shan said, "without beams or walls." Beston says in the initial chapter where he situates himself that "on its solitary dune my house faced the four walls of the world," but he was the solitary one when the storm engulfed his house, and the house of the world was now open to him because its walls had fallen.

The depth of imagery and the drama of Beston's cosmic adventure on being—and, of course, the literary craft—make *The Outermost House* a book of lasting value, a better book than such good books as John Hay's *The Great Beach* (taking its title from Thoreau's designation for Cape Cod's outer beach) and Robert Finch's *Outlands: Journeys to the Outer Edges of Cape Cod* (the title playing on Beston's). (All three describe the migration of alewives, itself a homing, a return, as much the advent of spring on Cape Cod as the melting ice of landlocked Walden.)

The Outermost House is a better book than those by Hay and Finch because its structure is not as loose and its source is deeper. The ten chapters—some of them admittedly catchalls for what Beston finds in his journal and sometimes patchy—transcribe the circle of the year from September to September. Beston seldom employs the expected spring-to-spring cycle—and in this instance marks the completion of his year with a sidereal phenomenon, the rising of Orion, the reason being, as Elizabeth Beston notes, his "love of the night sky . . . his strongest bond with the earth he celebrated." His first love, he told his sister, were the stars—for him, as for Emerson, the last outpost of God, a cosmological surety?—and he confessed himself that rarity among nature writers, a "noctamorist."

"By day space belongs to man," he explains in a letter from the Fo'castle to Elizabeth Coatsworth; "by night, space is his no more. He escapes, then, from his own world into the universe." His night country, however, is not of Loren Eiseley's Poe-esque kind; it opens to mystery but is not dark. He ends with the rising of Orion to underline the achievement of his year and the great moral Nature taught him: to disclaim possession, "to yield self life [ego] to the will of life universal." The familial and communal life that followed his solitary year answers to this imperative, and it puts in perspective the conspicuous Romantic gesture of entering on solitude. He derives the moral of yielding the self from the spectacle of Darwinian nature, but it belongs as well to the Enlightenment, which he gives preeminence by evoking the stars. Their *ritual* is processual, but not of the "overwhelming, relentless, burning" kind he witnessed in the return of the alewives; and the process he finally subscribes to is the all-inclusive cosmological one, an orderly one like life on the farm—"the ritual of the farm," William Carlos Williams says in "Rogation Sunday," "the wonder of continuous revival."

In *The Wheel*, Wendell Berry takes the epigraph explaining the never faltering perfect "Wheel of Life" from Sir Albert Howard's study of organic agriculture, where Howard says that "it needs a more refined perception to recognize throughout this stupendous wealth of varying shapes and forms the principle of stability [that] dominates by means of an ever-recurring cycle."

To read *The Outermost House* with *Walden* in mind is to note some omissions, perhaps the most significant the skirting of the biographical occasion and the elimination of the possibility of failure. It seems that it just "came about" that Beston was free to stay on for a year, and it seems that building the house, which he himself didn't do, was as effortless and smooth as the sentence, "so I built myself a house upon the beach." Though Elizabeth Beston refers to him as a "solitary Outermost Householder," he does not identify the self, as Thoreau does, with the house and so precludes the rich resonances Thoreau derives from symbol making. In the chapter on "Winter Visitors," where Thoreau is mentioned by name and the title abbreviates his "Former Inhabitants; and Winter Visitors," the striking of the first phrase accords with the absence of human history and, with it, a history of failure. (Thoreau provides a history of Walden woods, and Robert Finch, in *The Primal Place*, locates himself in the widening circles of the local history of Brewster, but Beston says little about Eastham or Orleans, where he went every week for supplies.)

Publicly, in a brief, noncommittal introduction to Dudley Lunt's edition of *Cape Cod*, Beston acknowledges the first (and still the foremost) of our nature writers. Yet, in keeping with what Scott says of Beston's admitted tie to Jeffries, that both were "poetic writers" where Thoreau apparently was not, Beston closes the introduction with an example of his own best prose: "The volutes of the breakers approach, rear, tumble, and dissolve, and over the glisten, the foam, and the moist, sea-fragrant air still fly the small shorebirds hastening." As he told Scott:

> I suppose that I do link up with Thoreau, but I do not read him and have never been under his influence. He is not a naturalist. What interests him and stirs him most deeply are the principles governing the individual life when that life is enclosed in a gregarious society. If I tie in with anybody, it is with Richard Jeffries. We are both of us scholars with a poetic joy in the visible world.

If nothing else, misprision shows the anxiety of influence. The Emerson-Thoreau award probably did not assuage it.

Elizabeth Beston reports that Beston never liked to have *The Outermost House* compared to Thoreau's *Cape Cod*: "'Thoreau had very little heart,' he would say." But what could he do, taking for his the region Thoreau occupied before him, his every book, with the exception of *Herbs and the Earth*, prompting comparison with Thoreau's? He could not have written *The Outermost House* without recalling the ritual of the year and "private business" of *Walden* and what Thoreau had done in *Cape Cod*. Nor in preparing *The St. Lawrence* could he have overlooked *A Yankee in Canada*. *White Pine and Blue Water* inevitably includes Thoreau's encounter in *The Maine Woods* with the very wilderness Beston prizes so much. And *Northern Farm*? A domestic *Walden*, an almanac if not all that Thoreau wanted in his "Kalendar."

Thoreau had very little heart. But then, Beston's experience on the beach ends in emergence and healing where Thoreau's remains throughout a crisis of belief, which may explain, as Federman notes, that Beston's "merciful" disclaims Thoreau's "voracious beach." The heart of the matter, of course, is metaphysical and linguistic, always troubling to Thoreau but never to Beston, who waives it when he claims to be a scholar with a poetic joy in the visible world. Thoreau put the matter in his first book, *A Week on the Concord and Merrimack Rivers*: "Is not Nature, rightly read, that of which she is commonly taken to be the symbol merely?" His question addresses a belief in "correspondence" and in the sovereign power of the symbolizing mind—a power no longer efficacious when encountering elemental things. Eyes were made, he said in *A Week*, "to behold beauty now invisible," that is, to see directly, without mediation, the face of God. But the visible world he saw on the outer beach resisted the mind's appropriation, would not confirm the desire to idealize it, had no invisibility, was what it was, predicated itself: The visible was all there was, voraciousness to be seen everywhere on the beach—heard, too, in the ceaseless roar.

Metaphysical concerns do not trouble Beston. He questions neither his perceptions nor his faith in language. Accordingly, his work wants the depth(s) we find in Thoreau's. Beston's aestheticism, grounded in the Romantic belief that beauty is truth, is already beyond the need to seek spiritual correspondences: Things as they appear to be are enough, to be enjoyed for their beauty and the sensuous delight we find in them. (*Mystery* and *poetry*, as he uses them, pay homage to the very dimension of experience he no longer plumbs.) This is not a superficial view easily dismissed because it is a way station to eco-stance and -sense. For one thing, it asks us to consider beauty and not merely economy as a measure of nature's value, the appreciation of beauty itself the result of yielding the sovereign ego and the atomistic sense of things. This view also belongs to Pragmatism and its critique of philosophical idealism, for Pragmatism abandons the hierarchical correspondential for a coherence (relational) theory of truth—

the truth of actual lived experience in which things are found to be together and not in need of the glue of the mind. Consequently, the symbol-making use of language no longer serves, giving way, in Beston's case, to what Ponge calls *adéquation*; and because Beston is a master of this linguistic mode he brings us as readily as anyone into the world and into a sense of the cosmos.

Though he loved paintings ("pictures"), Beston insisted that he was not a painter. Was this to deny connection with Ruskin, whose treatment of clouds he rivals in *The St. Lawrence*, or to set himself off from a near-contemporary verbal painter, John Van Dyke? Beston speaks up for all the senses, especially smell, which brings him the "interesting savours and fragrances" of the ocean world and tests the "foul blue air" of cities, the "stench modern civilization breathes." His book on herbs is a book of smells. But the eye, he knows, is "the master sense and chief aesthetic gate." In "The Headlong Wave," he says that he saw with the "outer rather than . . . inner eye" and that the "outer eye [had] the best of it." *Outer* and *inner* belong to the correspondential idealist view that demands, as Blake said, that we see through the eye, not with it. (Since Blake, because of this, was not a naturalist, maybe Thoreau, as Beston claims, wasn't either.) *Outer eye: outermost house*—this house of many windows is itself an eye, its vision directed outward to natural not inward to mental phenomena: "I like the seven windows of the larger room, and the sense one may have there of being almost out-of-doors." *Almost* tells us that he is self-aware and prefers to look out. The house is a site for sight.

Not a painter?

> I shall always remember this picture [of ruddy turnstones taking wing] as one of the most beautiful touches of colour I have ever seen in nature, for the three dominant colours of this bird . . . are black, white, and glowing chestnut red; and these colours are interestingly displayed in patches and bold stripes seen at their best when the bird is flying. The great dunes behind them and the long vista of the beach were cold silver overlaid with that faint, loveliest violet which is the overtone colour of the coast.

Beston is an engaging and seemingly artless writer. Bill Rueckert notes his purity. He opens his experience to us: "Walk through these grasslands . . . and you will see . . ." He situates us with him as he writes: "Writing here [now] this cloudy morning . . ." He exposes to us the construction of *The Outermost*

House, the house that he is building with words: "I will close my chapter with a few paragraphs on heavy surf." In these ways, among others, he reenacts experience.

The chapters of the book are composed of short sections which seem to have been written notebook in hand, paragraph by (sometimes disjunctive) paragraph. Observation in one may become meditation in another, the modulation keeping our interest. Paragraphs and sections often end in clinchers, as in this instance of a concluding paragraph: "The straggling beach peas . . . are in bloom; the west wind blows the grass and rushes out to the rippled levels of a level sea; heat clouds hang motionless on the land horizon, their lower rims lost in the general haze; the great sun overflows; the year burns on." Sharp declarative strokes in the present tense compose a simultaneous whole, a picture. Here is another instance: "The afternoon sun sinks red as fire; the tide climbs the beach, its foam a strange crimson; miles out, a freighter goes north, emerging from the shoals." The tripartite construction is not wavelike; the movement is not sequential but concurrent.

Just as good are Beston's images:

an orange sun floated up over the horizon with the speed and solemnity of an Olympian balloon

(Thoreau: "The morning wind forever blows, the poem of creation is uninterrupted. . . . Olympus is but the outside of the earth every where.")

geese settle at sundown *in* the golden skin of the western coves [my italics]

the solemn unrest of ocean

Every spatter was a crumb of phosphorescence; I walked in a dust of stars.

And then there is *adéquation*, the key concept in Francis Ponge's poetics, unknown to Beston, yet in some ways exemplified in his literary practice. *Adéquation* repudiates correspondence for equivalence: language is not to be used symbolically but only to define and describe, the "definitions-descriptions," Ponge says in *Méthodes*, themselves "aesthetically and rhetorically equivalent." Beston does not follow Ponge in wishing to make independent objects out of words (an aesthetic equivalent); he follows, or anticipates, him in wishing to make a "verbal representation . . . so close to the thing itself that it partakes of it" (a rhetorical equivalent). For symbolism displaces the things it uses where *adéquation* places them before us so freshly they claim our attention.

Adéquation accords with the outer eye and is the method Beston most often employs when he chooses to render the central fact of his elemental world: its motion. He knew before Olson stated the law that "there is only one thing you can do about kinetic, reenact it."

He does this brilliantly in "The Headlong Wave," his attempt, he told Elizabeth, to write the first "real study of the shapes and colors and tricks of waves." There he tells us as much about his normative syntax as about waves when he speaks of "the triple rhythm" of the latter, the fact that they come in threes:

> Three great waves, then an indeterminate run of lesser rhythms, then three great waves again. Every mood of the wind, every change in the day's weather, every phase of the tide—all these have subtle sea musics all their own. Surf of the ebb, for instance, is one music, surf of the flood another, the change in the two musics being most clearly marked during the first hour of a rising tide. With the renewal of the tidal energy, the sound of the surf grows louder, the fury of battle returns to it as it turns again on the land, and beat and sound change with the renewal of the war.

1, 2, 3; *thén, thén.* And more often than not in his work, *nów, nów.* Of the marsh hawk, he writes, "Now she hovers a second as if about to swoop, now she sinks as if about to snatch a prey—and all the time advancing." Threes again, the hovering enacted in *a second as if about,* the following clause parallel to the first, *swoop* fulfilled by *snatch,* the sentence itself *advancing,* the participle extending the motion beyond its close.

Motion and sound.

> Listen to the surf . . . : Hollow boomings and heavy roarings, great watery tumblings and tramplings, long hissing seethes, sharp, rifle-shot reports, splashes, whispers, the grinding undertone of stones, and sometimes vocal sounds that might be the half-heard talk of people in the sea. And not only is the great sound varied in the manner of its making, it is also constantly changing its tempo,

its pitch, its accent, and its rhythm, being now loud and thundering, now almost placid, now furious, now grave and solemn-slow, now a simple measure, now a rhythm monstrous with a sense of purpose and elemental will.

The rhythm of this syntax carries over to passages that are not intended to be equivalences—to passages of rich symphonic prose and passages that moralize his experience. His imperative at the end is: "Touch the earth, love the earth, honour the earth, her plains, her valleys, her hills, and her seas; rest your spirit in her solitary places." How wonderfully the biblical rounds out his sense of earth as Gaia ("The seas are the heart's blood of the earth")!

At the end, when he closes the door on his experience, he refigures his year by recollecting the sun and waves and storm (all inevitably having psychic resonance), and the turning of the year tells of his turning and the healing he has known:

> And because I had known this outer and secret world [outer = secret = mystery = poetry], and been able to live as I had lived, reverence and gratitude greater and deeper than ever possessed me, sweeping every emotion else aside, and space and silence an instant closed together over life. Then time gathered again like a cloud, and presently the stars began to pale over an ocean still dark with remembered night.

We might say, borrowing from Thoreau at the end of *Walden*, that Beston had "witnessed [his] own limits transgressed."

Did I say that he doesn't sound many notes? Like the sea, he has many voices.

Even though Beston dismisses the "moralistic fustian" of the New England literary tradition, he shares this legacy. It finds its place in the frequently tripartite structure of *The Outermost House*, a structure more discrete and fixed in *Northern Farm*. Each brief weekly installment of this almanac—its initial publication as "Country Chronicle" in the *Progressive*, from December 1945 through December 1946, was surely read by Aldo Leopold—is composed of three parts: an initial section of "small adventures" of observation in closely attending the accordant seasonal rituals of nature and agriculture; a "Farm Diary," its italicized sentences and sentence fragments punctuated by slashes, this catchall extending his observations beyond the farm to the neighborhood and community and admitting other voices and sources of information; and a concluding section, not so much philosophic (as Bill Rueckert notes in the margin of the edition I borrowed from him) as meditative-moralistic, turning repeatedly on the differences between nature and civilization, farm and city, preindustrial and industrial society, past and present, at-homeness and alienation. This structure, it seems to me, has a remote analogue in the New England sermon and a closer analogue in Emerson's anatomy of the soul, its three parts—the organic-practical, the aesthetic-intellectual, the moral—answering to Beston's several voices as well as offices of farmer, writer, and preacher.

Northern Farm belongs with such chronicles of country life as E. B. White's *One Man's Meat* (its first installment published in 1938, the book itself in 1942), Edwin Way Teale's *A Naturalist Buys an Old Farm*, and Wendell Berry's novels. Beston strikes the keynote of such books when he considers our obsession with size: "Who would live happily in the country must be wisely prepared to take pleasure in little things. Country living is a pageant of nature and the year; it can no more stay fixed than a movement in music, and as the seasons pass, they enrich life far more with little things than with great." His observations of this pageant are ordinary, but they delight us because we recognize in their exactness what we have seen but not so well.

Few of us are as alert or save what we see by style, as, for example, in this sentence concluding a paragraph on a winter storm: "Every now and then I could hear, even through the wind, the sound which snow makes against glass—that curious, fleecy pat and delicate whisper of touch which language cannot convey or scarce suggest." Style, adequate here, certifies what he sees; it is the register of an "I" (and ear) unobtrusively there.

The pageant of nature and the year is serene, its elemental moments few. Beston no longer lives at the edge. The empty house that he comes home to at the beginning has stood 150 years, the center of a settled life that he again resumes when he puts the pendulum of the clock in motion: "With the steady tick, the life of the house began to beat." No need to press for literary effect: We bring all that is requisite to such primary images as *house, kitchen,* and *hearth,* and stirred to reverie we recover our own lost lives in following his.

This installment also sets in motion the essential themes of the book. Its parts are more incremental than usual, the first bringing us from the city and the suburbs north to the snowy countryside. Whittier's "Snowbound" comes to mind, and the image of flying ducks secures the recollection of Bryant's "To a Waterfowl." Modern urban existence is likened to unaware comfortable life on a luxury liner bound nowhere on an unknown sea (see George Oppen, "Party on Shipboard," *Discrete Series*, 1934). "Farm Diary" marks the days until Elizabeth's arrival, when the "vital heat" (Thoreau's phrase) of the Bestons' house will be wholly restored by the domestic eros. Then the closing meditative paragraph:

> As I settle down in this familiar house, with lamplight glowing from its windows and the great planets crossing its chimney tops, I find I am shaking off the strange oppression which came over me when I lived by an urban sense and understanding of time. In a world so convenient and artificial that time is scarcely day or night, and one is bulwarked against the seasons and the year, time, so to speak, having no natural landmarks, tends to stand still. The consequence is that life and time and history become unnaturally a part of some endless and unnatural present, and violence becomes for some the only remedy. Here in the country it all moves ahead again. Spring is not only a landmark, but it looks ahead to autumn, and winter forever looks forward to the spring.

The life of the house in this chronicle of outer and inner warmth also beats to the measure of sidereal time. The house is not at sea, bound nowhere, but centered in the great, sure, unfailing round of the cosmos. With Beston, coming home, we know where we are.

Winter forever looks forward to the spring. This is true at the beginning but not at the end of the book, the cycle from winter solstice to winter solstice, among other things, making affirmation difficult. In October he begins the "housing up" in readiness for winter's siege; the days grow shorter, the light diminishes, the cold increases. He recalls in one of his meditative paragraphs the recent "carnival of death" (World War II) that still poisons the air. Deeply oppressed by this, and perhaps by the approaching winter of his age, we find him alone in the kitchen at night writing out, on the last page of what will be his last important book, his "unchanged belief" in the earth-life he has lived and, as he knows, almost all of us have forfeited, to become, as he says, "vagrants in space [he is referring to space travel], desperate for [because] the meaninglessness has closed about us." On this winter's night the planets do not wheel overhead: "*I open the storm door and gaze out into the night. It is pitch dark and utterly silent, and past the streaming lamplight falls the snow.*"

Life shuts down; it does, when there is no amplitude. We no longer live in an age of expansion but in an age of contraction.

"When we had moved to the farm," Elizabeth Beston says, "he seldom returned to the Cape. If he felt like going anywhere, we usually headed northward to Quebec and the French Canadian villages on the St. Lawrence. . . . The St. Lawrence was the last country outside of Maine that he felt like writing about." *The St. Lawrence* was not Beston's last book, but Elizabeth Beston had good reason to place it last in *Especially Maine* and to the end with "Indian Pilgrimage" and what Beston called "the Indian's America."

The St. Lawrence is Beston's only travel book, for this reason perhaps the uneven book it is. It is at once a guidebook, a children's book (when historical events, Indian captivities, and legends are recounted), and a nature book. But for Beston himself it is a reverie toward childhood, a pilgrimage (like Henry Adams') to the Virgin (of Bersimis, an Indian village), to *le vieux Canada* (the France of his childhood, visited with his mother), and "an adventure . . . into the older America of the forest, the cataract, and the shadow of trees" that for him recalls *The Last of the Mohicans*. Like Thoreau, it's Canada East he's come to see, an old world not the new, but his journey, unlike Thoreau's, which was downriver and back, is down, following, as he says at the outset, the "eastward resolution" that marks the rhythm of the landscape, the flow, "the great and continuous flowing which is the being of all things." He writes superbly of this as well as of the sky and the immense scale of the continent. When he writes of the Indians of Bersimis, whose village is the goal of his travels, he is a gracious seigneur. Superior to the Noble Savage, whom he considers both noble and savage, he nevertheless sanctions them by placing them where he does in his elegy of lost America. He is often sentimental and nostalgic, but this may be because he sees the present so sharply, the river "scummed" by industrial development, the surplus young men sent to the bush to cut wood, and the "commerce of pure destruction" that "Le Pulp," as he names a chapter, involves. "The pulp towns," he told Dr. Neff, "are the most hideous conglomerations of diseased ugliness that human beings have ever made to live in." Like the more recent settlement at Prudhoe Bay, these towns disturb his arctic dreams and prompt the only explicit ecological comment in the book: "Visible nature is not the immediate spoil of an age or its generation, but the timeless inheritance of man, the ancient mystery to be forever shared with those who forever are to come."

Note also that his historical motive is *culturally* ecological, to prevent the destruction of the past, and that his journey east, counter to discovery, is one of recovery. (Robert Duncan: "There is a hero who struggles east / widdershins to free the dawn.") As the river widens in its seaward course, it becomes "a sidereal stream . . . a part of space and the sky"; it restores "the earth's time, and the wheat's time and the time of the curé and the seigneur and the peaceful flowing of the days." And as he moves with it beyond the thin coastal strip of "frontier fishermen, farmers, and cutters of pulp," it brings him to both the "final blue of the sea" and "the north and the cold," the inalienable (as he thinks) northern half of the continent that shelters the past and allows primitive people to live undisturbed in timeless ways.

What he recovers imaginatively portends death. The fluxion of rivers is seaward, immemorially deathward, countervailing the alewives who (in *Northern Farm*) affirm "life pressing on, believing in itself, keeping the first faith." The northern cold also portends death. This, perhaps, is what it means to return to origin, yet this is a direction increasingly important as f(act) and imagination. The frontier is no longer west but north, a direction, if we will, for the old exploitation ("Nature . . . to be robbed greedily like an unguarded treasure," Beston says) or, for some, of redemptive purification. Nothing is more important imaginatively to Eiseley, for example, than the ICE, whose northern virtues of simplicity, physical work, and endurance Oppen claims as "primitive" and finds in the fishermen and craftsmen of Maine.

The sea, the farm, the river, and the garden. How is it I end with *Herbs and the Earth*? Is it because more than any other this small early book evokes his sentiment of being, tells how working in the garden helps his "soul . . . possess . . . her earth inheritance"? This manual and history of herbs is the most scientific of Beston's books, but also the most charming and tranquil. The elements and the solar round have a place in it but belong to the garden's orderly cosmos; and here he ends with spring (winter's plans made good), framing the book with his sense of all the lost things—earth, history/continuity, the poetic relation, spirit—that he has found and that the alienated may find again. "Stop . . . with me . . . / You shall possess the good of the earth and sun"—this bears repeating because *Herbs and the Earth* is his *Leaves of Grass*.

"What pleasant paths begin in gardens": Beston, not Bachelard, but even so Bachelardian. Matter, Bachelard says, and etymology bears him out, is the "*mother-substance*" of all reverie. To think of *earth* is to dream of mother, to recall, as Beston does, his childhood with her in France and remember the European earth he honors in this book by telling the folklore of herbs, "our most noble heritage of green." Moreover, by gardening at the farm, Beston acquires, as Bachelard explains, the fullness of vertical being. Beston says in *The Outermost House* that rain on the roof is a sound he has loved since childhood, and Elizabeth notes, connecting this with Beston's happiness, that the herb attic became his study, where on stormy nights he went to hear the rain. Tending herbs is thereby associated with the attic—and it may be that the attic is associated with the earth and that the tranquil solitude of ascent belongs also, in Beston's case, to descent. No other book finds him so secure and centered; none is so intimate. Elizabeth says that Beston "wrote well when he wrote from himself" and that he considered the last passages of *Herbs and the Earth* his best.

The Education of a Hunter

READING RICHARD NELSON

Nelson's way in *The Island Within*, his most recent book, is not ours: The education to which he would be true and the experiment on life it proposed stand our way on its head. Thoreau says in the chapter on "Higher Laws" in *Walden*, in what I think is still the best morality on hunting and fishing, that hunting had been one of the best parts of his education, undoubtedly, as he goes on to say, because it "is oftenest the young man's introduction to the forest [Nature] and the most original part of himself [the correlative island within]." He acknowledges that there is "a period in the history of the individual, as of the race, when the hunters are the 'best men'"; but in respect to the race this period is past and in respect to the individual, who recapitulates this period, it is to be "outgrow[n]." Though he had "fished from the same kind of necessity that the first fishers did," the argument from necessity (subsistence) has little force for him. Even now, he says, "in civilized communities, the embryo man passes through [should pass through] the hunter stage of development."

Yet in our civilized community I find, as William Carlos Williams says in "The Descent of Winter," that the hunters return to the city

135

empty-handed howbeit
for the most part
but aloof
as if from and truly from
another older world

William Carlos Williams captures the ambivalence and measure of the autumn ritual and grants the transformative power of an other, earlier world that itself is efficacious. "Empty-handed" tells us this, and placed initially and heavy-stressed, it carries for me the moral weight of Thoreau's determinative declaration: "No humane being, past the thoughtless age of boyhood, will wantonly murder any creature which holds its life by the same tenure that he does."

Is Nelson's education belated? Or is it, as with others who return to the "old ways," full of needed instruction for us?

Nelson never hunted in his youth in Wisconsin, where hunting (harvesting) deer, as Leopold learned, was always a heated political issue. "I loved animals only with my eyes," Nelson says, "and judged hunting to be outside the bounds of morality." This sentence tells us that he has since found that hunting is a way of loving animals and within the bounds of morality, and this is the heart of the matter which, for those opposed to hunting, may be beyond appreciation. Yet this is what we must try to understand and what Nelson's unusual education and its praxis in *The Island Within* may enable us to do.

(I choose *praxis* over *application* because I find it in the dictionary only a word away from *pray*, which is an aspect of sacralized hunting, and, homophonically, calls up *prey*. *Prey*, in turn, reminds me that hunting is predation and that of all predators human beings, as Nelson's ethnographic studies show, are the most skilled, the masters of the art.)

The love of animals moved Nelson to study zoology, which proved unsatisfactory because, as science sometimes will, it put a "barrier [of detachment and abstraction] between humanity and nature." *Contact, connectedness, intimacy*—these are what he wants and, by way of anthropology, which he went on to study, he found that hunting peoples, the Eskimos of the Arctic and the Athabaskan Indians of the subarctic, had achieved: "They had achieved the deepest intimacy with their wild surroundings and had made natural history the focus of their lives." He found this not so much from the traditional practice of observation and interview as by *entering* (he uses this word) the society of hunters, living their village life and, in demanding apprenticeship (often refused by the present generation of young men), participating in the hunt and thereby learning "their hunter's way." It should be noted that when he speaks of this, in the version of "The Gifts [of Deer]" published in *Antaeus* from which I've quoted, and elsewhere, notably in the appendix of *Shadow of the Hunter*, the biographical occasion is of the utmost importance. For, in 1964, when he left home for the first time, at twenty-two, to study the Eskimos of Wainwright, Alaska, the transition in his life had been as swift and disorienting as the flight from Madison to Barrow and the result of his year's initiation had been conversion. This, more than anthropological scruple, is why he feels the need to tell it. "The year I spent with Eskimos," he says, "changed the course of my life and made me a very different person."

Do I belabor this? Yet how few are changed by what they study and remain loyal to the teaching of their teachers.

Nelson fully and brilliantly records what he learned in his first apprenticeship in two books: *Hunters of the Northern Ice* (1967) and *Shadow of the Hunter: Stories of Eskimo Life* (1980). The first—his first book, and already the work of an accomplished writer—is thoroughly scientific, an impeccable anthropological study of "Eskimo methods of hunting, traveling, and surviving on the sea ice." It was funded by the air force with "the practical goal," Nelson says, "of gathering information for survival manuals." But his goal was otherwise, to study human ecology: to give an ethnographic account of the relationship of the Eskimos to their harsh environment—Eskimos, who, William S. Laughlin, his mentor, says, "have conducted the crucial experiment in human adaptability," one in which hunting, central to it, is a way of life, not merely a subsistence technique—and to come to this knowledge, it's worth repeating, by choosing, methodologically, to learn-by-doing, by entering the field. This is his distinction, and it grounds his defense of descriptive ethnography in "Retrospective, 1986," which, in the second edition, replaces the chapters on theoretical matters he had been compelled, in doing his doctoral dissertation, to add to *Hunters of the Northern Forest* (1973). Did reluctance to give primacy to theoretical concerns and a growing skepticism of scientific methods contribute to his decision to become a nature writer, to try a new life and career at mid-life? And earlier, isn't this turn prefigured in *Shadow of the Hunter*, in which he found a literary way of doing ethnography, a "counterpoint," he says, "to analytical scientific description" that too often omits "the sense of *life*"?

The sense of life is the desideratum, to be achieved by art, "the only twin life has," Olson says in "Human Universe," because art "does not seek to describe but to enact." So Nelson tells us that rather than "distilling and analyzing" events he here recounts them "as they actually occur": He enacts them. And he does this as a poet versed in recent poetics would, aware that there is no absolute truth but only the witness of the individual perspective: "In ethnography [he turns storytelling back on science] there are perhaps as many truths as there are observers." Military manuals of survival, moreover, are not now even a subsidiary goal, for what matters is that he find a way to teach us about a people whose way of life and environment are imperiled (by our need for oil) and to preserve "something of what was and might someday vanish entirely from the earth." He writes *Shadow of the Hunter* for the Eskimos. "This book," he says in the dedication, is for "the Ulgunigmiut, who taught me their life and so profoundly influenced mine; and [for] their grandchildren, who may wish to look back along the trail." They, in turn, would appreciate the traditional mode, the essentially oral intent, of his stories, whose written form may be said to be the shadow of the oral form, for words, as Nelson says, are only the shadows of experience, "shadows of the way we once saw the world."

Barry Lopez, who refers to *Hunters of the Northern Ice* in *Arctic Dreams* and comments approvingly on *Make Prayers to the Raven* in the annotated booklist of the special issue of *Antaeus* on nature writing, does not mention *Shadow of the Hunter*, and neither does Tom Lyon in the extensive bibliography of *This Incomperable Lande*. Of the people with whom I correspond, only Gary Snyder mentions it: "A lot of my thinking about these things [hunting] has come from considerations of subsistence and foraging in all their aspects, & sport hunting has not entered my calculations much so far. Dick Nelson is the liveliest contemporary thinker on these lines I guess . . . have you seen his older *Shadow of the Hunter?*" Snyder mentions the earlier book because, as he wrote in a previous letter, he is enthusiastic about *The Island Within*—from which, incidentally, Nelson read in Berkeley before coming up to Kitkitdizze. In this letter, where Snyder speaks of his present work on *The Practice of the Wild*, he says, of what turns out to be my present enterprise, that the "problem is [because *The Island Within* is not yet published] nobody in his right mind would want to do a piece on Nelson until *The Island Within* is out . . . because that is what Nelson will henceforth be known for." True enough: No one can now write about Nelson without taking account of this book, whose endorsement by distinguished nature writers welcomes him to their company. But whether or not this is the book for which he will be known, or should be known, remains to be seen. I am not sure that it is and am writing to find out. His ethnographic work is a splendid achievement, and it seems to me now, at this moment, that *Shadow of the Hunter* and *Make Prayers to the Raven*, because they also have literary merit, are his best work, that is, the work that anyone coming to Nelson should read.

I read *Shadow of the Hunter* before *Hunters of the Northern Ice* because the earlier book is out of print and took time to locate. This may account for my somewhat dutiful reading of it and for the displacement of my interest from the rich ethnographic detail to the use Nelson subsequently made of it. A few of my neighbors here still hunt primarily for subsistence rather than sport and many read the hunting stories that appear in sportsmen's magazines. The magazines that are delivered to our rural mailbox are not of this kind, though I have read hunting stories—Cooper's, Melville's, Faulkner's, Hemingway's—and being here, where sport hunters invade our woods, has given me a perspective on hunting. I mention this because it certifies my praise of *Shadow of the Hunter*, a book of hunting stories that passed Paul Goodman's test (more demanding than Emily Dickinson's tingling spine) of grabbing me by the throat. Without hesitation, I place it with the best books on hunting that I have read: I think that Sakiak, the oldest, wisest, and most accomplished hunter, the tutelary hunter, belongs in the company of Natty Bumppo and Sam Fathers. (He is modeled mostly, I suspect, on Kavik, "the old hunter . . . [who] never tired of telling stories of his exploits.")

The stories in *Shadow of the Hunter* are of the present time, noted by references to the *Tanik*, the white man who figures as a sport hunter, and by the Eskimos' use of such things as outboard motors, Coleman stoves, and nylon thread. But, essentially, they belong to another time, when survival depended wholly on hunting, and hunting, accordingly, was the primary occupation, the requisite ecological knowledge taking a lifetime's experience to acquire, its successful fulfillment conferring all honor and status. Alone or in small groups, the hunter in the vast arctic landscape of sea and sea ice is unquestionably heroic, and the large shadow he casts belongs to a heroic age when exploits of survival were "adventures." No way of life is so remote from ours, so readily felt as mythic, this established largely by *muthos*, what is said, the preliterate oral, simple and direct mode of the stories and by the fact that action, not introspection, is their chief concern. Their artifice is patent. These stories were not told by Eskimos, then "totally translated," say, in the manner of Dennis Tedlock's transcriptions of the narratives of the Zuni. Nelson composed them—the people and events are "collages based on what is real"—and he narrates them.

This way of doing ethnography is substantiated by our confidence in their credibility. If the stories are sometimes stiff it is because they are also the vehicle of the ethnographic information in *Hunters of the Northern Ice.*

> *Piqaluyiq* was just one of many different kinds of ice that Eskimos recognized and dealt with in special ways. In fact, elders like Sakiak used well over a hundred specific terms for sea ice, according to its age, thickness, topography, and other features. "There is so much to learn about the ice," he often joked, "that by the time we understand it we are too old to hunt."

There are other ways of introducing information ("'Thick clouds and calm weather can be dangerous so far out at sea,' he thought aloud"), but I cite this passage to indicate the third-person narrative point of view and to show how the white narrator acknowledges the authority of his Eskimo teacher and adds a significant detail to his characterization. Ethnographic studies usually have glossaries (that of sea ice terminology in *Hunters of the Northern Ice* is extensive), but the native words in *Shadow of the Hunter*, which also has a glossary as part of its authorizing frame, are used, as *piqaluyiq* is, for their authenticity, their immediate evocation of the Eskimos' world. The outstanding, because essentially structural, examples of this are the titles of the stories, which name the months of the lunar/hunting year, the "subsistence round." Each of these titles, with a cast of characters, is set off on a separate page whose verso features an appropriate drawing by Simon Koonook, an Eskimo artist:

Siqinyasaq Tatqiq
Moon of the Returning Sun
(JANUARY)

MAIN CHARACTERS
Sakiak (Sah-*kee*-uk) *an old hunter*
Kuvlu (*Koov*-loo) *Sakiak's adult son*
Nuna (*Noo*-nuh) *Kuvlu's wife*

Like children learning to read, we must sound the syllables of these strange new words. This is our initiation, and it prepares us to enter a strange old world.

I am reminded by *Shadow of the Hunter* of Barry Lopez's *Winter Count*, not because Nelson's stories are historical in the way of winter counts but because the predicament of the narrator is that of the anthropologist in the title story. Like Roger Callahan, he respects what he has learned in the stories he has been told and the experiences he has had and is unwilling to systematize them. That his ethnography is sound speaks well for his science but as much, or more, for his allegiance to the people who have permitted him to live among them. In the stories he tells he is present not as a *Tanik* but as Pamiuk and Patik, apprentice hunters, disciplined by the teasing of the elders, whom they "were expected to serve . . . to compensate for the burden created by their frequent mistakes." Yet as narrator he has authorial authority. This, however, is never preemptive and, as Roger Callahan would have it, is used to "defend them"—defend the people from both scientific inquisition and their own sad acculturation.

(Lopez's story, which appeared after the publication of *Shadow of the Hunter*, seems to have anticipated a crucial incident in *The Island Within*. The storm that finally breaks in "Winter Count," that "howled through his [Callahan's] room and roared through his head" and restored his earliest sense of well-being and the wild, has its counterpart in *The Island Within*, where the different context is of special interest. In the only chapter devoted to his home and to the work he does there as a writer, Nelson tells how the storm, admitted by him, enters the house and "put[s] some life into the still, imprisoned air." This breath of life, of all that he seeks outside in the island world and wishes to make an island within, challenges the vocation he has now twinned with his intense outdoor existence. Writing, it seems, does not fully engage him; he does not seem to have his being, as writers often do, in verbal space. And he seems to have found that doing nature writing—that is, being obliged to do it, even though it is done in defense of nature—is compromised by the need to use as verbal material the experience in nature to which his vocation may have predisposed him.)

Nelson does more in the stories than the prescriptive form of *Hunters of the Northern Ice* permitted him to do. He conveys much of the information—the formation, variety, and hazards of sea ice, the astronomical phenomena and climatic data, the kinds of fishes and birds, and the animals (fox, polar bear, whale, ringed seal, bearded seal, and walrus) and the ways of snaring, trapping, stalking, killing, and butchering them. But now this information belongs, as Olson says of enactment, to the "dynamic" of human life and is therefore constitutive of a way of life. In the stories, the hunters leave and return to homes in the village and have wives and children, whose lives Nelson depicts. The stories present an entire hunting society, its life structured by the calendar set out in designations ("The Moon When Whaling Begins") that denote the optimum time of hunting the several animals that Nelson had previously cataloged, its very life turning on the courage, hardiness, and skill of hunters and the fortunes of the hunt. And the stories, telling of *old, adult,* and *apprentice* hunters, concern transmission (the ancient way of learning upheld by Snyder in *Axe Handles*) and are themselves its instrument because, as Nelson says in "The Death of Hunting," the concluding chapter of *Hunters of the Northern Ice,* "the sadly beneficent government has made it easy for men to live without being self-sufficient" and young men now have only "a rudimentary knowledge of Eskimo economic culture." The measure of Nelson's concern with acculturation is the wish-fulfilling story that reverses it. In this story, Kiluk, who has left the village to go to school and refuses the old ways, is troubled by her identity—"although she was no *Tanik* she was not fully Eskimo either." But in the course of time, because of her grandmother's solicitude and teaching and her romance with Patik, Sakiak's grandson, himself a resolute apprentice hunter, she chooses to stay on in the fishing camp and to be(come) an Eskimo.

All of the stories, except the story of Kiluk, have the same pattern and involve male hunters. They are hunting stories; that is, the hunter or hunters go out, find and encounter their prey, kill it and sometimes butcher it on the ice, and, often after several days and from great distances, return home with meat and other necessities for their families. It might be better to call them hunting-for-survival stories, for that is what they are, and they should be distinguished from our hunting stories because most of the best of these are about something else, the withdrawal from "civilization" to "nature," this also paradigmatic (as we say) of much nature writing. The Eskimos do not travel to the wild, as the hunters do in *Go Down, Moses;* they are already there, where they have their lives. They do not chase polar bears with airplanes; they are not sport hunters and do not share "the *Tanik's* strange need to pursue the thrill of danger and to hunt for sport and trophy." For "hunting, after all," as Nelson says, "was the most essential and serious activity of their lives, the focus of all their intelligence and energy. It was not idle pleasure or pastime that brought them far out among the floes to kill walrus, but the harsh dictates of survival." Having learned to appreciate and accept this exigent pragmatism, even in the instance of infanticide, Nelson grounds his defense of hunting on the fact that "the practical dictates of survival held sway above all else." As much as the sacramental, this contributes to his sense of its mystique.

To live life on the edge (not just the edge of the ice) can be exciting, and *excitement* and *thrill* belong to Nelson's lexicon. Hunting is a primordial activity, and the emotions it, and stories about it, awakens may also be primordial and deeply satisfying. For psychologically, we are still hunters, easily engaged by the archetypal plot of hunting stories.

> Minutes passed. The glass fogged and he took the binoculars from his eyes, at the same time holding a warm hand on his numb face. Looking again, he saw it . . . move. "*Nanuq!*" he whispered. "*Nanuq!*" Watching its direction of travel, he projected his mind into the bear's, to predict where it would move and how quickly, glancing over the floes between to set his own pathway and find a place to wait. "*Nanuq!*" he whispered once more as he turned and hurried down from the hummock, charged with excitement.
>
> The old man had lived his entire life for these moments. The thrill never diminished. The times between were taken up only with waiting and with recollection of the times before.

In copying this I hear echoes of *The Old Man and the Sea*, but the story of Sakiak's encounter with the polar bear, equally good as a story, is to be distinguished from Hemingway's story and from Faulkner's "The Bear," which also comes to mind, because of Nelson's command of detail and knowledge of animals.

Eskimos seldom hunt alone, but Sakiak does in the stories that frame the book. The first, in which he kills a seal, prefigures the last: "He wondered about the bear whose tracks he had followed. It was a big one . . . he would like to walk out and look for the bear." Eskimos and bears hunt seals in almost the same way, the former probably having learned from watching the latter, and both are predators. This establishes an equivalence, the drama in the last story arising from the fact that "polar bears were among the few animals on earth that . . . stalk a man." Of the two, the bear, needless to say, is more formidable, larger (eight feet long), and much more powerful. But in this story, its naturalism recalling the stories of Jack London, the she-bear is not the equal of the famous old hunter. Nelson says that "there were few predators as cunning and deadly as this man," armed as he is with a lifetime's experience and trust in traditional lore. Both bear and man are moved by "the anger that lurk[s] eternally at the root of [the] predatory mind." Alternating sections tell their respective "thoughts," feelings, and behavior. At the close, these sections are as brief and quick as the mounting action, which culminates when "the two creatures [are] drawn within destiny's narrowing circle."

This story concludes, as none of the others have, with communal exultation and Nelson's own moving witness and eloquent subscription to the Eskimos' deepest sense of the world. The old hunter, who had killed the bear this very day, this quintessential hunter, now dances alone to the pounding rhythms of the drums. For this music, too, is part of the flow he celebrates, the flow which characterizes organic life: the food chain and the circulations of being, or, as here, appropriately, of blood—"fish and drifting plankton become the blood of seals, and the blood of seals became the blood of bears and of men." Life is taken and life is renewed; the "conversation of death," as Lopez calls it, makes sacred the necessity of killing.

Granted that we need to recover a sacramental sense of life, is there no other way to do this? Is the sacred, as René Girard tells us, always coupled with violence? Must civilization always rest on victimage?

The very titles pair them, name their common concern, and distinguish their locale: *Hunters of the Northern Ice* and *Hunters of the Northern Forest*. Both are studies in "Designs for Survival"—*designs* suggesting that we, too, may find something valuable in them. I cite from the subtitle of the later book, this one about the Kutchin Indians, an Athabaskan tribe living in Chalkyitsik, a small village on the Black River near the eastern boundary of central Alaska. Nelson speaks of this as a "companion investigation" and as "almost identical in every respect," meaning that his "second experience" again involved living with a native people in a harsh environment and learning their survival techniques of hunting, fishing, and trapping—and that his investigation took a similar form. *Almost,* I suspect, covers the difference in tone, this attributable to dissatisfaction (among those with whom he lived there were "no exceptionally knowledgeable and communicative old-timers") and to a greater sense of loss. *In the old days* and *in former times* are refrains; all of the things the Kutchin no longer do or know how to do are noted; and *Outside* and *Outsider*, verbally conspicuous, evoke an alien power that makes for change, for a "postcontact economy."

> Fishing has gradually declined over the past years as people have turned away from the land [subsistence economy] in favor of an increasing dependence upon the world Outside. But the rate of decline increased precipitously in the two or three years preceding this study because of the introduction of snowmobiles and the consequent decrease in the number of pulling dogs [who are fed fish]. . . . Now that reliance on dogs for transportation is fading rapidly, the only really significant summer activity, and one of the major fall occupations, has dwindled to only a fraction of its previous importance. . . . A major institution of native Alaska, the summer fish camp, has now almost disappeared. And soon the rows of drying racks, heavily laden with thousands of split and drying fish, will exist only in the stories of the old people.

The loss of abundance and independence evoked in the last sentences is the price exacted by the machine in the garden.

"By fish flakes and stages / on rocks near water with trees / against sea." The fate of America, according to Olson in *The Maximus Poems*, turned on fishing, "the newness / the first men knew . . . / dirtied / by second comers" who "knew [no] better / than to cash in on it."

There is another difference worth noting in *Hunters of the Northern Forest* because it prefigures the formal departures of *Make Prayers to the Raven*. Nelson employs the first person more often and is therefore more often personal. For example, he mentions his injured hand and the slowness in starting a fire, for which he was chided; he also speaks at times of his impressions and incorporates some of his field notes into the text. Increasingly he is present in his work, and in *Make Prayers to the Raven*, which complements *Hunters of the Northern Forest*, he accounts for this as a methodological decision that enables him to represent "the whole reality" of fact and feeling: "I use my own recollections and quotations from my journal to give an aesthetic sense of the world I am describing." The collagist mode he adopts makes it clear that there are two perspectives, the Koyukon and his own; and making himself "visible and explicit" in this way calls attention to the ethnographer's inevitable mediation of what he reports and thereby "expand[s]," he says, "the reader's total experience of my subject and my own reactions to it."

This method is even more conspicuous in *The Athabaskans: People of the Boreal Forest* (1983), an excellent, well-illustrated general study that supplements Nelson's work on the Kutchin and Koyukon people. Some of the considerable oral material in this study is set out as verse.

Make Prayers to the Raven: A Koyukon View of the Forest (1983) treats the Koyukon people of central Alaska, who live in the villages of Huslia and Hughes on the Koyukuk River. Like the Kutchin, the subsistence round shapes their lifeway, and their techniques of survival are much the same. These techniques, thoroughly described in *Hunters of the Northern Forest*, are no longer focal: *Make Prayers to the Raven*, as the title indicates, concerns another dimension of existence just as important for survival, "ways of understanding and interacting with the natural world." Hitherto, Nelson was chiefly concerned with techniques; now, in what I consider the inevitable deepening of his thought, he is concerned with beliefs ("belief system," "ideology") and behavior, with *their* natural history, nature as this people "whose lives emerged from the forest" understand it and with the eco-wisdom they have acquired over millennia. "The integration of subsistence into Koyukon intellectual culture," he says, was his primary interest.

This, surely, accounts for the distinction of this book—the book of his I value most. And just as surely, having superb teachers (neighbors, in fact, and never informants but always teachers and instructors) enabled him to do more than he had done in Chalkyitsik. The book, it seems to me, was written out of the unusual well-being of living further into existence, and it marks a second conversion experience, one of great importance to the life he has since chosen to live and to record in *The Island Within*. The formal means he adopted must also be acknowledged in the happy result, for they liberated him from the strictures of scientific writing (not, it should be said, from the discipline of science) and allowed him to enter his work and put himself on record.

The title, after the fashion of *Walden* and *Leaves of Grass*, is a constitutive metaphor for the entire book and, as with works of imaginative force and integrity, the book can be read out of it. Raven, the trickster-creator of the world, is a large presence in the book, not only treated at length in the chapter on birds and evoked in many stories of the Distant Time, but named where it matters, in the dedication ("to those who will find wisdom in a world Raven made") and at the beginning and the end. The introduction and epilogue, which provide a personal narrative frame, concern the raven. Nelson begins the book by telling of an encounter with a raven while traveling alone with his dog team—an *encounter*, as Buber speaks of it, because, having lived for some time with the Koyukon, he "had gradually begun to look quite differently at ravens . . . [and] to *feel* the further dimension in nature that was so preeminently important to my teachers." He had begun to enter a world which, as an initial chapter title names it, is "watchful," a natural world in which everything has spiritual power and animals are close to human beings because once, in the Distant Time, they were human. So much turns on the fact, not as with us, that humans are not like animals but rather that animals are like humans. This secures a human, ethical ground for animal rights, which are acknowledged by the Koyukon. But, then, everything in their world, even landforms and the booming ice on the lake (as here/now), has "rights," is to be respected because, as a Koyukon remembers his father's counsel, *"he said* EVERYTHING *has life in it."* The natural world is a community little different from and related to the human community; it is intimately experienced, and it requires, as the maintenance of any society does, the respectful (and reverent) behavior that comes of recognizing the I-Thou. *"It's just like talking to God, that's why we talk to the raven,"* a Koyukon tells him. And so, knowing this, Nelson makes this knowledge his own. He, too, talks to the raven, makes his prayer, asks for the luck which figures largely in this "belief system": "After a long, self-conscious hesitation, I shouted '*Tseek aal* [Old Grandfather], bring me luck!'"

The epilogue suspends his belief:

> I stood beneath the tall timber and watched a raven fly above me. . . . And I wondered what, or who, it really was. Certainty is for those who have learned and believed only one truth. Where I come from, the raven is just a bird [an It]. . . . But where I am now, the raven is many other things first . . . a person and a power, God in a clown's suit, incarnation of a once-omnipotent spirit. The raven sees, hears, understands, reveals . . . determines.
>
> What is the raven? Bird-watchers and biologists know. Koyukon elders and their children who listen know. But those like me, who have heard and accepted them both, are left to watch and wonder.

Taken together, these anecdotes are representative in Kenneth Burke's sense: They represent the book, that is, *Nelson's book*, the many other things that he has learned and that have brought him into the Koyukon truth. What he records—the impressive deep ecology of the book—belongs to *where I am now*, to an overwhelming present experience of inhabiting a reality different from any he had known. This, perhaps, is the deepest reward of inhabiting. He tells us that he "was suddenly confronted with the power of this reality," that never before had he "found access to this element" of the lives of native peoples, and that now, although intellectually prepared, he "was entirely unprepared for it emotionally, unready for the impact of *living* it." This experience challenged his assumptions but it did not, he claims, convert him, and this is why we find him *between*, certain only that no single truth is certain, knowing that we are limited by our speculative instruments—that reality is a construct, "not just what we see, but what we have *learned* to see." Nevertheless, the book is testimony to what he learned to see and feel, the latter often spoken for in journal entries. It is proof of the fact that the Koyukon "inhabit an ecosystem that can be *comprehended* from their perspective." His book offers us this perspective and the correlative ecological ethic, and its title is an imperative to adopt the Koyukon view of the forest. The considerable extent to which he has done this is evident in *The Island Within*, where he is *between* (in another sense, and because he prefers the Koyukon way), and concludes in the epilogue with another encounter with Raven. Here, by telling a story of the Distant Time, he tells us why we should make prayers to Raven. In this story, Raven restores light and life to a darkened world: "As light flooded over the earth the people celebrated, knowing Grandfather Raven had brought the world back to its proper order and saved them all from certain death." The moral, obvious enough, is underscored at the close, where Nelson speaks for all of us:

As I watch him [the raven] grow smaller in the distance, I feel a deep longing, pangs of uncertainty, and a sense of aching, overpowering loss.

Then the words come, without hesitation or self-consciousness, almost without thought:

"Grandfather Raven!
We've lost the light . . .
Toss it up [the sun]!
Toss it up again."

Raven

> *wha, wha, wha* flying
> *in* and *out* thru the smoke hole
> —Gary Snyder, "Through the Smoke Hole,"
> *The Back Country*

At the headwaters itself . . . ravens are meditating, and it is from *them* that the river actually flows, for at night they break down and weep.
—Barry Lopez, *River Notes*

As much as anything, my appreciation of *Make Prayers to the Raven* is owing to where I am now, at the very southern limit of the boreal forest, in a land, like that of the Koyukon, of rivers and lakes, where the weather deserves to be personified because the "cold [as this morning] comes with a dense and heavy calm that leans upon the land." I am here in the woods because in the woods I come to my senses. Here I attend some of the natural events of importance in the life and lore of the Koyukon—the migration of birds, the breakup of the ice—and much of what I see—the pine grosbeak, first seen this winter—belongs to a natural history that goes back to the Distant Time. ("*In the Distant Time, grosbeak-man made a long trip* [and met a giant woman with whom he made love]. . . . *He became a bird and escaped from her body, but ever afterward the grosbeak was colored red from her blood.*") Nelson's book is a native ornithology, botany, and zoology, in which the Linnean taxonomy is of less importance in ordering species than the Koyukon sense of their spiritual power and economic use. It might be placed with the other guidebooks we have, though it is preferable because, in ways they don't, it peoples my world.

There's the white spruce, of which I have planted more than a thousand. Nelson treats it in a section on "The Sheltering Forest," where "plants [are] born with a Protestant ethic," and he places it first, under the heading "Green Spires," because, spiritually and economically, it is first. The three pages he devotes to the spruce are typical of the collagist form he often employs: a composite of minimal scientific data, his own impressions and testimony, the Koyukon significance, a story of the Distant Time (indented, in italic, with an unjustified margin), and a journal entry (also indented and unjustified). The white spruce, as in the cover photograph, identifies the boreal landscape. Unlike black spruce ("muskeg gnomes"), "these are the tall and narrow spires so often silhouetted against the horizon, enhancing the slow transfiguration of sunset or piercing the clear depths of moonlit sky." Aesthetic impressions, his and those of the Koyukon, are always recorded because beauty is as important as economy; and here his impressions belong to a configuration that spells out benignity, for Nelson also tells of looking for the tree's rare golden-colored needles, his experience of the tree's healing pitch, and the evident pleasure he finds in "the beautiful log houses [made of spruce] most Koyukon people live in." The story of the Distant Time explains why spruce at lakeside have "long, skinny roots," and the journal entry at the close, depicting Nelson's repose beneath "the outstretched arms of a giant spruce," brings him home. ("The Koyukon are a people of the forest. . . . Home is in the forest.")

The variants of this composition include Koyukon riddles, oral comments and stories of present-day Koyukon, and supporting scholarly evidence, notably from the large work of Father Julius Jetté. The method is conspicuously one of conglomeration, an appropriate method for a particularist and someone who feels surer of what he's been told when experience itself gives it to him. The frequent admission that his teachers didn't tell him all he wished to know and that some things were not vouched for in his experience strengthens the credibility of what he calls "this beginner's account."

The riddles, some of which reappear in *The Island Within*, are, for me, the hallmark of the Koyukon imagination, a strict form of perception and playfulness. I choose an example from the section on grouse because this morning, walking in the woods with Flash, we flushed three.

> *Wait, I see something: It scatters little wood crumbs from the trees.*
> *Answer: The ruffed grouse, feeding in its high roosting places.*

And I choose it because the story of the young girl who was transformed into a ruffed grouse in order to escape Raven recalls the myth of Tereus and Philomela.

Few of the predatory or large animals of the northern forest live here, in my experience only the red fox and the black bear. Sometimes a moose is reported to have strayed this far, or a wolf may come down to inspect old haunts on Wolf Lake. The deer is *the* large animal of our far-from-subarctic woods, though today, at $-28°$ F, they are cold enough. Maybe that's why I think of the loon, whose return I await: *"Loons always come in after good weather turns cloudy and rainy, around breakup time."* But all along I had the loon in mind because Nelson's account of the *dodzina* tallies with my experience of the bird I'm most familiar with, the summer companion of my otherwise solitary swims, a partner in hide-and-seek. Its four inimitable calls are signature enough: "Heard at evening in the silent wildlands, from the shore of a lake surrounded by deep timber," Nelson says, "it is the essence and beauty of the north country itself." Yes, as Minnesotans know. But for the Koyukon the loon's call is also a manifestation of spirit power, the source of inspiration for their own songs. According to a Koyukon saying, *"When a loon calls on a lake, it is the greatest voice that a human can hear. . . . 'The loon's call is the one against which all others are judged.'"*

Two instances of the Koyukon appreciation of the loon are associated with Chief Henry, whose last days and death may be said to be a motif, his fading presence making him, imaginatively, the last of the Koyukon. Of the three concluding sections of the book (the chapter on "Nature and the Koyukon Tradition," the epilogue, and appendix 1), the first closes with a journal entry on the death watch at Chief Henry's house. We are many pages from the beginning of the book, where, by way of aerial flight to Huslia, we shift our minds "from the modern world of the outside to the traditional world of village, land, and nature." We have become insiders and soon will hear Chief Henry say: *"I know that my time is near. . . . But I have had a good life. I have camped many times beneath spruce trees, roasting grouse over my campfire. So there is no reason to pray that I might live on much longer."* Like the author, finding that "subsistence is a [pleasurable] way of life, not just a way to make a living," we defer leaving. Chief Henry represents the Koyukon way and "the greatest wisdom in a world Raven made," the fact that over millennia the Koyukon have been the "stewards and caretakers" of a vast land, the land itself, so little changed, their legacy. A *wildland* and not a *wilderness*. Nelson has waited until now to tell us this because we define wilderness as empty and uninhabited, and to think of the Koyukon "homeland" as wilderness "reflects [our] inability to conceive of occupying and utilizing an environment without fundamentally altering its natural state." *Fundamentally* is the keyword, for land is always altered by human presence, and "the oldest task in human history," as Leopold reminded engineers in 1938, is "to live on a piece of land without spoiling it." We have not often been wise in this way, and all reports from Alaska indicate that development is still spoliation. This may be why Nelson responds to the sad songs at the death watch with a vision: "A clear image of the future entered my mind, an image of beautiful green forest, lush and alive with summer, in a time when Koyukon people were long vanished from this land." The image is at once elegiac, apocalyptic, and optative. Acculturation may bring the death of the Koyukon lifeway, but as it proceeds the old men remain skeptical. One of them tells Nelson that "we never know how long we'll have all this white man stuff, so we might need a dog team if there's no more machines." What the old man doesn't say, and wishes, Nelson adds: "The white man, like all else in the northern world, is destined to ebb and flow." Over the course of time, the beautiful green forest will recover itself, such is the strength of the earth, the greatest spirit power. But meanwhile the beautiful green forest answers to the landscape of Nelson's future on an island off Haida Strait. The final journal testimony in appendix 1 also turns on the songs an old Koyukon woman sings to her granddaughter:

> I was transfixed, and for those moments there was no world beyond what I saw. My senses could scarcely contain the beauty around me. Sometimes I am over-whelmed by my feelings for this place and people, and I wish for a way to possess them in words and pictures. But neither will do, and the most I can hope for is a memory that is burned forever into the core of my mind.

Borrowing from Victor Turner, we might consider Nelson's ethnographic studies a pilgrimage that eventuates in an experience of communitas that measures all subsequent experience and is not fully recovered when sought for singly in the beautiful green forest.

> Go fish and hunt far and wide day by day. . . . Rise free from care before dawn, and seek adventures.
> —Thoreau, *Walden*

The Island Within begins and ends with Nelson's recollection of Grandpa William, a Koyukon elder; it rehearses considerable Koyukon lore; and Raven is a significant presence. All of this may be said to focus on the initial paragraph of the book, where Grandpa William announces one of its themes: "A good hunter . . . that's somebody the animals *come* to. But if you lose your luck . . ." The opening and closing chapters of the book, which follow the course of the year from one hunting season to another, are detailed accounts of hunting deer, not wantonly for sport but for subsistence and according to the Koyukon way.

For reasons that are creditable yet still, I think, insufficient, Nelson, who now lives on the Northwest Pacific coast and is engaged in nature writing, has chosen not only to live as the Koyukon people do, with respect, humility, and restraint in the watchful world, but to hunt, "to take a portion of [his] family's food from the land and sea." Necessity does not press him to do this; not even the desire to know where his food comes from so much as the desire to participate in the flow whereby death furthers life, to be an agent and locus of this fundamental transformation, itself a paradigm of how the world enters us, how an island without becomes an island within.

And then, more than anything he does in this book of exploration and adventure, hunting joins the two, usually unreconciled, "homes" that define its world, the *house* on the beach from which he leaves for brief visits to the *island* and to which he returns, as in the last chapter, with food for another year. These "homes"—he uses *home* for both—figure in the out-and-back/withdrawal-and-return of nature writing for civilization and nature, and though Nelson respects both, they are not equal. Of the many instances of his misgivings over their claims, the following is the most succinct: "She [Nita, his partner] looks ahead, toward the lights of the town, anticipating *her* cozy little house. I turn and watch longingly behind" (my italics). Here the domestic world, as we often find it in nineteenth-century American literature, is "feminine" and constrains men who look elsewhere for adventure. And all the more, it seems to me, when both homes answer to the need for security and love and when the freedom to adventure is a gift. Even as he acknowledges this, Nelson omits the adventure and notes the obligation: "and to Nita . . . for working full time so I could be at home to write."

In the societies he has studied, hunting (providing) is the measure of manhood and is its token here, along with the desire to teach his son Ethan the necessary skills and requisite attitudes. But Nelson has misgivings about hunting—these more than want of luck bring failure—and more often than not forgoes killing. Snyder speaks of hunting as "making love with animals," and this is true of the watcher that Nelson becomes. It may be, given the curious logic of betweenness, that civilization has made him a hunter. Never, to the extent exhibited here, has Nelson had to take account of competing allegiances. When he speaks in the preface of being guided in his daily conduct by the teachings of Native Americans and, at the same time, of remaining "deeply committed to the Euro-American culture into which [he] was born," these allegiances seem to be complementary. But they are not: His experience throughout is ambivalent, its contradictions unresolved. In fact, fidelity to this complex truth is a notable achievement of what he calls his "progress report." It saves it from much that otherwise might seem simple.

That he finds himself on a last "frontier" may explain the ease with which Nelson adopts (falls into?) the nineteenth-century way of thinking about civilization and nature. Another explanation, especially for a nature writer who equates the wild with adventure, is a reverie toward childhood (Bachelard's term) that finds its historical ground in a time when nature was unspoiled. (As the unnamed island is, the few scars of military occupancy and clear cutting setting off all that is still pristine. Imagine finding such an island now, at one's front door!) For me the touchstone of this is Leopold's remark, "I am glad I shall never be young without wild country to be young in." Leopold was fortunate, and so is Nelson, who says of his apprenticeship to the Koyukon people that he had "the privilege of experiencing again a child's discovery of the world." This might also be said of his experiences on the island, especially those, contrary to Koyukon wisdom, that are adventures because they involve unnecessary risk. Of these, surfing alone in the cold waters of the northern Pacific is probably the best example, offering, as it does, the occasion of being "thrilled by the wildness of it all." I take the phrase from an account of two vicarious adventures, one in which Ethan is nearly seized by an eagle, the other in which he must swim in rough water to the skiff. Nelson's response to the former is to wish his "childhood had been filled with such experiences," but then, reflecting on the latter, he realizes that there was "no need to envy his [Ethan's] youthful adventures": "The mistake I made was in defining myself out of his childhood and assuming my own had ended." Childhood is a desideratum, and the watery (temperate) world he has chosen to live in belongs to it.

In "The Island's Child," the central adventure of birding reminds Nelson of Joseph Grinnell, the only naturalist he mentions. In 1896, Grinnell visited this very place in search of bird eggs, and his writing ("laced . . . with delightful asides") represents the kind of nature writing that inspired Nelson in his youth and, having turned from scientific writing, now defines his own "richly descriptive field reports." Here, too, the desire to enter a sea cave, resisted only because the price is death, hardly needs explanation. To be physically at home (in nature), to enjoy "the elixir of the senses," to seek the intimacy of contact with all that surrounds him (who but Whitman is more sensitive to and desirous of touch?) is always erotic. So now, as he fronts the rebounding wave, he is kissed ("I've never been kissed so vehemently"), as he will be again simply by breathing ("I breathe in as the forest breathes out; we press our opened lips together and pass the air back and forth between us").

Love, a key word, enables him to assimilate nature to home—to make nature home—even as it is the word he employs to speak of the "conflicting absolutes" of his recurring sense of being between. He tells us that the "human love" of Nita and Ethan "sustains" him but that "deep inside" (the island within) he feels "an ache, an emptiness" because their love of the island does not match his ("we cannot share in the same way or with the same intensity"). Desire—he speaks of a "shapeless desire" that brings him to the island, where he finds "an elemental comfort much like shared human love" and "revel[s] in the absence of purpose"—desire prompts him "to give more of myself to the island" when "need" (work, perhaps guilt) prompts him to give it less. These are the "two compelling loves" he is torn between, a psychosocial conflict that he attributes to history, to "the accident of being born to a culture that separates nature and home [civilization]."

But the home on the beach is not *home* to him, is never realized in that way or even as a social place, a dwelling in a community. The only representation of town is economic, the fleet of boats competing to empty the sea of fish, taking advantage of nature's flow as loggers too have done in this wonderfully wooded region. Town means work, and the work of writing that Nelson does there seems to be done reluctantly. (This is why I think of Hart Crane's apt commentary on Rip Van Winkle in *The Bridge*.) Nita and Ethan, for whom town is home, are not realized either and more often than not are figures for conventional sentiment; they are the only significant Others, in a book characterized by merger, with whom he does not merge, and they serve as foils in much the same way that Topaz, a fishery biologist of Zennist persuasion, does. The domestic concern of greatest importance, the death of Nita's mother, is also treated, it must be said, in a sentimental way and may have been included, when other domestic events were not, because death is a pervasive theme of the book, and Mrs. Couchman's death, accepted by the family in Christian terms, moves Nelson to state his own essentially Koyukon view.

Nelson's Koyukon teachers believe, as he does, that "Christian teachings offer little guidance on how to live with[in] the whole of creation," and they "kin-

dled," he says, his "interest in searching for answers on this island." By answers
I think he means confirming experiences: The experiment he undertakes on the
island tests the Koyukon view, the "ancestral wisdom" he would now, at this
stage of civilization, like to recover for us. The experiment requires that he
inhabit the island and thereby achieve a sense of place, for place is not his by
privilege of birth, a native place, as with the Koyukon, but only his by virtue
of the transformations told in the book, the all-essential transformation being
from (hostile) space to (intimate) place, from *out* to *in*, from world alienation
to worlding. The external world, the indifferent Other for most of us, is usually
thought of as hostile and becomes a friendly or intimate place when we *make*
our dwelling there. For Nelson, as for Thoreau at Walden, the chosen site,
because of the deep reasons that prompt the choice, is not considered hostile; it
is a case of love at first sight, and what Nelson wants is to become *more* intimate. He does not live on the island in the way that Thoreau lived his seasonal
round at the pond, but his frequent excursions bring the needed familiarity. He
follows the Koyukon way of knowing, through experience—through "direct
intercourse and sympathy," as Thoreau said, and to the end of "Indian wisdom." But knowing for him may also be construed in an erotic sense, and the
search, so often dreamlike, may be romantic, a quest for love, for the anima, for
the ultimate gift of ensouling. (Others, understandably, do not participate in this
profound monodrama.) In the chapter devoted to town, Nelson "treats" himself
to an evening view of the island, which he describes as "lovelier and more
mysterious than ever, like a beautiful woman seen from afar." The emotion he
feels is "an elemental love much like one shared between people," and he asks
us to consider it in terms of the affection the Koyukon feel for their homeland,
an intimacy, he says, he is beginning to understand. But the many instances of
his closeness to the natural world, especially to animals, go beyond anything we
find in *Make Prayers to the Raven*. The Koyukon, at home in the world as he
will never be, do not make such demands on nature: "Perhaps I want more
closeness than could ever exist for me, wishing away barriers [of culture] that
will never disappear." And the Koyukon do not, as he does in providing a clue
to his motive, harbor secret dreams of touching deer (caribou). The complete
sentence needs quoting: "Over the past year, I've kept a secret dream, that I
would someday touch a full-grown deer on this island." The book culminates in
the realization of this dream. In the context of hunting, this much-prefigured
episode is the crucial dramatic instance of intimacy, the doe, in *her* "amorous
confusion," choosing his attentions rather than those of the buck. This, as well
as the foregoing, may make less farfetched my recollection of Hudson's *Green*

Mansions. Thoreau speaks of marrying nature as a way of engendering the imagination. Nelson literally wants nature to love him, and he uses imagination and art to this end. "Closeness," he says, "is my talisman," and his fable is of an eros that only nature can satisfy. In this way he fulfills the possibilities of being.

> My purpose, which has emerged gradually and of its own accord, is to under-
> stand myself in relationship to the natural community of which I am, in some
> undefinable way, a part [and apart]. I've come seeking a better sense of how I
> fit into this place, not only as a visitor and watcher, but as a participant. From
> the beginning I've had a nebulous idea of "studying" the island or of exploring
> a world that seemed external to myself. But the exploration has turned inward,
> and I have slowly recognized that I am not an outsider. . . . I am an inhabitant,
> a member of the [all-inclusive natural] community.

The title of the book, another constitutive metaphor, asks us to attend this in-ward exploration, which becomes necessary because the natural world *is* external to him, and only language, which mediates self and world, can bring it to him. *The Island Within* names the process of its making and the end result: "The island and I," as he says, "turning ourselves ever more inside out"—this, in the manner of projective verse, using the *out* to tell the *in*. The book itself is his island, the fullest transformation of *out* to *in*. It is the verbal representation of fully contextualized experience, everything an event related to the whole it helps to create. Having chosen to experience the world directly, nothing, he finds, is "a splintered fact," and, in one instance, a brown creeper is "a living, borderless thing, mingled with the place that made it, shaped by my own senses and thought, and woven into what is becoming the island in my mind." And *of my mind*: the island set down in words.

Probably nothing geographical is so easily equated with the self as an island and nothing so gladly followed by those who make such equations as the advice Thoreau gleaned from William Habington:

> Direct your eye-sight inward, and you'll find
> A thousand regions in your mind
> Yet undiscovered. Travel them, and be
> Expert in home-cosmography.

Waiving all other expertise, Nelson, as I read him, is on the way to finding that he must become expert in home-cosmography. Writing itself, in now being open, discovers more than he knows. It has taken him into hitherto uncharted places, to a wilderness/homeland within.

Nelson writes best within established forms, as in *Shadow of the Hunter* and *Make Prayers to the Raven*. Now, moving beyond such forms into the freer form of the personal essay, he seems suddenly awkward. Not that he doesn't write well; the very merit of his work recalls Whitman's "The Dalliance of the Eagles," Muir's exhilarating experience of storms and the story of Stickeen, Beston's attention to the movement of the ocean and Carson's to life at its edge, Eiseley's star-thrower and Franklin Russell's birding in *The Secret Islands*. And not that he doesn't give the chapters of the books a sound cyclic and dramatic structure, but that the essays—composed of experiences told in a specious present tense, of autobiography and other recollections, of meditation on nature and ecology, and of fantasy—are protracted and do not easily keep. Nelson seems to be aware of this because he gives the chapters metaphorical titles and ends them with set pieces that answer to the heightening of closure. (The briefest: "I ask no heaven but this Raven's world." The most suspect, reminding me of Annie Dillard: "There is far too much, and the distance is too vast. I've left everything of myself there, and brought everything I am away. I stare at my own hand, trembling in the twilight, and find a mountain inside.") More troubling because fundamental is the linguistic means he employs, the correspondential method that appropriates the world and turns everything into self, that displaces things with mind, a proprietary way of seeing at odds with Koyukon propriety. The simplest unit of such displacement is the simile, the figure of speech most frequently used by Nelson. Nothing is gained, I think, by asking us to see a moss-covered stump in terms of "a hunched man in a green cloak"; we do not need the preemption of literary sensibility, a common fault of nature writing. Far better, attesting to attentive observation, is this depiction of a raven in flight: "There is no bird, only a shadow, a flat, soaring silhouette, a magic indigo hole contorting its way across the membrane of sky." Or this: "Insect swarms scribble on the slate of light." Both examples are still markedly literary, and I'd be happier with something as directly recorded as this: "Cold, clear, and calm in the pale blue morning. Snow on high peaks brightening to amber. The bay a sheet of gray glass beneath a faint haze of steam."

Some similes work the interchange that here accords with correspondential vision:

> The forest surrounds us like a great, warm creature, the trail coiled through it like an intestine. The heat of its body smolders in decomposing leaves and needles. Its chest heaves and sinks with the undulating earth. Its voice is the drawing in and pouring out of wind. . . . I breathe in as the forest breathes out; we press our opened lips together.

> The more I look, the richer [Kanaashi Island] becomes, the more deeply penetrated with life, like a stone colossus touched and made animate. Last night I listened to the island chant with myriad voices. This morning I felt the island shiver when the swells broke powerfully against it. At midday I looked in the island's throat, heard it shout, and took the cold wind of its breath against me. And now I float like a speck in the island's opened eye. Adrift between sun and rock, I gaze down inside the eye that watches and contains me.

Verbal means touch and make animate, and make possible the verification of his response in a way similar to "I touch a spruce bough and sense it feeling me." Nelson does not usually use correspondence to bring objects into the mind, where they signify symbolically as ideas, itself a means of appropriating them, but to merge himself with the objects he anthropomorphizes. And he never questions this, recognizes correspondence as a problematical manner of seeing, except perhaps for wishing that he "could see a fragment of the world as it really is." Bill Rueckert, who has been sharing my reading of Nelson, unerringly sees that the crucial problem in *The Island Within* and other nature writing is one of metaphor, and he puts it in terms of Kenneth Burke's dramatistic pentad:

> His title is a metaphor collapsing agent and scene into each other and preparing the way for his later I am the island the island is me. . . . His metaphor . . . anthropomorphizes the island rather than the other way around—that is, naturalizes him. He might better have used some terms from ecology which suggest symbiosis, interdependence, rather than an exchange of identities, or, rather, identical identities—something that is impossible. However deep his yearnings, he is not nature nor nature him, and his yearning for the primitive, for a return to earlier ways made impossible by both history and his education, is just that—a yearning.

Yes, yearning, which belongs with the honesty, truth, and detailed experience of nature that Bill appreciates in the book. The "Nelson" the author presents is engaging and admirable, seriously involved in the exuberant exploration that over the course of the year brings the accordant maturation of his autumnal meditation on death. He yearns not only for the gifts of deer (of food and love) but for what he speaks of as his ecological niche, his place in the community of nature. This, too, is part of his reverie toward childhood inasmuch as childhood, as Edith Cobb points out, is the time when we possess an "ecology of imagination" and an imagination of ecology. And only the naturalistic understanding of death as part of the flow of life, which also legitimates for him the predation in the world, makes it possible for him, finally, to feel at home, to be at home in the cosmos. His home-cosmography, which Bill questions as merely self-justifying, serves the larger end of home-cosmology. And Nelson's yearning—"how acutely alone he seems," John Haines remarks in a recent issue of *American Book Review*—is representative, for we, too, are homeless and wish to be at home.

Stephen Toulmin, in *The Return to Cosmology*, says that the "program of cosmology," once fulfilled by means of the correspondence of things celestial and terrestrial, "has an intrinsic connection with the ideas of 'natural status' and 'home.'" (Correspondence is a grand construct, a way of seeing to the end of cosmological at-homeness.) He believes that now ecology, not the "pure science" but the "practical philosophy," furthers this program. To be "at home in the world of nature," he says, ". . . means making sense of the relations that human beings and other living things have toward the overall patterns of nature in ways that give us some sense of their proper relations to one another, to ourselves, and to the whole." To be at home, then, does not require that we merge with nature but rather that we consider, in terms of our science, "the character and demands of our . . . adaptation" to evolutionary history and recover a natural theology comparable, say, to that of the Koyukon and an ethics of responsibility to nature such as Holmes Rolston III argues for in *Environmental Ethics*.

Merger, in any case, belongs to daydreams ("I drift off in daydreams, as if I've sunk into the island itself"), and such naturalizing merger, to amend Bill's statement, nullifies the self ("I become smaller and smaller, and vanish forever beneath the tide"). The death of the self in the flow is the ultimate participation in the community of life that constitutes the world, and in these terms Nelson says that it is not death but an illusion. Whitman, who subscribed to similar views, comes to mind, all the more so because Nelson's evolutionary cosmology might have been taken from Whitman's book:

Before I was gathered together . . . , I was many things: infinite and unaccountable things, unknown and unnameable things, as far back as there were rocks, before water, before this quick life that covers earth. What has coalesced to become me was in the parasol of an ancient jellyfish, the wing of a coal forest dragonfly, the eye of a Mesozoic reptile.

His sense of cosmic sustenance is also as great as Whitman's: "We are all one child," he says, "spinning through mother sky."

Another cosmological image summons the Emerson of "Circles." Nelson's inward exploration culminates in his ascent of Kluska Mountain, where, in fulfilling another dream, he comes to "the core [the heart] of the island" and finds himself ensphered in water: "The horizon is an enormous circle, surrounding the irregular circle of the shore, with the perfect circle of the mountain's base within it, converging to the innermost circle of the summit. Above it all, the cloudless circle of the sky looks as if the ocean had lifted up from beneath the horizon and circled overhead to enclose us." Being, Bachelard says, is round, and indeed it is.

That Nelson's climb to the "unhanselled" nature of the summit of Kluska Mountain neither puts in question the enterprise of correspondence nor threatens the self as Thoreau found it did when he climbed Mount Katahdin suggests the extent to which Nelson writes under the sway of reverie. Bachelard reminds me of this profoundly active imaginative work, this supremely correspondential way of coming home to the cosmos. Reverie enables Nelson to take the "spirit journey . . . [the] shaman's flight" he had not taken in his childhood in Wisconsin and to make good an otherwise difficult ontological possibility. This book discovers in him a writer of unusual imagination whose further spiritual journeys will perhaps be poetry.

What Thoreau said of himself at Walden may be said of Nelson: "[He] dwelt nearer to those parts of the universe and to those eras in history which had most attracted [him]." Yet having done so fills him with "sadness for what is lost." He says that "sometimes I feel like a survivor from that age [of discovery], a figure on a faded tintype, standing in a long-vanished, pristine world." The very ontological possibility he sometimes realizes contributes to the elegiac undertone of the book, which we read as he says he reads his island notebooks, "as if they had been discovered in someone's attic, recollections of a lost way of life." Considered now, from the present, his notebooks awaken a sense of "romance" and prompt the feeling that his experience is a "miracle."

No one among the nature writers I've read is so little political, and "an ecology apart from politics," Bill says in yesterday's letter, "is absurd, unless you just want to escape from the modern world." We can neither wait for the intercession of Raven (if we were disposed to make prayers to Raven we might improve our luck) nor "sink down into the earth and wait" for nature to renew itself, as Nelson wishes to do. His only political statement is personal: "The most I can do is strive toward a separate kind of conscience [separate because of inevitable complicty with his own culture], listen to an older and more tested wisdom, participate minimally in a system that debases its own sustaining environment, work toward a different future, and hope that someday all will be pardoned." He does not tell us how he will work for a different future. But inasmuch as he recovers the old ways he may be said to be doing this, and even elegy and reverie toward childhood may have their political uses. John Dewey reminds us, in *Art as Experience*, that literature works the most penetrating criticism of life when its "imaginative vision [addresses] imaginative experience . . . of possibilities that contrast with actual conditions": "It is by a sense of possibilities opening before us that we become aware of constrictions that hem us in and of burdens that oppress."

For most of us, the hunter's way is not an ontological possibility. Leopold's husbandry of the wild, Snyder's inhabitation of the San Juan Ridge, and Berry's settlement of America are more useful and demonstrably political models. This is not to say that we have nothing to learn from the ancestral wisdom of hunting peoples. They have taught Nelson to be watchful in a watchful world, and this is a fundamental lesson that we too must learn. Then, perhaps, it will be enough if our imaginations, as William Carlos Williams says, strain after deer; if deer, as Wallace Stevens says, "walk upon our mountains"; and if the "wild deer" unseen by us, as George Oppen says, "startle, and stare out." We might begin again by asking no more than Oppen does in "Psalm": "That they are there!"

A Letter from Richard Nelson

[*I began to correspond with Richard Nelson when, having spent a futile day in a map library, I wrote to him to find out the exact names of the places mentioned in* The Island Within. *He noted in his reply that in the original introduction to the book he had explained that all the place-names were fictitious but had decided against informing the reader of this because it might awaken curiosity and threaten the right of privacy he believes belongs to the landscape. Besides, he would have us discover, study, and care for our own places, those where we have our daily lives. When I completed my essay I sent it to him, and he replied in the letter that follows. This letter has been edited at the expense of its felicity in order to delete corrections of fact that could be incorporated in the essay, exact place-names in* The Island Within *that I sometimes knew, and encomiums consonant with the generosity of response and always gentle argument. It should be noted that the letter is a commentary that follows the exposition of the essay.*]

You correctly surmise that parts of the essay concerning *The Island Within* are troubling to me. . . .

I am especially concerned about passages that draw conclusions about my personal values and feelings, based on the glimpses I've provided in writing. This brings to mind a feeling I've often had about my own ethnographies—especially how they're viewed by the people about whom I have written. I believe the best we can do in ethnography is to create something like a caricature; the subject's identity is clear enough, but the image is distorted because the ethnographer stands outside the culture and is limited by time, experience, information, language . . .

In my later work I have responded to this problem by asking for readings and corrections from Native people in the communites where I lived. Koyukon villagers also did this for me, with wonderful results, in the "Make Prayers to the Raven" television documentaries. With this same hope, I am responding to your . . . decision to allow me to read your essay before it is published.

. . . After several rereadings, I begin to see how Thoreau's view of hunting influences the essay's perspective on *The Island Within* and by extension affects its view of my character and values. This starts with Thoreau's interesting twist on the idea that "ontogeny recapitulates phylogeny," here the assertion that individuals recapitulate the history of human culture as they go through a childhood hunting phase, which they eventually outgrow as adults.

In response, I would like to say a few words about how the outdoors fits into my life as an adult member of my society. The idea, if I understand correctly, is that my outdoors activities—especially hunting—may be grounded in a quest for adventure and a reaching toward childhood. In my opinion, both points are bound to a specific cultural milieu. I believe this because I would have thought similarly before I experienced the lifeways of Eskimos, Athabaskans, and some Euro-Americans in northern communities.

In our Western tradition, removed from day-to-day working relationship with our surroundings, we often regard the outdoors primarily as a source of adventure, play, pleasure for the senses, and other pursuits commonly associated with the freedoms of youth. Hunting is strongly perceived as a form of recreation, not as a kind of legitimate work or a way of life to be undertaken by responsible adults. As a serious endeavor, hunting and the intensely outdoors lifeway associated with it are conceived as the realm of "primitive" or "archaic" peoples, whom we may respect but also believe we have evolved beyond. (Anthropologists, of course, recognize that these cultures are as highly evolved in their own direction as we are in ours, just as biologists recognize that all organisms are equally "advanced," though on separate evolutionary courses. I suppose this is why anthropologists and biologists are becoming increasingly cautious about concepts of hierarchy and "stages of development.")

I remember when I first lived with the Inupiaq people in Wainwright, thinking how odd it was that these *grown men* spent all their time outdoors—traveling around with dog teams, camping out, fishing, hunting—doing what I regarded as play or recreation. At first it seemed as if their lives were suspended in an endless adolescence. With time, I recognized how thoroughly my perceptions had been conditioned by the culture into which I'd been born. These men were *working*. They were making a living, as surely as adults worked for a living in the community I'd left in Wisconsin. But I had grown up with a set of cultural values that led me to an ethnocentric view of the Inupiaq people and their lifeway.

The outdoors-oriented life which I pursue in my home community centers around *work*. One element of this work is fishing and hunting, by which I provide a substantial part of my family's food. In recent years we've had very little money, so the work that produces fish and venison for our household has been extremely important to us. Other activities—such as traveling, camping, learning the land and water—are also thoroughly integrated into the work I have chosen.

Like many people, such as my neighbor, who is a commercial and subsistence fisherman, I love my outdoors work and it brings me great pleasure. That my work falls into a category identified primarily as recreation and often associated with childhood is an artifact of culture. Rather than having aspired toward childhood, I believe that I have *matured into* these pursuits, assuming in my chosen way the responsibilities of adulthood and drawing from the education I've received in several cultures. As an adult, well beyond "the thoughtless age of boyhood" in Thoreau's declaration, I find any "wanton murder" of other creatures personally and ethically appalling.

. . . If my choice of words led to a conclusion that I see hunting as a "way of loving animals," I regret having created a fundamental misperception. I have written that I love animals *as they give me life*, which is a different matter. I do not see hunting as a way of expressing love toward animals, but as a way of depending upon them and as another means of *coming to love them*.

When I lived with the Koyukon people I was struck by how deeply and on how many different levels they expressed a love for animals. And I know from inside myself what it is to love animals both as a watcher and as a hunter. But it's also easy for me to understand that persons who had never experienced hunting, or who were strongly opposed to hunting, would have difficulty accepting or comprehending this.

. . . None of the place-names in *The Island Within* are found on maps. . . . I have worked with my publisher and others to keep the island's location and the identity of my home from being publicized. Mostly, this is to protect the island's wildness and solitude, to emphasize my belief that all places are equal, and to preserve my own sense of privacy. . . . My choice is to say that I live on the Northwest Pacific coast.

. . . It may be correct to say that I am not "fully engaged" with writing, in the sense that my interests and attention are divided. I have always struggled with the sacrifices necessary for writing, but until the island book never had a reason to discuss them. For me, the problem is that writing must be done *indoors*, and that I always want to be outdoors. On the other hand, if I did not love to write, I would never consider making the compromises it requires. These compromises include the extreme financial insecurity that has been a way of life for my family because of my desire to write. An attractive teaching option has long been available to me which would involve only a few months' work each year, would do away with our economic problems, and would allow more freedom for outdoors activities. Nonetheless, I have still chosen to write.

So, it would be correct to say that I struggle with mixed feelings about writing. But I am profoundly engaged with writing; and from what I know of myself, I believe that my being is deeply immersed in "verbal space." Also, I am *far* more emotionally and personally engaged with writing now than I ever was while at work on the ethnographies.

. . . I disagree with the assertions that I was obliged to write and that I was "compromised by the need to use as verbal material the experience in nature." The truth, I believe, is exactly the opposite. While I was working on the island book, I felt that writing about those experiences significantly heightened and intensified them for me, integrated them more deeply into my life, and allowed me to relive them as I never could have done otherwise.

These thoughts lead me to an aside: One thing that has sustained me through the uncertainties and sacrifices of writing is the encouragement so generously given by others. Since I started work on the island book, I've been treated to the most inordinate kindness by friends, both personal and professional, who have taken it upon themselves to guide and affirm my work. What has impressed me above all is the support that has come from other "nature writers," including people whom I'd never met.

My only explanation is that we are all working, in our different ways, for the same thing. Rather than compete, I think these writers unite around their sense of collaboration in the cause of protecting the environment and their emphasis on doing service toward their subject. Their efforts are devoted to something larger and more important than themselves, and I believe they recognize that nurturing each other's work—in all its diversity—is a way to further that cause. I interpret the recent Burroughs Award for the island book in this light.

I never experienced anything like this while I was writing the ethnographies. To my knowledge, your essay is by far the most extensive and appreciative review of my ethnographic work. I don't think my writing is particularly well known in anthropology, and it's my impression that few anthropologists (other than the ethnobiologists) really understand what I was trying to do in *Make Prayers to the Raven*.

The story of Kiluk and Patik's growing interest in Inupiaq ways is based on my later experiences in Wainwright, where I saw some younger people learning to hunt and becoming more interested in tradition. Earlier on, I had believed the young Inupiat would never make such a choice, an opinion I set forth in a section called "The Death of Hunting" in *Hunters of the Northern Ice*. Events since 1969 have shown that my predictions about the imminent demise of hunting were incorrect. In the introduction to *Shadow of the Hunter*, I said there is nothing in the book that either has not happened or could not happen exactly as described. I still believe this statement is correct. Incidentally, Patik's story is based on a young man I knew in the 1960s and last saw about ten years ago.

I take up this point largely on behalf of the Inupiat, who are struggling with enormous forces of cultural change and should be spared the added pressure of ethnographers like myself prematurely forecasting the end of their culture.

I've had little interest in, or awareness of, hunting as a political issue until the past few years. If it was discussed in Wisconsin during my childhood, I don't remember it; and here . . . the debate over hunting is heard far less than in other states. When I wrote *Shadow of the Hunter* and the other ethnographic books, I was not interested in a defense of hunting, nor was I particularly concerned about the philosophy and politics of hunting per se. My principal goal was to document the intellectual achievements of Eskimo (and later Athabaskan) people as they related to hunting and to convey the emotional power I felt in the hunting experience.

On the other hand, I was indeed motivated to defend the rights of Native people to pursue their traditional subsistence lifeways, which center around hunting. For this reason, I sometimes compared sport hunting to subsistence hunting (although I had little direct knowlege of what is generally called "sport hunting"). Behind these discussions is a long and complex political history involving Native "subsistence" and land rights in Alaska.

A minor point of accuracy regarding the statement that "Eskimos seldom hunt alone." If I wrote that, a correction is in order. Eskimos often hunt in groups and with partners, but men commonly go out on their own for seal, caribou, and polar bear and for other activities such as fox trapping.

The essay asks Girard's question, "Is the sacred always coupled with violence?" I believe this is true only if "violence" includes the killing of plants by gatherers and the destruction of natural communities by traditional and modern agriculturalists, many of whom surround their plant-focused activities with sacred beliefs and religious rituals. The further question, about civilization resting on "victimage," is an interesting one. Perhaps the most elementary of all ecological principles is that life sustains itself on other life. If we accept the idea of "victimage" and the moral judgment it implies, then worms are the victims of robins and mice are the victims of foxes, as surely as goldthread and flowering dogwood are the victims of deer.

I believe that, as a culture, we have drifted away from the deep, insightful understanding of organic life that emerges from a daily working engagement with the natural environment. I was fascinated by the book *Man and the Natural World*, by Keith Thomas, which documents the Western history of discomfort regarding our own biological nature and our deep ambivalence toward what is wild both around and inside us. Is it possible that these values from our European history are woven through contemporary discussions about the morality of one means of procuring food versus another?

. . . I assume the use of "wanton" [later in the essay] refers to the quote from Thoreau. . . . Does this mean that hunting for sport is by definition "wanton"? It sets me thinking of Audubon, Chapman, Seton, Grinnell, Pinchot, Baird, Marsh, Merriam, and many other naturalist-conservationists who were hunters or fishermen. I say this with utmost respect and from a conviction that we desperately need unity among all people concerned with protecting the environment, regardless of their differences. While we divide over issues like animal rights, eco-tactics, and management of national wildlands, our neighbors in industry have a freer hand to destroy the natural communities that have made all of our interests possible.

Although I do not consider myself a sport hunter or sport fisherman, I have much more in common with those who are than with the leaders of Exxon or Dow Chemical. To me, our shared purpose of keeping natural communities intact is more important than the differences in how we choose to engage ourselves with those communities. As an environmental activist, I believe in promoting coalitions among recreationists, commercial fishermen, sport hunters and fishermen, tourism officials, cruise ship operators—*anyone* who has a vested interest in saving the land from wholesale destruction.

. . . Regarding the phrase *"her* cozy little house," I must say that I disagree with the essay's analysis. I consider this, in every sense, *our* house, in which Nita, Ethan, and I have a shared and equal stake. It is the place where my life is most strongly rooted. I intended the phrase about "her" house to emphasize the particular circumstances of coming home from somewhere else, a situation in which Nita and I probably felt differently. This is a subtlety of language that I'm hard-pressed to explain. Perhaps you have heard the same figure of speech in similar circumstances, where someone is trying to emphasize another person's relationship to something. For example, sometimes I'll also refer to our automobile as "Nita's car" when I'm talking about a situation in which the use of it relates to a special interest of hers.

This might be a good place to acknowledge my own culpability, lest it seem that I am holding someone else responsible for impressions I have created myself. It was my choice to write about my personal life and feelings, and I alone carry the responsibility for selecting whatever information is available in the books. So I must apologize for the times when I have misled readers by my own clumsiness or poor judgment.

. . . It may be true that "civilization has made [me] a hunter," but my choice most fundamentally came from the experience of living in Eskimo and Athabaskan communities. I doubt that I would ever have become a hunter otherwise; and I assert again that while "adventure" accompanies my outdoors activities it is not their prime motivation. If "a nineteenth-century way of thinking about civilization and nature" means that I am guided by the quest for adventure, what I comprehend of myself leads me to disagree.

Earlier, I discussed the question about returning or clinging to childhood. It is true that I live intensely and actively, in a way people often abandon as adults. But again the assertion seems culture-bound. If we accept the lifeways of traditional people like Eskimos and Athabaskan Indians as one valid measure, my focus on active, outdoor living is appropriate for a mature adult.

Of course, it was I who brought up the words "child" and "childhood" several times in the book, and this requires some explanation. There is an apparent misapprehension of my sentence about "experiencing again a child's discovery of the world." I meant this not in the sense of "childish" or of recovering a lost childhood but in the sense of rediscovery, of openness to the rewards of seeing things anew, and especially of the intense learning that is our gift as children. This is not to deny that I love adventure, because I do, as the stories you mention illustrate. However, I believe it would be a tragedy to reserve the joy of adventure for childhood, and it is in this spirit that I have written.

. . . Return to the question about my relationship to our home in town: My error, I believe, lies in what I have not written. A friend once took me to task for writing almost exclusively about men in *Hunters of the Northern Ice*. It's a valid point; but after all, I set out to study what *men* do. I asked, would a writer be equally wrong to focus on women in a book about women's work? *The Island Within* is mainly about my life AWAY from town. Had I chosen to write a book about my life with family and friends inside the house and around town, I might equally be seen as having an inadequate relationship to the island.

I did not set out to write about every aspect of my life in this book. . . .

. . . From the book, it probably appears that the main values of town for me are "economic," "work," etc. But I hope that adding information to what is available in the books will broaden the picture of me and my life, beyond the "me" that is accessible in those pages.

An interesting question is brought up about people like the Koyukon seeking intimacy with animals, such as the suggestion that Koyukon people "do not . . . harbor secret dreams of touching deer (caribou)." I cannot be certain because I am not Koyukon, but I believe that many of my Koyukon teachers would go to considerable lengths to touch a deer or caribou, given the right situation. I have been with Koyukon people when they stalked within a few yards of animals, having no intention to hunt them, wishing only to be near them and to see them closely. During those times, every evidence indicated that their motives and feelings were essentially the same as mine.

The essay is correct about my emphasis on loving the natural world and the island. On the other hand, I feel that one should not ask or expect nature to love him. On page 277 of the island book, I tried to make this explicit in describing the "special wisdom" of Koyukon teaching: "to expect nothing of nature, but to humbly receive its mystery, beauty, food, and life."

It is true I put much emphasis on seeking intimacy with nature, which I unfortunately described (on page 274) as "craving inhuman love." Perhaps I should have chosen more accurate but less poetic words like "craving to fully experience my love for a being other than my own kind." I did not mean, here, a desire that such love or intimacy should be *given to me*, but a desire to experience it *within myself*, to sense in the fullest way my own love for the inhuman. Note the words immediately following: "torn between the deepest impulses . . ." I am referring to my own emotions, which are sometimes in conflict because I am both a hunter and a watcher. Here I am somewhat comforted by the knowledge that many writers have occasion to regret a misleading choice of words.

In any case, if at some deep level I want nature to love me, then I am not in close touch with my own sensibilities. Looking at it another way, what I do want is to feel that I *belong* here, as a member of this community . . . and that I have earned the right to membership by living here respectfully.

What the essay interprets as a purely verbal excercise, I must in all honesty say that I do not. I accept that my words are probably inadequate to describe my belief in the merging and borderlessness of things. But . . . the words do have real meaning for me. Perhaps I've simply not been fluent enough to express what is for me the most important lesson of these island years. Nevertheless, I am sustained by the old and widespread traditions regarding connectedness and borderlessness among things, which are embedded in Native American and other cultures around the world. Having said in the book's introduction (and in later chapters) that I am only trying to pass along ideas borrowed from other teachers and thinkers, I truly hope that I have not been guilty of "waiving all other expertise."

I am troubled by the apparent suggestion that I might have borrowed words or thoughts from Annie Dillard. The passage mentioned is one of my favorites in the island book. I don't know where Dillard has written something similar to this. I must admit that my reading of her work is extremely limited, and I've had cause for embarrassment that I could not list any of it among the books cited in the reading list at the back of *The Island Within*. In any case, honesty and integrity are among the values I treasure most, and to my knowledge I took neither the inspiration nor the substance of that quote from anyone else.

. . . My own belief is that we are all nature and that nature is us, whether we reside somewhere on the wild edge or in the middle of a city. Each of us lives in constant interchange with the natural environment—the process which keeps us alive. I believe this makes us by definition a part of nature, and it's this ecological principle that underlies the phrase "island within." Perhaps what the essay intends here is *wild* nature . . . yearning for closeness to wild nature. In any case, my emphasis is not metaphorical when I talk about being a part of nature—I mean something literal, physical, ecological, physiological.

Perhaps I've created the impression that I am "acutely alone," but if so I have seriously misled. It would be correct to say that I am at times *lonely*, a fact that I often made clear in the island book. My loneliness comes because I have an incredibly rich relationship with my family and with a group of very close and loving friends, who flow in and out of the house almost every day and who share meals with us several times each week. These friendships are the center-point of my daily life.

The responsibility for this error is mine, because I chose to write about my times of solitude, when I am lonely for the companionship that nurtures my social life. I wrote honestly about those feelings to emphasize that while I love nature I also love the company of other people. I had hoped that by writing openly it would be clear that I am not homeless, nor do I long to find a place I could consider home. I *am* at home, in a place I have no desire or intention to leave, among the closest group of friends I've ever had. . . . Perhaps only in the book's acknowledgments could a reader gain some sense of my attachment and grati-tude toward the people with whom I share life.

. . . I am concerned about the phrases a "spirit journey" and "shaman's flight," which are quoted out of context—they occur in a different chapter and in quite a different situation. Of course, I meant these words only as metaphors. This may seem a minor point, and I apologize for troubling you with it; but I prefer to steer a wide course around "New Age" thinking, and this means great caution in making reference to shamanism or spirit manipulations.

The thought about "figure on a faded tintype" is also out of context, and I disagree with the interpretation here. I used this image to describe my feelings about living in a place that remains largely pristine when so many other places have been changed. If I am attracted to historical eras, it's only because the natural environment was less fragmented and disheveled then. I assume that many others who appreciate the natural world share this sentiment.

I am also attracted to many things that are only possible in the present era, such as the privilege of looking down at the earth from 30,000 feet and of choosing a home so far from my birthplace. And like many others I might not be alive—and I would surely be blind in one eye—if it weren't for the technology of present-day medicine. This gives a temper of practicality to my romanticism.

I would like to consider the interpretation that the island book is "so little political." From the start, I saw *The Island Within* as a thoroughly and fundamentally political book, and I still see it that way, though it is not political in the traditional sense. Except for the material on clearcutting and commercial exploitation of herring, it does not reiterate themes of ecological destruction, which are thoroughly and insightfully evoked in numerous other books about nature and the environment. My political agenda in the island book has to do with changing the way we think; and the way we think underlies the way we behave—the usual realm of politics. I also consider *Make Prayers to the Raven* a similarly political book.

Outside my work in writing, I am much involved with environmental politics. For a long time, I've been on the board of directors of an environmental organization, and for the past few years I've served as its president. Whenever possible, I attend gatherings of environmental activists. . . . I am also working to gain protection for the island from the continued threats of large-scale logging and other developments.

I believe the connections between hunter and animal are fundamentally identical to those between gatherer and plant, agriculturalist and crop. What has changed in our culture, and in others like it, is the development of intermediaries between ourselves and the source of our sustenance. This has allowed us to forget that we are no less dependent on our environment than an Australian Aborigine, an African Pygmy, or an Alaskan Eskimo. I hoped, in talking about my own connections to animals and plants, that others might better recognize how they connect to the animals and plants that sustain them.

What I have not yet explored in writing, but will in the book about deer that I'm working on now, is the way all of us are engaged with the lives and deaths of wild animals. In our society, we can easily forget that the agricultural process begins with elimination of the natural community of animals and plants in the place where our crops are grown.

We can also buy our food unaware that hundreds of thousands of wild animals—notably including deer—are killed each year to protect the crops that feed us. For example, in much of Wisconsin, farmers' economic capacity to tolerate crop losses is the principal factor in setting annual hunt quotas, which keep the deer population at about twenty per square mile, where it would otherwise reach about one hundred per square mile. Throughout the United States, farmers and ranchers also acquire permits to kill (or have others kill) wild animals causing damage to crops. The harvests protected in this way include almost every food we eat—from corn, alfalfa, lettuce, and broccoli to wine grapes, apples, snap beans, strawberries, and many more. The list also includes Christmas trees.

All of us who live by the products of modern agriculture are ecologically, if not ethically, connected with the deaths of these animals. I intend no moral judgment here. It is simply another element of the living process that we have delegated and overlooked.

In my view, we have difficulty in comprehending our relationships with the environment because our ecological connections to nature—including animals like wild deer—are so convoluted. The supermarket is an agent of forgetfulness. We have forgotten our own biological selves, which we sustain in one way or another at the "expense" of our fellow organisms. We have also forgotten, or at least abandoned, what traditional people like the Koyukon believe—that not only animals but also plants and the earth itself have spirit, awareness, and full stature in the moral universe. Anthropology is a rich source of reminders that our perceptions of biological life and our constellation of moral judgments concerning it are created by a particular cultural milieu.

People like the Koyukon inherit the same moral and ethical obligations toward *all* the living things that feed them and share their world, while we limit such obligations to certain culturally favored organisms and suspend them with regard to others. I address these issues with great respect toward persons whose beliefs differ from my own or differ from those of traditional peoples. My goal is to nurture a sense of common ground among those of us who love nature. Again, I am concerned about the issues that divide people who are otherwise in fundamental agreement about the need to protect our environment.

Shifting the topic slightly, I should make clear that Athabaskan Indians and Inupiaq Eskimos have long had access to imported agricultural foods. Even in the mid-1960s, when I stayed in Wainwright, people could have lived on groceries from the village store. They would have considered it an extreme hardship, but it was a possibility. In other words, the boundaries between people like Alaskan Natives and people like me are somewhat hazy. There is a great political debate over this issue in Alaska concerning the definition of "subsistence" and the legal rights accorded to those who follow a subsistence lifeway. The town in which I live—with a mixed population of eight thousand Natives and non-Natives—is presently granted the special rights of a subsistence community.

On a related question: Does the element of recreation, adventure, or pleasure enter into the morality or ethics of hunting? The Eskimos and Athabaskan Indians experience great pleasure and something akin to adventure—if not adventure itself—as an integral element of hunting. While a prime motive is to provide food, it's extremely difficult to sort out and rank the motivations in something so emotionally bound as hunting. This brings to mind the matter of biology, the connections between people and their sources of food, the human animality that has been so long perplexing to Western culture. A similar challenge of sorting out motivations with regard to biological processes seems to underlie the religious edicts deeming sex for procreation conscionable while sex for pleasure is not; as if it were possible to carry out the act of procreation without pleasure. . . .

. . . I gain from the essay a sense that the island book is flawed by the fact that I've hunted while living in my own cultural community, where other sources of food are available and the motives of pleasure and adventure might be perceived as having a different role. When I worked with the Eskimos and Athabaskans I also hunted—although I could have gotten by on commercial foods purchased at the village store or shipped in from Fairbanks. In the earlier books I wrote little about my own engagement with hunting, which was both my primary source of food and my fundamental method of learning, just as it was for the island book. But in every case, whatever choices I have made regarding sustenance, I have tried to understand how I am engaged with the lives and deaths of wild animals, whether direct and near-at-hand or indirect and distant. . . .

. . . Above all, I am striving toward a life centered around respect toward others, toward my surrounding environment, and toward myself. . . .

Sincerely,
Richard Nelson

Eiseley

Back and Down

LOREN EISELEY'S *IMMENSE JOURNEY*

Turn to any of the figures about whom Eiseley writes: Bacon, Darwin, Emerson, Thoreau, Jeffers. These "representative men" are all self-characterizations, partial portraits in the conspicuous self-presentation of his work. He speaks in *All the Strange Hours* of the "concealed essay," a modification of the personal essay in which "personal anecdote was gently allowed to bring under observation thoughts of a more purely scientific nature." But *concealed* does not conceal the accommodation he found for the tension he had been made to feel in the double claim of science and literature. "Science and Humanism," a rubric in *The Star Thrower*, puts these claims in current terms. There Eiseley addresses them in respect to C. P. Snow's *The Two Cultures*, only to deny the opposition, which he says—and his work notably proves—is an illusion. Nor does the curious word *concealed* conceal his predilection for the essayist's trying out of autobiography. "Nature and Autobiography," another rubric, puts the issue in these terms. It may be that *concealed*, which awakens suspicion, answers to and reveals the condition stated in what immediately follows his definition: "That the self and its minute adventures may be interesting every essayist from Montaigne to Emerson has intimated, but only if one is utterly, nakedly honest and does not pontificate."

I am not alone in feeling troubled by Eiseley, not because I would have him tell me more than he does or speak otherwise, but because, as Robert Finch says in a review of *The Lost Notebooks of Loren Eiseley*, he is often "stagy and sentimental." Fred Carlisle, who had several interviews with Eiseley, says in the preface of his book that he had been wrong in assuming that Eiseley would "reveal things about his life that he did not carefully control or stage." Eiseley's concern for his "public image," he found, was impregnable. Staging the self and making it the focus of feeling may account for his popularity (popularity, I suspect, is what his scientific colleagues held against him); this, and the somber prophecy against which he raised his hope, which reminds me of Lewis Mumford, with whom he corresponded. In every sense, Eiseley is a truer autobiographer than Mumford, his autobiographical impulse primary, deep and genuine, prompted from the start by a desperate need to create and confirm his identity and forestall the nemesis that he figures as the Other Player. Even so, he inordinately dramatizes himself and stages over and over the scenario of his life. He takes life, as all of us must, by the handle of the self, but the self noticeably plays this role. I speak of *scenario* because, as James Olney observes in a review of *All the Strange Hours*, Eiseley's avowed autobiography, he "has written this same book, under various disguises and titles, more than half a dozen times before." But I cite what he says only for its general truth: *All the Strange Hours* is not the same book, being at once fuller and more masterful than the "oblique autobiograph[ies]," as Olney calls the earlier work, and dependent on them for its overwhelming resonance.

My appreciation does not cancel my criticism so much as show what comes of reading all of a writer's work and sharing his "inner galaxy." Years ago, when I dismissed Eiseley, it was on the evidence of brief acquaintance: this, contrary to the way I read. And since my dismissal took the form of refusing to direct a dissertation on him proposed by a very good student, contrary to my willingness to follow a student and participate in new work. This is the single instance (and I regret it) of not accepting an invitation to enter on work suggested because thought to be congenial with my interests, and I think that I rejected Eiseley then for the very reason that he engages me now, his use of the idea of correspondence. By the time I was asked to consider Eiseley, I was more critical than I had been of this idea as it enters so centrally in the work of the Romantics—no longer pleased with the symbolic displacement of the world (the things of the world) by the mind and its symbolic appropriation to the end of aggrandizing the self, as if self-culture were the ultimate vocation. I had thought often of Emerson's dream of eating the apple of the world and had noted in his journal his remark that the universe is pendant to men, and I was no longer ready, even in behalf of spirit, to share the confidence in an age-old way of thought that permitted him such dreams and ideas. Eiseley simply crossed my path at the wrong time, and later, when he crossed my path again—this time by way of a volume of late poems I found in a secondhand bookstore—I was still critical but more disposed to take the trouble to see what he made of this fundamental idea.

To begin with Eiseley's poetry is to begin at the beginning because at the outset he was a poet—and in a more auspicious time would probably have remained one. (Of course, in his way, he remained one.) And at end, in the homing of the later poems, he returned to his beginning. He closed his life and the circle of time in a most significant way for autobiography, and with poems themselves markedly autobiographical. In fact, it was during the time he was writing *All the Strange Hours* that he published *Notes of an Alchemist* and *The Innocent Assassins*, the first of the three volumes of poems published in his lifetime, a fourth volume, mostly of early poems, published after his death. This turning back, it seems to me, was prefigured in 1965 in the foreword that Eiseley wrote for *Not Man Apart*, a Sierra Club book commemorating Robinson Jeffers and the Big Sur coast. During his apprentice years as a poet, Eiseley responded most deeply to Jeffers, whom he met at Carmel and with whom he corresponded, and his best literary reviews of this time were those on Jeffers. Some of what he said then he incorporated later in the foreword, not, I think, because he found it expedient, but because it was so essentially true for him it had weathered time.

One may take as a measure of what is important to Eiseley the degree to which he works by identification and assimilation. He found agreeable the idea that we see what we are, that we follow our temperament, the iron wire, as Emerson said, on which the beads of our moods are strung. "The poet's peculiar temperament," he wrote in regard to Jeffers in 1932, "is the master of these [natural] forces and uses them for its own ends." Eiseley accords temperament more than Emerson initially does in the essay "Experience," where it is said to be a limitation. And citing from Thoreau's journal entry on the superiority of the "wild" in literature as the gauge of Jeffers' strength, he says that the peculiar temperament he has in mind is rare. (*Peculiar* calls up *peculium*, the word Sampson

Reed defined in *Observations on the Growth of the Mind* as the divine legacy of the unique individual self, a word Emerson adopted as synonymous with *temperament* and associated with *genius*. We are more likely to think of *peculiar* as the dictionary defines its first meaning: "Unusual or eccentric; strange; queer," words sometimes used to characterize Eiseley.)

For Eiseley the rarity of Jeffers' temperament is owing not to divine legacy but to the integral relationship of the self and the environment. "It is that very rare phenomenon," he explains, "which happened once at Walden and a few other places"—Big Sur for one, and for another, as all of his work insists, the *altiplano*, this final word in *All the Strange Hours* bringing him home at last to the high plateau of his native Nebraska. This rare phenomenon comes about with "the complete identification of the individual with his environment, or, rather, the extension of the environment into the individual to such a degree that the latter seems almost a lens [Emerson's image in *Nature*], a gathering point through which, in some psychic and unexplainable manner, is projected a portion of the diversified and terrific forces of nature that otherwise stream helplessly away without significance to humanity." The lens is doubly important, an inner result of relationship that enables the poet to project outward what Eiseley later called the "inner galaxy." *Inner galaxy* (so nicely cosmological) is a metonym for correspondence, which Eiseley may have already learned from Emerson and Thoreau—his denial of their early influence only confirms it—is a doctrine of sympathetic relationship and reception as well as of expression.

In some psychic and unexplainable manner. Eiseley later speaks of this as *alchemy*, taking the term from Jung. When he concurs with Freud's view of the unconscious sources of creativity, he cites Emerson: "I conceive a man as always spoken to from behind, and unable to turn his head and see the speaker." Charles Olson, also indebted to Jung, speaks of this transformative miracle of relationship when he says, in "Proprioception," that "the unconscious is the universe flowing-in, inside."

What should be noted, since the passage speaks for Eiseley's sense of this relationship, is that the agent, the active force, is not the self, sometimes said by others to be co-extensive with the world, but the environment. In the foreword, he says that both Thoreau and Jeffers were "profoundly 'imprinted,' as the modern biologist would say, with their natural environment . . . and they drew their literary sustenance from it."

At the outset, then, when he was very much involved with the *Prairie Schooner* and writing poems and reviews for it and other little magazines, some regional and some not, such as the *Midland* and *Voices*, he was familiar with the idea of correspondence. As with Emerson, this idea enabled him and his associates on the *Prairie Schooner* to hold to geography rather than tradition. Regionalism, a powerful movement at the time, reaffirmed the transcendentalists' belief in indigenous art: Place was the ground of individual talent. This, if you will, is the "tradition" to which he subscribed in his earliest criticism and in the important essays he later wrote on Emerson and Thoreau. Even Darwin, whom he placed with the "parson-naturalists" in *Darwin's Century*, belongs to it—belongs in the "more gracious, humane tradition [of the study of nature that] descends through John Ray and Gilbert White . . . to . . . Thoreau and Hudson."

Eiseley used the idea of correspondence to distinguish the writing of Thoreau and Jeffers from "mere 'nature writing' in the ordinary sense." *His* Jeffers, moreover, is always linked with Thoreau, "one of the first great writers truly indigenous to America"; linked in respect to place and also because of their aversion to society and their solitary being. Speaking for himself again, he says that Jeffers "embodies the restlessness of a wandering, adventurous and essentially active stock now turned inward upon itself"; and he characterizes himself when he reminds those more optimistic than Thoreau and Jeffers that "there will still be lonely minds surveying the night heavens, or casting forward toward our end, or lonely in lonely places finding the doctrine of acceptance and easy pleasure somehow unsatisfying."

The essential scenario is already here, for he had resumed the pioneering of his ancestors by riding the rails during the early years of the Depression, and his mind, lonely from childhood in a strange household, was confirmed in loneliness by the time he spent in lonely places recovering from tuberculosis. (If he insists on the scenario, which in full is the story of a wandering, homecoming man, it is because he appreciated the paradox of his birth. As he says in *The Lost Notebooks*, "I was born seven years after the start of the century in the wrong time, the wrong place, and into the wrong family. I am not insensible of the paradox: It is this which made me." In this instance of his art, the patent attitudinizing of the first is saved by the recognition of the second sentence.)

Eiseley does not neglect Jeffers' dark side, but the Jeffers he endorses first and last is not the poet of the long poems that tell the terrible stories of the mind turned inward upon itself. He admits in the foreword his familiarity with the dark side but chooses to remember Jeffers' "gentler aspect" and to recall the lyrics "concerned with waves and sea-fog, the small hoof-prints of deer, the clay homes of swallows under the eaves, the passages of hawks or mountain lions." He anticipates Robert Hass' recent judgment that "Jeffers is strongest in the descriptive and meditative lyrics," seeing in them, I think, the needed thing, "some gesture of love toward the universe all outward." (Hass cites from *The Tower beyond Tragedy*, as others have, Jeffers' declaration, spoken by Orestes, "I have fallen in love outward," and Jeffers' explanation of the love and reverence we owe the beautiful world, "one being, a single organism, one great life that includes all life and all things.") Eiseley's touchstone remains "The Loving Shepherdess," from which he had cited earlier in the review as an example of seeing with the heart:

> The beetle beside my hand in the grass
> and the little brown bird tilted on a stone,
> The short sad grass, burnt on the
> gable of the world with near suns
> and all winds, there was nothing
> there that I didn't
> Love with my heart . . .

To see with the heart is to see correspondentially, sympathetically. "He cannot be a naturalist until he satisfies all the demands of the spirit," Emerson says in *Nature*. "Love is as much its demand as perception." Such seeing, which Eiseley knew was "symbolic reading," may be disparaged as anthropomorphizing, but he defended it because we thereby relate ourselves to the things of the world and by doing this affirm our humanity.

Eiseley gave his heart to the hawks, and Jeffers entered his work. A sonnet written in 1935 evokes the hawks, but I cite it because this typical early poem plays on, or helps to create, the scenario and is answered within a page or so of the *Prairie Schooner* by a sonnet by Mabel Langdon, who became Eiseley's wife.

> L. E.   Terror of loneliness is over now.
> Sharp in the early morning, once the cry
> Of birds in the low pastures, or a plow
> Poised on the empty furrow, were a pry

Turning the heart clean over. As a stone
Rainwashed and sunwarmed is reluctant turned
Upward to show the darker undertone—
The blind side from the sun—so I have burned
Under the summer of too many years
Stark in the open starfall and the drouth
Not to have peace, not to be free from fears,
Done with the lonely memory of your mouth.
Desires as fierce as hunger—one by one
They all grow still—like old hawks in the sun.

M. L.   These things are ancient and betray us still:
Maps of far lands, the evil colored chart
Devised with cunning to seduce the heart
And make it transient beyond its will;
Songs in strange keys, too subtle for the ear;
Legends of women beautiful and cold—
Such tales as wanderers bring—Oh, learn to fear
These sly and stealthy enemies of old.

Darken the window that looks out to sea,
Bolt the strong door—build up a fire for night,
Quell the strange song, let map and atlas be
Hidden forever from the wanderer's sight.
Be strong in witchcraft, artful, and your guile
Shall triumph against these things . . . a little while.

(Did Eiseley remember this poem when he was writing "The Palmist" in *All the Strange Hours*? There, after the fashion of Hart Crane in "Cutty Sark," are the strange songs luring the mariner on. There never seems to have been *la belle dame sans merci*, though for Eiseley-Odysseus there seems to have been a Calypso. His homecoming, in evolutionary terms to the "first world," seems also to involve eros. "Poet or scientist, he will come home sorrowing not to Ithaca," he says in *The Lost Notebooks*, "but to the now vacant waters of his youth, yearning for what he abandoned in his youth, Calypso, the immortal one." Doesn't the perfect cadence of this sentence authenticate it? And in *The Unexpected Universe*, perhaps the book most moved by "hunger for home" and "the green world," he says: "Odysseus in his death is carried by the waves to Calypso, who hides him in her hair. 'Nobody' has come home to Nothingness.")

The imprint of the wasted, bitter land of the Great Plains is sharp and clear in the many poems he published during his long association with the *Prairie Schooner*. Almost without exception, the outer figures his inner landscape, so much so that this seems to be the only way this son of the middle border can declare himself. And there are two more imprintings that may be considered fortunate, these, again, of Nebraska: the literary apprenticeship on the *Prairie Schooner* that confirmed him as a writer (his early success was acknowledged) and the concurrent scientific apprenticeship in paleontology that extended his landscape to the Wild Cat Hills and the Badlands. Under the auspices of the Nebraska State Museum, Eiseley had been one of "the bone hunters of the Old South Party, Morrill Expeditions 1931–1933." This is how he puts it in the dedication to *The Innocent Assassins*, suggesting again that both poetry and science were necessary to him, science itself not opposed to poetry but essential to it, as much as anything part of his ground, his secret mythology. Indeed, the Badlands figure for him as the place of vision quest. In the preface of this volume of poems, he says that "as a young man engaged in such work, my mind was imprinted by the visible evidence of time and change of enormous magnitude," and he adds what every reader of Eiseley knows, that for him "time was never a textbook abstraction." "The Great Plains," Olson remarks in "A Bibliography on America for Ed Dorn," "enforces ["some millennial sense"] on everyone."

I take *secret mythology* from Roland Barthes' *Writing Degree Zero*, where he speaks of the "subnature of expression . . . where the great verbal themes of [a writer's existence] come to be installed." In his account, which is so much to the point of Eiseley's work, *style* is "a vertical dimension of thought . . . its frame of reference . . . biological or biographical, not historical." This vertical dimension plays against the horizontal dimension of *language* and brings the writer to "the threshold of power and magic." As readers of literature, we already know that imaginative writing has this depth and power, but Barthes' reminder helps us see the conflict as one in verbal space between poetry and science. Eiseley's epigraph from Thoreau in *The Immense Journey*, his first book, states the issue: "Man can not afford to be a naturalist [scientist], to look at Nature directly, but only with the side of the eye. He must look through and beyond her." And another epigraph from William Temple adds to the necessity of correspondential seeing the condition of symbolic expression: "Unless all existence is a medium of revelation, no particular revelation is possible." Eiseley believes, as he says in this book, that there is a "mysterious shadow world beyond nature, [a] final world." The vertical reaches into this final world. The *inner*, Emerson claims, answers to the *above*—or, in Eiseley's case, the *below*, to what is back both temporally and psychically.

When Eiseley uses *imprint* he always addresses what mattered most in the creation of his identity. (*Identity*, I forgot to say, is the focus of Fred Carlisle's study of Eiseley's development.) But it should also be noted, as the previous instance shows, that when he found his identity as a bone hunter he found his identity theme. Or one of them. For as he continues to set out the record in *The Innocent Assassins*, he tells us that by "some strange osmosis these extinct . . . creatures merged with and became part of my own identity." We remember, as he does elsewhere, the Whitman "stucco'd with quadrupeds and birds all over," and remember that in an evolutionary perspective this is the case. But he has more in mind when he says that he had assumed "the animal masks of many ages" and cites by way of explanation the following verse from *Notes of an Alchemist*:

> The wind has stolen my coat away,
>   my thoughts are becoming animals.
> In this suddenly absurd landscape I find myself
>   laughing, laughing.

The laughter here is of "the old ones," much needed, Eiseley believes, for "balance," Surely, to find himself laughing is a rare satisfaction, all the more so, the verse suggests, because thereby he finds himself (the me myself).

Eiseley often found himself in the guise of animals, and not only or chiefly because he saw in them the fugitive and victim he believed himself to be. In "Let the Red Fox Run," a poem published in the *Ladies' Home Journal* in 1964, not an early poem but very much like them, Eiseley identifies with the fox whose flight from the hunters redeems him from his own death.

> But somewhere still in the brain's gray vault,
> Where the light grows dim and the owls are crying,
> I shall run with the fox through the leaf-strewn wood.
> I shall not be present at my own dying.

This poem, reprinted in *The Star Thrower*, represents a substantial portion of Eiseley's early poetic universe. Obviously flawed, it is saved by what we come to recognize as Eiseley's authentic voice and by this remarkable closing stanza, in which the "I" becomes the still-living fox in the "first world" of nature and so, no longer present, is now beyond dying.

The animals, of such prominence in his work, belong, as he says in *The Innocent Assassins*, to "that haunted country"—the night country or underworld of his deepest imagining, where the poet acquires power and magic and becomes a shaman. This is what anthropological study under Frank Speck enabled him to become, what, in fact, in his early poems he was practicing to become. To Speck, he dedicated *The Invisible Pyramid*, a book of fathers. It begins with a recollection of Clyde Eiseley, who showed his son Halley's comet and, in promising him that he would see its homeward turn, gave him a primary figure of thought. It ends with Speck, who helped him find his way home to "the green world," the "old first world" that Speck himself had known as an "Indian." One, he says of these imprintings, gave him the inheritance of time and space, the other "set his final seal upon my character" and made him what he was to be. This is reason enough to call Speck "the last magician," but *magician* here also means shaman, whose ways Speck had written about in, among other studies, *Naskapi* and *Penobscot Shamanism*. *What he was to be*: not a professionally narrow scientist, never that, but a poet whose science sometimes became magic and whose task, in the words of another poet, was to "dance us back the tribal morn."

Eiseley claims our attention as a nature writer because he is a poet of science of the kind he believed Jeffers to be. He recognized Emerson's wide reading in science and advisedly used *vision* in entitling an essay on Thoreau. His lineage is clear enough, and Whitman, Melville, Hawthorne, and Poe also belong to it. No other recent nature writer I know owes so much to the writers of the American Renaissance, as much perhaps as the poet William Bronk, whose *The Brother in Elysium*, begun as an undergraduate during the years in which F. O. Matthiessen was writing *American Renaissance*, establishes his own stake in the territory. Eiseley is a nature writer of visionary power, a poet who found in science, as Yeats found elsewhere, metaphors for his poems—and essays. Mabel Langdon told him to be strong in witchcraft (this, at the time of Speck's tutelage), but in identifying with animals he had already become so. He answers, if any nature writer does, to George Fowler Appel's definition of the ideal modern animal poet: "The 'ideal' modern animal poet would be a master shaman-scientist. . . . [He] would . . . imaginatively recapture our lost sense of identity with the non-human world without sacrificing our new scientific knowledge about that world" (I cite from "Modern Masters and Archaic Motifs of the Animal Poem," Ph.D. dissertation, University of Minnesota, 1973). In fact, this new scientific knowledge, when imaginatively "read," as, say, the writers of the American Renaissance had read Nature after the example of Champollion's decipherment of hieroglyphic writing, would recover the lost world, the "timeless inviolable world," according to Appel, "of unfallen [undifferentiated] 'reality.'"

Nature writers might be identified and placed by their concern for animals.

Eiseley confirms Appel's observation that "out of nostalgia for paradise, wholeness, and timelessness, the vocation of the shaman arises." His life story might be read as preparation for becoming a shaman: the call from an animal helping-spirit, the period of mental and physical disturbance (the moratorium, to use Erik Erikson's term, of his troubled young manhood), the instruction (by Speck), the solitude (his deafness). The story, of course, would not be simple because Eiseley knew that to find Eden you have to go back and then, unless in death, can't have it. "There is no road back," he says in "Man the Firemaker," "the primitive is no longer our way." This does not alter the fact that we should respect animals and love the world but tells us that our nostalgia will have to be satisfied in, of all places, our inner galaxies, that is, in verbal, imaginative space. Poetry, for Eiseley, provided this space, an archaic space to be shared with animals.

Were it not that so much of what I find in the early poems persists—belongs to Eiseley's secret mythology—I'd write it off as attitudinizing. Spring is not this young man's season; his are the melancholy seasons of autumn and winter, of frost and snow, seasons in their nature lonely and empty. In "Nocturne for Autumn's Ending," he says that "the frost begins to crawl / On summer honey" (an arresting image), but in his belated world there never seems to be much honey. Not that there isn't passion ("mad," he says, "with the lava's flow") but too much restraint even when he knows that where transience rules one should seize the day. Many of his sonnets are love poems in which he declares love by expressing desolation: "Responsive still to unforgotten springs," now, in November, he is "brave but lost / Under the cold blue pole star of the frost." One of the sonnets, "Poem to Accompany a Poem," develops a conceit (he knows the "metaphysical" poets) in which his formal means, by way of *box*, becomes a casket, appropriately so for someone who claims, in "Portrait," that he "loves [death's] taste" and whose use of *dust* and *mold* is obsessive. The animals with whom he identifies, among them coyote, wolf, fox, deer, hawk, owl, and lark, are as lost as he is; as much victims, with only courage to endure, like the lark, "the homeless, the embittered, the lost one / On the last ["frosty"] wing." He sympathizes with "small things" that exist by flight, by *fleeing*, for even birds seldom take wing, seldom image ascension, the joyful condition of lightness that Bachelard tells us belongs to youth and its soaring spirit. (The exceptions in his later work are notable: the released hawk in "The Bird and the Machine" and the pigeons in "The Judgment of the Birds.") His imagination is seldom aerial. Among much that is suggestive in Bachelard's *Air and Dreams*, consider this: "In the realm of the imagination, as in paleontology, birds develop from reptiles."

When his imagination is aerial, it is challenged, as in "Earthward," published in the *Midland* in 1931, by the terrestrial and descendental. In the octave of this sonnet, he describes an abandoned ranch where the brown water still flows in the irrigation ditch and the larvae of a dragonfly are transformed, "shed / their tight water-shrunk skins for a crystal and gold expansion, / the unquestioning flight / along the blue air." In the sestet he *reads* what he has described:

> Men have said this before, but some few
> must learn for themselves: I find it suddenly good
> not to think any more but to mix with brown water and earth smells,
> to split the confining shell of the mind
> and relax on this oldest,
> most certain breast.

The imagery of this open, quietly meditative poem is complex, the analogy turned to wholly unexpected ends. The larval self will shed its mind, not its skin, not take flight but sink down to mother earth, *mix* (the strongest word in the poem) with the elements and thereby achieve its "expansion." For Eiseley the descent beckons chiefly as a movement toward cessation and secure rest (*relax* and *certain* are similarly strong) and not, as with Williams, toward self-recovery, the kind that Eiseley will increasingly find in memory. The downward pull of his poems is of such intensity I find myself taking the figurative literally: It *is* death he seeks, to be "safe at last in earth's darkest burrow" and glad for "the covering snow."

His vision is of extinction, confirmed by evolution and current history. Writ large in "Star Cycles," the coming extinction will call us back to what we are losing. In this poem he speaks from "the first of those deserts which will later / engulf the whole earth" and thinks of

> how, in Time's future, the people in cities clustering
> > our dying ice cap
> will yearn from a myriad housetops
> > toward that silver embodiment [Venus]
> of green woods, and the lost, unforgettable seas.

The Tennysonian echo of the closing phrase is in keeping with Eiseley's view that for us, on a dying planet, Time's past is the place of green woods.

In "Remembrance: Cape Ann," Eiseley depicts himself as a "small quick bird" in need of love, which the appositive tells us is a "crevice deep" that defends him from the "fiercer wing" of death. The axis of his imagination, as in this instance, is vertical, putting in polarity ascent and descent, sky and abyss, the latter terms of these pairs usually having the positive value we associate with the former. For an archaeologist, of course, temporality is spatial and figures vertically, as in "The Slit," the essay with which Eiseley introduces his work. Time is recovered by digging down, and autobiography, the art of memory that annuls it, is excavation. ("There is an exact analogy," James Olney says in his review of *All the Strange Hours*, " . . . between Eiseley's practice of archeology/ anthropology and his practice of autobiography.") Eiseley speaks in *The Lost Notebooks* of "the black abysm of forgotten time," recalling Shakespeare's "the dark backward and abysm of time." In defining *abyss*, the editors of *The American Heritage Dictionary* cite Eiseley's "lost in the vast abysses of space and time," thereby acknowledging one of the foremost explorers of these depths.

He knew this darkness early, and it was formative. He recalls in *The Lost Notebooks* that as a child he was "closer to the darkness under beds and sofas than my parents, whose minds *floated* high above me in the light of lamps" (my italics). Just as this home-faring man saw himself as Ulysses, so, in respect to darkness, he saw himself as Dante. The *selva oscura*, the dark wood of the *Inferno*, Eiseley says, was what he "saw . . . as a child under the bed"; and when he says that Dante saw it "when he encountered himself," he makes clear that the homophone, *dark self*, also applies. Somewhat later in *The Lost Notebooks*, under "Of Bones and Searches," the staginess of "I am a college professor and a castaway" doesn't alter the fact that for him the inner space of the mind, its darkness called time, is "the most dreadful of all deeps" and that his profession has taken him "as far into that darkness as any man alive," deeper even than the "ancient caverns, haunted tombs, and . . . great libraries" he has inhabited.

The titular poem of *All the Night Wings* is a late poem interesting for its recollection of a night visit to a graveyard with a girl who weeps when matchlight discovers "Our baby" incised on a tombstone. (Here Eiseley weeps for his childlessness.) Whoever entitled the book chose well because *night wings* is a primary poetic image in the Bachelardian sense of bringing together the polar terms of the vertical axis. In this way the dark/abyss may be said to acquire the values of flight, albeit *descendental flight*. The dedication to Mabel, written much earlier, is also fitting. In it, Eiseley asks Mabel to remember the young man who had been "Glitter Wing, the blue dragonfly"—"Remember Glitter Wing," he says, "like us betrayed by summer, his destiny to forsake the sun-paths and shiver to a pinch of jeweled dust at the first touch of frost." Remember, he implores, "his dust was jeweled!," the image once more of the authentic primary kind. The secret mythology of the poems is one with this inscription, and Mabel, who guarded his privacy, shared it.

"I have found animals in me when I stroll in the forest," Eiseley writes in "The Old Ones"; "I hesitate before a large dragonfly." Referring to this late poem in a letter to Howard Nemerov, Eiseley comments on his love of dragonflies and significantly substitutes *bow* for *hesitate* in the above line. He is, it seems, now at home in the dark wood, and his gesture is the reverential one that others have found requisite.

Not only is his imagination of the night country, it takes flight, like the owl, at night, *in the dark*. Perhaps this representative verse is an analogue:

> Consider the sly fox
> that in each season knows

the best way through the dark
though toward the dark he goes.

With Eiseley, as Emerson says in *Nature*, "Nature always wears the color of the spirit." He might have written in defense of his vocation what Emerson wrote to Lidian: "I am a poet in the sense of a perceiver & dear lover of the harmonies that are in the soul & in matter, & especially of the correspondence between these & those." Correspondence was so essential to his conception of the poet that he adhered to it even when he recognized that the cosmology it assumed was no longer tenable. The crux, I think, is the statement in the essay on Thoreau that he wrote in 1974, that is, near the end of his life, when he demonstrably settled the quarrel between science and poetry by resuming his early vocation: "He had, in the end," he says of Thoreau, "learned that nature was not an enlarged version of the human ego, that it was not, to use Emerson's phrase, 'the immense shadow of man.'" This disclaimer, according to Eiseley, tallies with Thoreau's turn, in his last years, from literature to science, a turn, it should be noted, neither as drastic nor as dramatic as Eiseley makes it out to be in behalf of his own turn from science to literature. He says categorically in *The Lost Notebooks*, which glosses the published essays on Thoreau, that "Thoreau began in literature and went to science, and I began in science and went to literature."

The insistence of this statement questions its truth. For Thoreau did not, Eiseley admits, ever give over correspondential seeing. Indeed, he could not because "the [inner] eye persisted." There was no denying this mysterious and, as Eiseley would have it by sometimes employing a capital *E* (for Eiseley? already told in his name?), this divine organ. And there was no denying the necessity of its seeing—its symbolic reading of nature—when science was already beginning to reduce everything to "a universal vortex of wild energies." This phrase recalls the "terrific forces of nature that . . . stream helplessly away without significance to humanity" of which he had spoken some forty years earlier in regard to Jeffers' saving role as a poet of science. The eye was especially prominent now because he worked from an entry he made in 1957: "'Always [Thoreau says in *A Week on the Concord and Merrimack Rivers*] the laws of light are the same, but the modes and degrees of seeing vary. . . . There was but the sun and the eye from the first.' Use this for start of nature book?" Once the eye, equally mysterious, has been a lens, not attributed to God. Now, in the substantiation of Thoreau's early belief, "the eye has many qualities which belong to God more than man."

Eiseley denies Thoreau's testimony in *Walden* that "the Visitor . . . never comes." He claims that in the guise of Thoreau himself the Visitor had come and had looked out upon the world. Moreover, the Visitor still comes; we, too, are visited: "We [are] all the eye of the Visitor—the eye whose reason no physics [can] explain. Generation by generation the eye [is] among us." An adjacent entry on Whitehead, the philosopher Eiseley most frequently mentions, suggests to me that he appropriates Whitehead's conception of God as the subjective aim, the ideal whereby each of us, in the ever-creative open of a process world, strives to actualize its possible, though always deferred, order. This may account for the definitive declaration in which Eiseley speaks for himself as well as Thoreau: "His life had been dedicated to the unexplainable eye."

And to the *I*, its spiritual correlative, for which autobiography searches. This, it seems to me, is borne out by the remarkable passage in "The Star Thrower," where, confronted by the eye in a photograph of his mother, Eiseley protests his love for the small, beaten things of the world and, himself "a creature born of Darwinian struggle, in the silent war under the tangled bank," thereby moves beyond the species boundary. This crossing is truly supernatural, and he accounts for it in the supernatural terms of a creative myth:

> Out of the depths of a seemingly empty universe had grown an eye, like the eye in my room, but an eye on a vastly larger scale. It looked out upon what I can only call itself. It searched the skies and it searched the depths of being. In the shape of man it had ascended like a vaporous emanation from the depths of night. The nothing had miraculously gazed upon nothing and was not content. . . .

> Some ancient, inexhaustible, and patient intelligence, lying dispersed in the planetary fields of force or amidst the inconceivable cold of interstellar space, had chosen to endow its desolation with an apparition as mysterious as itself. The fate of man is to be the ever-recurrent, reproachful Eye floating upon night and solitude. The world cannot be said to exist save by the interposition of that inward eye—an eye various and not under the restraints to be apprehended from what is vulgarly called the natural.

Gathered here is much that is essential to Eiseley's vision, especially the vertical of being, the negative (a theme of *All the Strange Hours*: "behind nothing / before nothing / worship it the zero"), the dimensional universe, and the belief that out of necessity evolution itself produced the organ of correspondential seeing.

Much earlier, sometime toward 1966, two entries not far apart in *The Lost Notebooks* confirm his dedication to the unexplainable eye.

> The writer's creativity is to open men's eyes to the human meaning of science . . . to prevent his relapse into "aloneness in the universe."

> I should note [having entered the title of his autobiography] this could be the *first* volume . . . ending where I abandon science disillusioned and turn to literature like the bull at the wall, realizing at last that the esoterics and magicians, if foolish, at least have known the other road was hopeless and that something more desperate had to be tried.

All of the disguised autobiographies postdate these entries and may be said to explore the way of hope, to open a vista of at-homeness only to be restored by returning to the first world, the world before its disenchantment. Literature gives us the human meaning of science, and this, too, as Eiseley's reiteration of *turn* tells us, involves returning—to an earlier way of seeing, that of the esoterics and magicians (shamans). His way of putting the issue—the volte-face it demanded of him—suggests that both he and the measures he took were desperate. He argues the issue in almost all he writes, and in the volumes of poems he published in his last years and the collection of essays and poems he had ready for publication at the time of his death offers a demonstration and provides a defense of poetry and correspondential seeing.

This collection, *The Star Thrower*, is a very special *Loren Eiseley Sampler*, as it was initially called, because it is not perfunctory, got up simply for the sake of continued publication, one of those capstone volumes with which weary and needy writers capitalize on their fame. It does not sample the full range of Eiseley's work. Omitted altogether are examples of his studies in the history of scientific ideas, although his own thought is always interwoven with and set in the perspective of what he learned in searching the seventeenth- and nineteenth-century intellectual worlds of Bacon and Darwin. Instead, *The Star Thrower*, the title naming his ultimate stance, gives us the conclusive portrait of a man who wished to be remembered as a writer for whom the eye persisted. This apologia pro vita sua is a thematically coherent and consonant book, much better, I think, than Andrew Angyal, the most discerning critic of Eiseley's work, believes it to be.

Eiseley presents and defends his vision, is himself the figure of his thought, the representative of his ideas. The book, its final version arranged by Kenneth Heuer, is framed by the vision quest of "The Judgment of the Birds" and the summary vision in "The Inner Galaxy" of what might be called evolutionary love. At the outset, Eiseley tells us that to "resuscitate [a] waning taste for life" it is necessary to experience "marvel[s]," to seek in the wilderness for "a natural revelation." He is such a seeker, someone who sees "in the flow of ordinary events the point at which the mundane world gives way to quite another dimension." He speaks of the "border of two worlds" (Emerson: "The visible creation is the terminus . . . of the invisible world") and how sometimes they "interpenetrate and one sees the miraculous" (Emerson: "The invariable mark of wisdom is to see the miraculous in the common"). He reports some of these "miracles of experience" (Emerson again), the first, of pigeons in New York City, a happy example of his imagination of flight, of how his vision mounts from the void. He sees from his hotel window birds "pouring upward in a light that was not yet perceptible to human eyes, while far down in the black darkness of alleys it was still midnight" (*pouring upward* is miraculous); and imagining the besiegement of an "immense snowfall," he wants to take flight, "to launch out into that great bottomless void with the simple confidence of young birds." (Does he learn to take the leap, to have instinctive faith?)

The other miracles he recalls are variations of this central figure for death and life: the warblers, whose flight into the "oncoming dark" prevails against the "dead world at sunset," the fifty million years beneath him in the Badlands; the sparrows, who sing "under the brooding shadow of the raven"; and the spider, unperturbed, who spins a web on a streetlight. The last example is whimsical where the others are not, though all, in the Coleridgean sense, exhibit Fancy rather than Imagination and expose the artifice of Eiseley's revelations and a predilection for moralizing. Much that is obsessive in his work is evoked: the autumn evening, the beginning snow, the spider (hitherto most often defined in Gothic terms), the shadows. Projected by the streetlight, the shadows create a Platonic correspondential world, a little cosmos that Eiseley investigates by climbing a ladder. He oversees (like God?) a universe of Darwinian struggle that he likens to the mind. No analogy is left unturned. (Emerson: "Man is an analogist, and studies relations in all objects. . . . [Marry natural history] to human history, and it is full of life.") Even though the universe around the spider is "running down," she continues to spin her web, for she embodies the "life force" that does not yield to "frost or stepladders" and represents "a kind of heroism, a world where even a spider refuses to lie down and die if a rope can still be spun on to a star." Eiseley reads these meanings for the sake of those of us "who will fight our final freezing battle with the void"—reads them even though he questions such literal reading or fixing of symbols. He knows that it is better "to record the marvel [than] . . . define its meaning," better not to allegorize but let the symbol reverberate and set minds "grasping at that beyond out of which miracles emerge." To create this dimensional world is the human need that symbols satisfy. He says in "The Golden Alphabet," a chapter on Thoreau and Darwin in *The Unexpected Universe*, that symbols compensate for our fall from the "grace of instinct." They belong to what, in another context, Thoreau calls our *instinctive* transcendentalism.

Works of Fancy may be affecting but their force diminishes on successive readings. Writers who do our reading of symbols for us, as Eiseley frequently does, no longer startle us. They tend to become predictable and we soon learn to anticipate them. In *The Lost Notebooks* we can see how practiced Eiseley was, how he gathered ideas and worked them up for literary ends. His initial paragraphs usually give him away, and his format, as in "The Lethal Factor," is often that of a (good) college lecture, or, as in "The Illusion of the Two Cultures," of a sermon. Whatever the format, the tone is much the same, which is what we expect of voice but not of the tone that, as Emerson knew, authenticates it. Eiseley's tone accords with his literal reading of correspondences, his admittedly profound themes (nature and human nature, our origin and destiny), and his wish to succor us. The sonority, and sometimes his discourse, is "religious" and may be said to date his work. When he pushes too far, as with the spider and the star (evoking Emerson's time-worn "hitch your wagon to a star") or the rainbow within whose arch the star thrower stands, he risks, as popular writing does, being corny.

All along I've been thinking of Barry Lopez because "The Judgment of the Birds" calls up his "The Passing Wisdom of Birds," which also has a profound moral for us. In addition to being an essayist, Lopez is a storyteller who is as familiar as Eiseley with the night country of dream and surreality. So when I read the representative story in *The Star Thrower* ("The Dance of the Frogs," in which what the skeptical young scientist says of Naskapi belief is enacted in the older scientist's batrachian ecstasy) I thought of Lopez and of how his finesse measures Eiseley's work. Generational difference matters here, and it's not just that Lopez is a better writer but that this is the case because he is truly less self-occupied. This is not to say that his imagination or "vision" is superior. I read on in Eiseley, critical of his means as I often am, because he has a significant vision, and this vision—call it a reverie toward the primitive—and the life story of what occasioned it remain compelling. I remember William James' remark that "a man's vision is the great fact about him"—that vision is always personal. Eiseley believes this: "Each man," he says, "deciphers from the ancient alphabets of nature only those secrets that his own deeps possess the power to endow with meaning." And to this he adds, "The golden alphabet, in whatever shape it chooses to reveal itself, is never spurious."

The idea of correspondence not only enables Eiseley's vision, it is part of it, the speculative instrument of the cosmological and ontological view he asks us to (re)consider. Many of the essays allude to or explicitly develop it. In "The Innocent Fox," it graces childhood: "I am not the first man to have lost his way to find, if not a gate, a mysterious hole in the hedge that a child would know at once led to some other dimension at the world's end." ("Through the first gate, / Into our first world," Eliot says in *Four Quartets*.) In "The Dance of the Frogs," it belongs to the childhood of man (Frobenius' term), to the Naskapi belief in "a force behind and above nature." Speck figures here because he had written about scapulimancy, "the cracks interpreted by a shaman on the incinerated shoulder blade of a hare," as Eiseley explains in "The Golden Alphabet," the chapter itself framed by his endorsement of the ways and wisdom of the Eskimo. In *The Lost Notebooks* he remarks on this "unconscious search for symbols," this early attempt "to 'read' nature" to other than economic ends. This story, however, puts the central question in terms of belief and vocational choice: "'The Indians believe it,' pursued old Dreyer relentlessly, 'but do *you* believe it?'" The younger scientist disclaims it, and we know where Eiseley stands when he pits a young against an old scientist. In "The Hidden Teacher," he recalls Speck and their common interest in shamanism, and he speaks of an "ultimate Dreamer who dreamed the light and the galaxies," of the human search for a transcendent realm, of the hidden teacher Nature herself is since her teaching is often "hidden and obscure." Yet in keeping with the uncertainty at the heart of his work, he questions "the Plan" in the story "The Fifth Planet," and in the story of Dreyer spares him the "demonic possession" of actually crossing the species boundary by having him invoke Christ's help.

Eiseley's own fables are "The Last Neanderthal" and "The Star Thrower," personal essays separated by some early poems, both taken from *The Unexpected Universe*, the book most frequently represented in the collection. In "The Last Neanderthal," the idea of correspondence is variously set out as he ponders meaning, time, memory, and death. He tells us at the start that "the same incident may stand as a simple fact to some, an intangible hint of the nature of the universe to others, a useful myth to a savage. . . . The receptive mind makes all the difference, shadowing or lighting the original object. [The receptive mind also *projects*, the word he invariably uses.] I was an observer, intent upon my own hieroglyphics." Correspondence, accordingly, is a function of the receptive mind; it does not exist apart from the brain, *the* evolutionary miracle. It comes about in time, and its symbol making allows us to keep time and have a future. This preeminently human faculty creates a second nature, "the invisible world drawn from man's mind," the "hidden world" that Eiseley considers most fully in *Francis Bacon and the Modern Dilemma* (enlarged and revised as *The Man Who Saw Through Time*).

Correspondence, therefore, belongs to what Emerson called "the natural history of intellect." Eiseley knew Emerson's lectures under this title and surely noted this epigraph: "Bacon's perfect law of inquiry after truth was that nothing should be in the globe of matter which was not also in the globe of crystal; that is, nothing should take place as event in life which did not also exist as truth in the mind." Emerson sees correspondence as the grand fact of symbolic appropriation, where Eiseley, troubled by the extent to which this creates a second nature (culture) that threatens the first nature, is not so certain. It is necessary to distinguish between an invisible world behind nature and the invisible world of the human mind, for the latter may not correspond with the former, or even with the visible world; and it is just as necessary to distinguish between history, as we sometimes speak of evolutionary process, and the history that evolution, with the emergent human brain and hand, introduces, the history that Eiseley reminds us gave us Faust and Captain Ahab and, in our time, the endangerment of species, the spoliation of the earth, and the death camps. Correspondence, then, is determined, for good or ill, by another duality, that of human nature. In "Easter: The Isle of Faces," Eiseley mentions Dr. Jekyll and Mr. Hyde as an example of *Homo duplex*, considered earlier in "Man the Firemaker." So correspondence, finally, depends on what we are and how we see, whether, as Eiseley puts it, we project *on* things or *to* things.

> The problem of restoring to the world original and eternal beauty [cosmos] is solved by the redemption of the soul. The ruin or the blank that we see when we look at nature, is in our own eye. The axis of vision is not coincident with the axis of things, and so they appear not transparent but opaque. The reason why the world lacks unity, and lies broken and in heaps, is because man is disunited with himself. He cannot be a naturalist until he satisfies all the demands of the spirit. Love is as much its demand as perception. Indeed, neither can be perfect without the other. . . . there are patient naturalists but they freeze their subject under the wintry light of the understanding. . . . But when a faithful thinker, resolute to detach every object from personal relations and see it in the light of thought, shall, at the same time, kindle science with the fire of the holiest affections, then will God go forth anew into the creation.

This passage at the end of Emerson's *Nature* asks the naturalist to become a poet, that is, to see also as the poet does. The eye is so much the soul for Emerson (and for Eiseley) that redemption itself depends on seeing rightly. Since this involves seeing things and their relations, it, in turn, restores the unity of the world, gives us again a cosmos; and it may explain why Eiseley prefaces what he says was lost to Thoreau when he turned to science with Thoreau's belief in "'the possibility . . . [by virtue of correspondential seeing] of being all, or remaining a particle in the universe.'" To kindle science in this way renews the creation, summons God to his evolutionary task, which is what, among other things, the rainbow in "The Star Thrower" signifies.

The essays introduced by "The Star Thrower" in the closing section of the book concern the ethical nature of seeing. Both scientists and artists (and literary naturalists believed to be outmoded) employ symbols, generative ideas, as Susanne Langer calls them, among them those that Eiseley cites because he is indebted to them: evolution and the more recent idea of an expanding universe, to which he owes the foreboding of extinction as well as the happier open prospect of his thought. Even so, he usually denigrates scientists, probably because as a university administrator he knew too well the kind fostered by "big science" and "big government." In "The Star Thrower," his spiritual crisis turns on abandoning their perspective and practice (in this instance, collecting) and overcoming the accompanying vastation. As in other essays, Eiseley charts the way to our present emptiness by rehearsing the history of evolution and recalling the dismaying aspects of the work of Darwin, Einstein, and Freud. He measures the homelessness and jeopardy to which their thought has brought us against what he believes to have been the safe and sheltered life of hunters in the distant time of the "enchanted forest." And when he learns to affirm life by following the example of the man who returns stranded starfish to the sea (for a likely model, see Rachel Carson and her account of the basket starfish in *The Edge of the Sea*, and for an analogue, see Barry Lopez's "Drought") he appreciates the "primitives" who knew the "empathy for life" he has been so troubled to learn. By closing the rift in Darwin's tangled bank he may be said to repossess the first nature, and this is why he also despairs of the inordinate power we have since acquired in the creation of a second nature. Perhaps this is reason enough to remind us that the "inward eye" may see beneficently and to wish to believe that there is a Star Thrower as much in love with all of life as he is. The title names this correspondence.

The hitherto unpublished essay that follows confirms Eiseley's subscription to correspondence. "Science and the Sense of the Holy" conjoins the seemingly opposed and calls attention to the fact that Eiseley employs the discourses of both science and religion. This may be unusual now but not, as he learned in preparing to write *Darwin's Century*, in the seventeenth century (his favorite century, I think), when the "feeling that religious insight could be obtained from the observation of God's work . . . led to a great proliferation of works upon natural theology." This is still the assumption of Emerson's *Nature* and, as in the instance of Einstein noted by Eiseley, an assumption not yet abandoned by modern science. Scientists, then, also appreciate the *mysterium tremendum* and, if only as the experience of children, as Freud maintained, acknowledge the "oceanic feeling" of oneness with the universe. It is not adventitious that the most personal and crucial essays of *The Star Thrower* have the ocean for their setting.

Eiseley professes no creed. His religious sense, so heavily nostalgic, derives from his temporal sense, at once archaeological and autobiographical, the correspondence here between the primitive and childhood. He mentions "'the terrible archeology of the brain'" in considering Freud, who believed that "'all the earlier stages of [human] development have survived alongside the latest.'" But this terrible archaeology also confirms the love of animals Eiseley knew as a child. "Nowhere," he says of the Ice Age hunters, "does that wonder [of the world, the sense of the holy] press closer to us than in the guise of animals in the caves of our origins, or, as in Darwin's sudden illumination [that animals "partake of our origin . . . we may all be melted together"]." The latter, of course, is Eiseley's reading of Darwin's reading of the golden alphabet, and it supports what he says of Odysseus' homecoming and the necessity of the dog Argos' recognition: "One does not meet oneself until one catches the reflection from an eye other than human." Eiseley's religious sense was conferred in childhood by such a meeting. Like Buber, he learned that he was surrounded by being(s).

At the end of "The Star Thrower," Eiseley evokes Dante in saying that "we have lost our way" and reminds us that "the hunters in the snow, making obeisance to the souls of the hunted, had known the cycle ["the perfect circle of compassion from life to death and back again to life"]." Then: "The legend had come down . . . that he who gained the gratitude of animals gained help in need in the dark wood."

Eiseley's wide learning in the humanist tradition also serves his parti pris. Among American writers, he cites Whitman on the need for sympathy and Melville for the prescient eco-fable of *Moby-Dick*, and he writes an essay on Emerson and two on Thoreau, about whom he had intended to write a book. The conspicuous tradition of *The Star Thrower* is the indigenous American one. Yet it is strange that in treating these focal figures someone as scholarly as Eiseley, digging, as he represents himself, in great libraries, could dispense with so much significant scholarship (much of it purchased by him) and confidently pursue his own singular interpretations. He was, it seems, curious rather than thorough, mentioning, for example, Olson's *Call Me Ishmael* probably because Ishmael was another figure with whom he identified, and thereby finding among much that he too believed that "Ahab is full stop. . . . END of individual responsible only to himself."

Eiseley pairs Emerson and Darwin in order to show the importance of their common Romantic heritage and to claim them as process thinkers, but chiefly because Emerson challenges Darwin's faith in "progress toward perfection."

(Ideas for Eiseley belong to their place and time; he knows that "evolution," like "nature," is a construct.) The dark Emerson he depicts is a melancholic, as Auden said of Eiseley in the introduction to the book. Emerson knows the vertical of being(s), the stair on which he finds himself in the essay "Experience." "Couched midway on that desperate stair whose steps pass from dark to dark . . . Emerson," according to Eiseley, "saw, with a terrible clairvoyance, the downward pull of the past . . . the weary slipping, the . . . entropy, the ebbing away of the human spirit into fox and weasel as it struggled upward while all the past tugged upon it from below." In *The Lost Notebooks*, Eiseley comments approvingly, in reading "Poetry and Imagination," on Emerson's symbolic rendering of correspondences. But this transcendental practice serves a descendental vision no one but Eiseley ascribes to Emerson, a descendental vision that Eiseley in his own practice adds to the transcendentalist legacy.

His Thoreau is equally dark, his fullest self-portraiture, his way of making sure that someone will note the consanguinity and say, as his editor does in *The Lost Notebooks*, that he is the "heir apparent to Henry David Thoreau." Though Thoreau is the rare, indigenous "night hunter," a "genuine Concord lynx," he is also, like Eiseley, a "fox at the wood's edge," the correspondential boundary. Eiseley dismisses previous literary critical interpretations to depict an elusive Thoreau, whose experience (of tuberculosis, loneliness, journeying) and temperament (response to vastness and mystery) tally with his own. His Thoreau, early "imprinted . . . by his home landscape," journeys across the altiplano, his "austere uplands," and, as might summarily be said of Eiseley, pursues "the summer on snowshoes," preferring "to the end his own white winter spaces."

This late essay, the one in which Eiseley treats Thoreau's science and the persistent inner eye, proposed a companion essay, hitherto unpublished, on Thoreau's unfinished business—*unfinished* because Eiseley's business was not yet done and he wished to answer "*What* business?," the query of his friend Wright Morris in the chapter on Thoreau in his hyped-up, Lawrentian (and suspect) *The Territory Ahead*. Seeing remains the primary business, associated now with alchemy (a proto-science and art of transformation) and archaeology. Both join in the characterization of Thoreau as an "artist-scientist who . . . pursue[s] the future through its past," who sees in arrowheads the "mindprints" left behind for our deciphering. (*Mindprint*: a concept imprinted on Eiseley's mind, thereafter central in his thought, as when, having mentioned Jesus' unfinished business on Calvary, he says of "acts which justify creation or annul it" that they are "mindprints, the symbols that keep the present from falling into the abyss.") Eiseley's own transformative art, intent on the business of salvation, turns on Thoreau's (and his) paradox that "the greater order known as nature" is civilization—Thoreau: "Wildness is a civilization other than our own." Nature thus becomes the civilization from which, in the biblical sense, we have fallen, or, as more often with Eiseley, the "great ice" of the Pleistocene that had made us and from which we had wandered. The still unfinished business is to "civilize [us] . . . back into that titanic otherness."

Eiseley says that only "the artist's mind"—the symbol-reading-and-making mind—can, alchemically, so to speak, "change the winter in man." *Winter* cancels the previous value of *ice* but belongs with it because death promises return. In writing about Thoreau, Eiseley meditates on his own death, as glad as Thoreau said he was to "fall into some crevice along with leaves and acorns." He recalls his visit in 1973 to Thoreau's grave and links it with a subsequent visit to the "dinosaur-haunted gulches of Montana." Here he ponders mindprints and the "great journal" spread out before him and concludes: "Like Thoreau, we had come to the world's end, but not to the end of nature, not to the end of time." The corruptions of time are what he wishes to redeem—he speaks too melodramatically perhaps of the "utter cleansing" that either art or science (atomic explosion) may provide. He also sees how time frees us, how the clean archaic quartz knife he finds had "aged out of human history, out of corruption" and was "free at last." Moreover, in the course of time the mindprints themselves (the only vestiges of time) "were joined to that other civilization, evidence of some power that ran all through nature." No wonder this insomniac reports that he slept soundly among the petrified logs and under the great sky!

But the alchemist is also "the eternal traveler," and there is more to his story. In the mountains of New Hampshire, Thoreau is said to have wandered "back into the time of the first continental ice recession" out of a secret wish "to come to a place of no more life, where a man might stiffen into immobility as I had found myself freezing into the agate limbs of petrified trees in Montana." Thoreau was not content with his Walden experiment, Eiseley claims, because he was "storm-driven" and "like a true artist dredge[d] up dreams even from the bottom of the pond." Having taken *alchemist* from Jung, Eiseley heeded him, and what he says here, by way of conclusion, is truer to him than to Thoreau—is, in fact, his own finished business.

(But his business was also *the reenchantment of the world*, to borrow the title of Morris Berman's book, where alchemy figures largely as an example of "participating consciousness," the kind of consciousness enabled by a correspondential sense of the world.)

Eiseley also considers Thoreau a "rural Robinson Crusoe" because he himself, as a boy, had read the story of the castaway and made it his own. Whenever he evokes the beach and the ocean, his childhood Crusoe is there, confirming Thoreau's belief, cited here, that "truth strikes us from behind, and in the dark." The distance from Robinson Crusoe to Thoreau's *Cape Cod* is therefore short, traversed by a comment that privileges Eiseley, who, by way of explaining his attention to this book, says that previous students of Thoreau had not been "men of the seashore"—*seashore* also including "the dead lake beaches of the west."

Eiseley overlooks the questioning of the idea of correspondence at the heart of *Cape Cod*. He treats only the episode of the Charity House, which exhibits Thoreau's habitual skill as a symbol reader and, as Eiseley would have it, his "final perception." Final perception or not, it may be that Thoreau's questioning of correspondence informs Eiseley's use of the anything-but-charitable Charity House to explain his own lack of basic trust. His bitter reading of this symbol pays off old scores. It tells how far we have "fallen out of nature" and the rancor at "the heart's hot root" (Hart Crane's exact phrase). It reminds us of one of Eiseley's earliest stories, "The MOP to K.C.," about riding the rails with a homeless dying boy (a double), this, in turn, surely remembered by him when, in "Science and the Sense of the Holy," he walks a railroad spur, sees a freight train being made up, and thinks of "travelers like Ishmael and myself," though Ishmael here no longer rages against the heartless world. By this time, he has learned from Queequeg, as Eiseley interpolates to tell us he has learned from the Eskimo, "the people of the ice," that sharing is redemptive. He has also learned, as he frequently declares by evoking the sunflower, to have a faith, like Thoreau's, in seeds.

Writers share by leaving their mindprints. Thoreau's final contribution may not be, as Eiseley says it was, "to [have seen] with eyes strained beyond endurance man subsiding into two wrinkled gloves grasping at the edge of infinity." This vision may not even be Eiseley's final contribution, though it belongs, in his case, to the "inexorable lens" he says is unalterable. For coexisting with it is a vision of nature "transcending the reality of night and nothingness," a miracle, he believes, each of us repeats. Nature, he might have said, is miraculous in whole and part, and for us nothing is so miraculous as whatever it is (here is mystery enough) that aligns the axis of our vision and the axis of things and thereby secures the correspondence of true seeing. Perception is the miracle that Emerson says it is. "Inner galaxy" is not hyperbole. In concluding with an essay of this name, Eiseley not only turns inward but asks us to consider all that we have read as *vision*, not necessarily the ultimate truth of things but a personal reading of things. Poet that he is, he has faith in vision and a visionary faith; and his vision, unusual in being so full and imaginatively complete, is, as William James said of visions, a mode of "feeling the whole push, and seeing the whole drift of life, forced on one by one's total character and experience."

The inward turn is understandable in a book moved by a sense of oncoming death, and the wonder of it is the concern with outward acts, with sharing and love, especially the love of animals as felt by the cave painters, who show us, he says, the "door of [the] true kingdom." In turning inward he found the central beliefs he recorded in *The Lost Notebooks* in 1957 in a proposal for a book: that we can "live only within the web of nature and by observing her laws" and that happiness comes of "grow[ing] outward into the world." In this proposal, he also speaks of our need, as orphans, for "a new kit of instructions upon how to live." He never wrote this book because he knew that a book of this important kind could not be done single-handedly.

At the end, Eiseley grew outward by dying into the world, thereby exemplifying a love "without issue, tenuous, almost disembodied." He often imagines his dying (death may be the sun of his galaxy), and here it occurs at the seashore, "where everything is transmuted and transmutes, but all is living and about to live." The castaway is now at home; his flight, imaged in the disappearance of an old seagull, is done. His dissolution speaks a love whose object is all of life, life itself so prodigal of love that the final imagination of this loser is of winning "if not in human guise then in another."

He says earlier, in "The Lethal Factor," where Jesus figures a salutary dying, that by dying we pass "beyond the reach of time into a still and hidden place." Here we find "an ancient and undistorted way," undoubtedly the way of primitive people who live, he tells us in *The Invisible Pyramid*, in the prelapsarian "green world," the first world of nature that he bids us enter. This lost world belongs to the shaman's dreamworld, where we are still animals, still happy and untroubled; it belongs to a dream Eiseley himself dreams only to experience the fall that Emerson says comes with consciousness. He knows that we will never again follow the way of hunters and gatherers, consume so little energy, and do so little to despoil the world. But we will, as his persistent imagination demonstrates, turn backward to protect the human spirit. He enters this thought in *The Lost Notebooks* along with a quotation from Thomas Love Peacock: "A poet in our times is a semi barbarian in a civilized community. . . . The march of his intellect is . . . backwards."

So the poems of his last years march backwards, and as a part of his dying. He "begin[s] dying," to use Ursula Le Guin's way of putting how it is when we live in the experience of dying, and this enables him, as she says of the Kesh people in *Always Coming Home*, to die *to* the soul, to enter and know the inmost place.

In his last years Eiseley wrote more than twice as many poems as he had written during his poetic apprenticeship. The poems collected in *Notes of an Alchemist, The Innocent Assassins, Another Kind of Autumn* as well as in *All the Night Wings* and *The Lost Notebooks* speak for the weight of time and for the virtue of integrity (versus despair) that Erik Erikson assigns to old age. Many of these poems, as one title has it, are songs for weeping, time purged by tears when memory, stirred by yearning, evokes the irrecoverable past, the home that never was (except in the heart), and the girls who now come to mind because of what can only be called erotic grief. The measure of these poems, too easily dismissed as sentimental, is their true feeling. When Eiseley says in "The Office" that being asked to leave the "green darkness" of his old office "broke [his] heart," the statement is literally true, and its lineation in a single line supports it.

After the analogy of the Judas tree, these late poems are also a late flowering:

> I come the closest
> to blossoming and sunlight
> now toward the end of winter
> when all I cherished is lost
> and I have no heart
> for summer leaves.

Like the Judas tree, in "one slow shower of petals without leaves," he will "condense" all he has to say, meaning that what he has to say will be poetry (after Pound's definition) as well as wisdom, his *Dichtung und Wahrheit*. The latter, according to Erikson, is the strength of old age. In defining wisdom as a *"detached concern with life itself, in the face of death itself,"* Erikson describes these poems, which, it should be noted, are unusual in making a personal concern for one's lifetime a concern with *life itself*, with life as evolutionary time reveals its process and in the all-inclusive sense in which Eiseley read Bacon's ethical injunction to put learning to "the uses of life." It should be noted, too, that they exemplify one of the uses of a life and show that generativity is not foreclosed by its closure and that, even then, generosity of being, perhaps the ultimate wisdom, works this miracle.

The number of poems alone indicates the remarkable creativity—and release—of this late flowering and perhaps the fact that only poems could do what Eiseley wished to do. For just as remarkable is the open form he adopts, one enabling him to set out the phrasal units of direct speech and slow the poem to its essential deeply meditative work. Auden considered the poems of *Notes of an Alchemist* free verse, but they, and all but a few in the other volumes, seem to follow a more recent spatial poetics. In a letter to Howard Nemerov about the first volume of poems, Eiseley explains that "I . . . excluded . . . my more formal poems because I thought they would appear odd [old?] in juxtaposition with *the more free-flowing things out of my later years*." Not *of* but *out of*, flowing freely from: What I've italicized answers perfectly to the poems, links their form to their occasion; and *formal*, indicating the kind of poems Eiseley had hitherto written, establishes the divide that prompts Andrew Angyal, who subscribes to the neoclassicism of the New Critics, to underrate the late poems. "The poems," Angyal says, "are analogous to journal entries: they are in fact verse notes of a continuous verse journal, comprised of deliberately unfinished poems." No, the poems are finished—Eiseley is a master of closure—and what they comprise is a serial poem, a poem, once begun, that is relinquished, as here, only with death.

The poems have the same urgent necessity as *All the Strange Hours*. By means of both he would assuage the "cold furies of time," unburden himself *and* hold to the self. The alchemist evoked in the title of the first book is intent, so Eiseley says in the preface, on transmuting "the sharp images of his [scientific] profession into something deeply subjective." Verse, he finds, gives him "a sense of release." He recovers here, as in the excavation of his autobiography, some of the "broken shards," some of the things that come to mind, like the derelict of "The Blizzard," that his art of memory fashions into artifacts as time-defying and permanent as a flint knife or a stone axe. But he knows that the extinction he foresees will obliterate these mindprints, that though "memory is / the mortal enemy of time that flows," it is *mortal*, and he can "defend these things [only] so long as memory lasts." This is why remembering, as Hannah Arendt reminds us, is a hinge of civilization, and the evolutionary time that Eiseley remembers is as important to us as the historical time Arendt remembers.

The title of a poem puts it well: Memory is "not time calendrical." Memory, as Thoreau said, belongs to "the lapse of time by which time recovers itself"; belongs to and shapes the circle of a life and asserts itself, in the first instance, in behalf of the continuity of self. "I am that I am," Eiseley says in "Not Time Calendrical," speaking God's words, defiantly, yet remembering, I think, the words of Meister Eckhart that Kenneth Heuer chose for the epigraph of *The Lost Notebooks*: "That *I* am, this I share with other men. That I see and hear and that I eat and drink is what all animals do likewise. But that I am *I* is only mine and belongs to me and to no one else; to no other man, not an angel, not to God except in as much as I am one with him." Immediately following this declaration of self, Eiseley acknowledges the paradox of dependence at the heart of his work:

> I did not will
> the notes on the piano that resound
> when all the house is quiet;
> I did not will
> the loneliness that follows room to room,
> the bird upon the windowsill
> that I must feed—
> or must I?
> Did my own will create
> that which I suffer from?
> I am that which came
> from a far province
> and another dust.
> I beseech
> return into a silence and sufficient ending.
> But still not yet, not now.

A sovereign self no longer speaks, an "I," an ego, does, beseeching a return it is not yet ready to embrace, though this is the very work these poems propose.

The title of *All the Strange Hours* comes from Swinburne's "Ave Atque Vale": *"Now all the strange hours and all the strange loves / are over, dreams and desires and sombre songs and sweet."* But the sentiment that moves both the autobiography and the poems is deeper—*deeply subjective*, as he tells us in the initial preface to his poems, *excavations*, as he suggests, out of the deep that is the abysm of time. Eiseley recalls several episodes of his life in both the autobiography and the poems. Of these the most crucial, I think, is his first dying, when, determined to take an examination (which he succeeded in passing), his ego-driven sick body collapsed upon the stairway. If Eiseley may be said to have had a conversion experience prior to that of the star thrower, this is it. His recollection of the episode in "I Am a Stranger Here" is especially significant because the title of the poem glosses the title of the autobiography—gives us its perspective—and the poem, as I gather from its publication in *The Lost Notebooks*, is among his very last.

"I climbed the stairs," he says, surely recalling the "desperate stair" of his essay on Emerson and Darwin—returned home, that is, knowing how far in the social sense he had climbed ("risen") to get his degree. But the light associated with the apex of the vertical belongs to the mind, "the tower of light in the mind," and when the body collapses it goes out. Then, as he tells it, he was "swept / . . . down to the dark," to death. Yet he finds, as all he will learn of evolution teaches him, that this death is not ultimate but only, as he says in the companion poem "Adder's Tongue," the "I [ego] dispersed, dispersing / in a multiplicity, a congregation." For "below me in the dark, but not myself nor my will," he says, the cells of the body, a "toiling congregation," all the while worked to raise him out of nothingness, "till"—the syntax puts it exactly—"till up from death I came."

No, not myself. The reiterated negative declares the most important lesson of Eiseley's descendental vision. Recall the early poem "Earthward," where he speaks, as so much of his work does, of the sudden good of "split[ting] the confining shell of the mind," of mixing with the elements, of "relax[ing] on this oldest, / most certain breast." The basic trust recovered in this early poem informs the gratitude he feels in the later poem:

> In all the years remaining
> I know, and am grateful to them, those secret alchemists
> of void and stardust who, when my will had failed,
> relit the light.

The work of the "secret alchemists" remains the deepest mystery of life even as it teaches him that the ego is singular and other: "I am the stranger here, the construct. I am the lonely one." For the stranger does indeed come from "a far province / and another dust." And when, as he says in "Adder's Tongue," "I have found myself," we will not find him, for then he will have "dispersed that ego, vanquished it forever." He will have become "worm," no longer, as with Emerson, the worm that "striving to be man . . . / Mounts through all the spires of form."

This is his immense journey, a journey back and down, as startling as Whitman's ascent a century earlier because the evolutionary *scene* (and *agent*, in Kenneth Burke's terms) belongs for Eiseley to a vision of death and dispersal rather than of birth and identification (*I*-dentification).

> I am an acme of things accomplish'd . . .
> My feet strike an apex of the apices of stairs,
> On every step bunches of ages, and larger bunches between the steps,
> All below duly travel'd, and still I mount and mount.
>
> Rise after rise bow the phantoms behind me,
> Afar down I see the huge first Nothing, I know I was even there,
> I waited unseen and always, and slept through the lethargic mist,
> And took my time, and took no hurt from the fetid carbon.
>
> Long I was hugg'd close—long and long.
>
> Immense have been the preparations for me,
> Faithful and friendly the arms that have help'd me.
>
> Cycles ferried my cradle, rowing and rowing like cheerful boatmen,
> For room to me stars kept aside in their own rings,
> They sent influences to look after what was to hold me.

Before I was born out of my mother generations guided me,
My embryo has never been torpid, nothing could overlay it.

For it the nebula cohered to an orb,
The long slow strata piled to rest it on,
Vast vegetables gave it sustenance,
Monstrous sauroids transported it in their mouths and deposited it with care.

All forces have been steadily employ'd to complete and delight me,
Now on this spot I stand with my robust soul.

—§44, "Song of Myself"

The truth of this cosmic-evolutionary account of human emergence is not in question so much as Whitman's aplomb—a touchstone of the progressive, optimistic reading of evolution that seemed to Eiseley to compromise Darwin's vision.

Eiseley belongs with such cosmic poets as Whitman and Jeffers but is to be distinguished from them because his inspiration is chaos. Angyal says of *The Innocent Assassins* what is just as true of all the later volumes of poems, that "the muse . . . is *Mu*, the primeval voice of chaos." In "I Heard It Breathing in the Lizard Dark," Eiseley tells us that *"Mü, mythos, mystery"* is the voice of the thunder of dinosaurs, the "beast sound," and that mythos "call[s] the dread forms of chaos back." There are other definitions of *Mu* closer to human need; for example, that it is the sound we make when we "murmur with closed lips," when we "mutter" and "moan" and "suck in," as in nursing. (I cite Liddell and Scott, *Greek-English Lexicon*.) It may well be our first sound and, by way of the subconscious, which Bachelard says is "ceaselessly murmuring" and "murmuring memory" (and memory of murmuring), the inspiration of our reveries toward childhood. Reveries of this kind are conspicuous in the late poems and share the impulse of Eiseley's longer journey back, the reason being, as he cryptically says in an early poem, "Song without Logic," that *"The honey of chaos is the honey of love."*

This early poem anticipates "Hence Chaos Is Your Name," a late poem in which chaos replaces Logos: "In the beginning chaos was, then form." The preference Eiseley expresses here for formlessness (asymmetry) over form (symmetry) explains the deep significance of the open forms of the late poems, whose literal activity enacts the inescapable paradox, that in trying to lose the self he holds fast to it and in seeking formlessness creates form. Even so, the poem declares his present yearning to "spew myself out"—the subsequent poem begins, "I have borne much to reach this thing, myself." The chaos of his very being is "restless, grown tired / of playing *Homo sapiens*," and he wishes to break out of his "tight prison." (This image always evokes one of his earliest memories, that of the prison break of Tom Murry in a blizzard, the chaos of snow and the correlative chaos of mind vividly reproduced when, searching the newspapers in an archive, Eiseley rapidly runs the microfilm through the viewer.) "I'll have myself outside this cage of bone, I'll be away," he says, the echo here of Roethke fitting because he, too, is moved by the powerful descendental urge of what Kenneth Burke, in an essay on Roethke, calls "vegetal radicalism." He knows, as he says in "That Vast Thing Sleeping," that "time's stairway ends upon a rail-less balcony / for all of life," that everything that lives "exists in chaos who can take it back"—*back* in time and in death. He knows that we belong to chaos, are forms of life serving it, but now, acknowledging the limits of poetry, he can only think of this welcome possibility of being:

> I think that I will go
> back to the half-liquid light
> before the deep was split, before form was,
> back, back beyond hot lava flows, bird cries, to utterly empty seas,
> lurk there interminably, have peace, be empty of
> all movement, all desire. Try that awhile, let mind
> delete itself, rest, rest.

A way station on this journey back belongs to Eiseley's preferred time, to the last ice, the caves, the hunters. As he says in "The Green Lion," he is a "throwback": His life has been filled with animals and he "see[s] with the hunters." He gives his allegiance to the "alchemists of the heart"; he belongs to the "most ancient brotherhood [of shamans]," having "long, long ago . . . joined another craft / in the red sunset on a badland hill." He realizes this now because he measures "our mortal illness" from the "first ice," when we were "habitants" and hadn't built ourselves out of the natural world nor probed outer space. In "Pioneer II," he appreciates the fact that

> This cosmos of a little band of hunting Indians
> has meaning.

Every rock, every stream, every animal
is accounted for
and the deep underlying
rhythm of things
can inscribe the message of the forest
on the cracked bone of a hare.

For the Naskapi shaman the axis of vision is coincident with the axis of things, not because, as Emerson believed, in the mythic time before the "degradation" introduced by history man "filled nature with his overflowing currents [of spirit]." No, the shaman, Eiseley says, is "reading"

something permanently bound into his universe
that he can decipher,
a code that can be read by the informed seer,
a voice from the universe reassuring for man,
hungry, enfeebled,
but knowing
there is a message to be read and one can find it
any time in the fire.
The world is held together
and man has his place:
that is the message.

We are not so fortunate. We no longer have a cosmos, and we hear "nothing but the echoes from a deserted universe." Deservedly, because lacking forebearance, we no longer keep the balance. In a poem commemorating the Acoma Indians, who "shall outlast / these United States of America because they know / proportion, limits, dignity," Eiseley says that

There is a boundary, a boundary
between us. This is the secret, I think, of the world,
the unseen necessary balance.
We have broken it.

The unseen necessary balance. This phrase, upon which so much of the eco-wisdom of his old age turns, occurs again in "The Aboriginals," where Eiseley longs for the way of life lived in the dreamtime, when "time dreamed itself"

and the ships that awakened time and history had not yet arrived to destroy the world.

Eiseley is not the first person to believe that "the blind world [is] swerving to its end, all balance gone," nor the first to consider our extinction merited. "The Fifth Ice," he believes, "would be cleansing if it moved, / but will it move in time?" But he may be among the first to have such thoughts not because of personal spleen but because of evolutionary guilt. The innocent assassins, the animals, have given way to a guilty assassin:

On these lost hills that mark the rise of brain,
> I weep perversely for the beauty gone.
> I weep for man who knows this antique trade [of predation] but is not guiltless.

Eiseley shares this guilt and speaks for it in the poem in which he remembers Wounded Knee and Mylai as instances of our "obscene malice." He says here that natural violence, "the march of glaciers," may be "cleansing" but that "in man / genocide is a pettiness." The gun is its instrument, the image in his poems of the deliberate killing that will cease when we learn pity and compassion for "our other selves who wander, / rabbit and fox, still tangled in the briars" of Darwin's tangled bank. On the day he lost his youth, Eiseley remembers, he "laid the rifle aside for the sake of the hiders." This and the fact that sometimes "the leveled cross hairs / on the rifle / are not followed by the finger's twitch" are instances of an evolutionary leap in which nature brought forth

> a creature not accounted for . . . ,
> [who] suffers the pangs of all, forgives all innocents,
> trapped in the living web by fang and poison,
>> tiger and strangler fig,
> does not believe death easy, will not gloss
> what came with the first amino-acid chains,
>> the steaming witches' broth,
> hears every scream and shrinks, yet loves
> in ways unvisioned, crosses the species barrier in this grim
> struggle beneath the bank, the tangled bank of time.

For Leopold, we remember, this radical change was more recent: the "ethical sequence" he considers in *A Sand County Almanac* in social/communal terms as a movement from "anti-social conduct" to "modes of co-operation," as a development in citizenship in the biotic community that depends on his nice distinction between the cognate words *property* and *propriety*. In a memorial address on the extinction of the passenger pigeon, Leopold confirms Eiseley when he says, "For one species to mourn the death of another is a new thing under the sun." We owe this, he reminds us, to Darwin's thought, "new knowledge," he says, that "should have given us, by this time, a sense of kinship with fellow-creatures; a wish to live and let live; a sense of wonder over the magnitude and duration of the biotic enterprise."

Leopold's admonition explains the elegiac burden of Eiseley's poems, the earlier to be distinguished from the later by another kind of autumn, his own autumn in the "final sun" and the final autumn of humankind, that brief season as evolutionary time is figured between the withdrawal and return of the glacial ice. In *Another Kind of Autumn*, Eiseley meditates, somewhat to Bronk's purpose, on the extinction of great civilizations. And in this volume, at the end of the end, so to speak, he returns to the scenario, identifies with outcasts, and accepts extinction by repossessing the "derelict" self he had for a time outlived. The derelict self belongs to the open world and is the deepest, most permanent and harbored self he knows. This self, he says in *The Innocent Assassins*, has "lain in the place outside" and "can never go back" if only because Eiseley had learned, as had Oppen, the bitter weather of our century. Eiseley calls it a "skewed century" and, thinking of humanity, almost uses Oppen's words when he says, "It is hard to pity / what is too numerous." He learned early what the Oppens wanted to learn *out there*, and his sympathy is with the drifters. But he also learned the weather of eons, and his sympathy is for the drifters in the place outside, all of the extinct and endangered species to be joined by going back. In doing this imaginatively, he sees, to borrow the title of a poem on Darwin, with an "Edenic eye."

Eiseley imagined his death many times, but the instances that most impress me are of his last years and his imminent death by cancer. "Before Surgery," a noteworthy poem, is a testimony to integrity that I remember because the dying man in "an old chair in the red sun [the sunset] of September" has been reduced—or better, has found his way back—to the beginning, when, as he may recall Thoreau saying, "There was but the sun and the eye." Even more memorable, inescapably because so much that is obsessive figures here, is his imagination of snow, the "ultimate snow" of the last poem in *The Lost Notebooks*, where defenseless, on a gurney, it is not the sun that fades but the white gowns of the surgeons. Now there are "only the white gowns fading, merging in darkness, fading / into the silence of an ultimate snow."

To cluster and chart all that Eiseley associates with snow would tell his story. But now, at the end, it is enough to recall his identification with the derelict in "The Blizzard," where he says that "snow is a beautiful white way into death, / more beautiful, I think, than spring." And enough to recall "Prison Break," in which Tom Murry is said to have taught an "impressionable child" the unintended lesson of "how to die well / in the snow." There is also "The Snowstorm" in *The Innocent Assassins* in which Eiseley meditates on a text from Thoreau: "It is the first and last snows—especially the last—that blind us most." Here he remembers his childhood awakening to beauty and death and speaks, much as William Carlos Williams does in "The Dance" in *Pictures from Brueghel*, for his present awareness of the "eternal storm" that has always enveloped us. In "The Face of the Lion," Eiseley remembers the small stuffed animal that solaced his childhood fear of parental quarrels and "blizzard[s] dark" and anticipates his most telling instance of dying. He says that now

> The lion's face is slowly changing
> into the face of death
> but when I lie down
> upon my pillow
> in the final hour
> I shall lie quietly and clutch
> the remnants of his mane.

Whether stuffed lion or the snow leopard in the zoo, who, freed, figures for him his own "treading / deep, deep and ever deeper, into snow," the animal whom he cherishes most and sometimes becomes is the "dire wolf," the kind that "had been dead for ten thousand years." In many pages of *The Lost Notebooks*, Eiseley tells the story of this "wraith of the snow time" who, he suggests at the end, "because of his Ice Age memories" might go up "into the high cold." He planned a book to be called *The Snow Wolf* but never completed it, probably because he tried to tell too much, imposing on the wolf not only the history of the species since the Ice Age but his own life story, his lifelong contest with the

Other Player, and the escape and hunting down of Tom Murry. The story, clearly, was deeply his. It had its inception as early as *The Unexpected Universe* and persisted in the late poems and *All the Strange Hours*.

Eiseley introduces "The Angry Winter," a chapter on the Ice Age in *The Unexpected Universe*, with an anecdote of a shamanistic (imaginary) encounter with a shepherd dog called Wolf, whose feral instinct is revived by an Ice Age bone that he had left on the floor. Wolf, who refuses to give up the relic, speaks in warning the veritable *Mu*, the "beast sound," but when summoned to walk in the snow leaves the bone behind. This bone ("his bone—our bone, rather") is the bone spoken of in the dedication of this book:

> *To Wolf*
> *who sleeps forever*
> *with an ice age bone*
> *across his heart*
> *the last gift*
> *of one*
> *who loved him*

But there is another bone, this one, we learn in the final pages of *All the Strange Hours*, that Eiseley finds in a satchel left to him by his mother. It reminds him of Wolf and serves as the talisman of the dream in which Wolf helps him cross the species barrier and thereby escape the Other Player and the terrible fate of Tom Murry. We know from his poems that he will dream this dream again, but no sentence in his work is more resonant and moving than the concluding one in which he declares his assurance: "They wait for me, the dog Wolf and the Indian, muffled in snow upon the altiplano."

Muir

Muir's Self-Authorizings

You read from the end and not from the beginning, that is, from knowledge of what Muir became—such minimal, perhaps common, knowledge as the following, Muir's last entry in *Who's Who* (1914):

MUIR, John, A.M., LL.D., U.S. Explorer and Naturalist; b. Dunbar, Scotland, 21 April 1838; s. of Daniel and Anne Gilrye Muir; m. 1879, d. of Dr. John Strentzel of California; two d. Educ.: Grammar School, Dunbar; University of Wisconsin. After leaving Wisconsin University made long journeys afoot, mostly, and alone in Canada, the Eastern and Southern U.S., California, Alaska; also long canoe voyages in south-eastern Alaska; in 1903–4 travelled in Europe, Russia, the Caucasus, Siberia, Manchuria, Japan, China, India, Egypt, Australia, and New Zealand: in 1911–12 in South America and Africa; interested chiefly in botanical and geological studies; visited the Arctic Regions in 1880, on the U.S. steamer "Corwin," in search of the De Long expedition; laboured many years in cause of forest preservation; Member of Washington Academy of Science; National Institute of Arts and Letters; National Academy of Arts and Letters; Fellow American Association for the Advancement of Science; President of Sierra Club; Hon. degrees: A.M. Harvard, LL.D. Wisconsin, LL.D.

California, Doc.Litt. Yale. *Publications*: The Mountains of California; Our National Parks; Stickeen, The Story of a Dog; Yosemite; My First Summer in the Sierra; My Boyhood and Youth; numerous articles on the natural history of the Pacific coast, Alaska, etc.; edited Picturesque California. *Address*: Martinez, California. *Club*: University, San Francisco.

Your vantage, then, is Muir's, who dictated *The Story of My Boyhood and Youth* at Edward Harriman's lodge in 1909 and labored hard, as he told John Burroughs, over the book that was finally published in 1913. And you read in the expectation of finding—for a primary aim of autobiography is to connect a later to an earlier self—that the end was already there in the beginning. This is the very thing that Muir himself masterfully establishes in the opening sentence of the book: "When I was a boy in Scotland I was fond of everything that was wild, and all my life I've been growing fonder of wild places and wild things." Even now, he indicates, this is the case, which is to say that the love of wild things is for him a sign of the self's continuity—and of its *willedness*, the self-determination and freedom that in Thoreau's etymology (out of R. C. Trench's *On the Study of Words*) are its psychic correlatives. The mark of maturity is not to put away childish things but to persist in them, to find them ever more attractive. Inevitably so, we concur, because we know that what he loved as a child has been despoiled and what remains is precious.

Muir's perspective, accordingly, is a "perspective by incongruity," to use Kenneth Burke's term for a displacement of categories that "'remoralize[s]' by accurately renaming a situation demoralized by inaccuracy." Muir's work, all of it devoted to transvaluation, employs this perspective, and, for that matter, this is the essential perspective of significant nature writing.

There is no better motto for nature writing than Thoreau's declaration in "Walking": "I wish to speak a word for Nature, for absolute freedom and wildness, as contrasted with a freedom and culture merely civil—to regard man as an inhabitant, or part and parcel of Nature, rather than a member of society. I wish to make an extreme statement, if so I may make an emphatic one, for there are enough champions of civilization." Nature writers, more or less, accept this melodrama of ideas, probably none quite as much as Muir, who set out its terms in "Wild Wool" and never moderated them because the wild defined the acme of being, the inalienable right and value of existence-in-itself, the intrinsic life of things never to be yielded to use. Whether small or large, ordinary or grand, every thing declared this organic mandate—yes, the chickadees and nuthatches that he vividly remembers seeing on the Wisconsin farm and that now, on this winter morning, are still to be seen from my study window.

Aldo Leopold, who had reason to know *The Story of My Boyhood and Youth* because he tried to restore the ecotone it celebrates, employs the same perspective. In the foreword to *A Sand County Almanac* he declares that "there are some who can live without wild things, and some who cannot," and speaking for the latter, a minority, he asks us to consider "the question whether a still higher 'standard of living' is worth its cost in things natural, wild, and free." (*Natural, wild, free*: Any two of these terms defines the third.) His example of a thing natural, wild, and free is the pasqueflower, second only to the lily in Muir's admiration and noticed by him for more than a page in the story of his early life, which in large part is the story of the rich flora and fauna of south-central Wisconsin and the avaricious, ignorant, pioneer culture that did not know how to value them.

Muir and Thoreau make "companionable" reading, for if ever there was a saunterer it was Muir. "I loved to wander," he says in the first paragraph of the book, ". . . to gaze and wonder," announcing right off his chosen way of being in the world and its correlative sentiment. This anticipates the single remark of his mother, who speaks the wish of his deepest self: "'Weel, John, maybe you will travel like [Mungo] Park and Humboldt some day.'" ("Be rather the Mungo Park . . . of your own streams and oceans," Thoreau says in *Walden*, turning exploration inward; and he mentions Humboldt in "Walking," probably the work of his of greatest importance to Muir.) To wander, which is to go astray, to leave the straight and narrow path of the true Christian, is not the way Daniel Muir chose for his son, and though Muir may be said to have fulfilled a pilgrim's progress, his father, who on his deathbed addressed him as "my dear wanderer," did not think so.

Muir and Leopold are just as companionable, their Wisconsin books best read together. Muir fills out the local history that Leopold only sketches, and both commemorate the same wild things and sometimes, as with the passenger pigeon, their extinction. Now that I am here I read both books with special attention, as I also read Thoreau's journals, in order to tally the many things natural, wild, and free that, remarkably, we still have in common. These books help me *world*.

It may be that Muir's consummate passion for and joy in things natural, wild, and free accounts for what I always feel immediately prompted to say about him: that I know no writer more exhilarating. Turning now to check the adjective in *The American Heritage Dictionary*, I find under *exhilaration*, "'*Few Yosemite visitors ever see snow avalanches and fewer still know the exhilaration of riding on them.*' (John Muir)." And just below I find *exhort* and *exhortation*, which cover the other voice, so stern and patriarchal, that we hear in *The Story of My Boyhood and Youth*.

Muir's art, it seems to me, is a practiced artlessness, close to speech, achieved by directness, sincerity, and enthusiasm, qualities that he would have attributed to a glacial stream, such streams having a "fountain" source. (Muir confirms Bachelard's conclusion to "Water's Voice" in *Water and Dreams*: "The stream will teach you to speak; in spite of the pain and the memories, it will teach you euphoria. . . . Not a moment will pass without repeating some lovely round word that rolls over the stones.") This artlessness befits the innocence of his persona, especially in *The Story of My Boyhood and Youth*, where he recovers himself as a child. Not, of course, the little viper of Calvinist thought that his father sought to scourge (*scourge* follows closely on *Scottish* in the dictionary) but the uncorrupted child of nature of nineteenth-century Romantic thought ("*as innocent of evil as a child*" is the example of *innocent* in the dictionary).

In recovering this child, Muir repossesses what Edith Cobb calls "the ecology of imagination of childhood." He repossesses his earliest intuition of cosmos, his sense of niche in the natural economy (the *oikos*, the house of the world), and his original perceptual wealth, much of it told in this glorious natural history of Wisconsin, albeit informed by scientific and ecological insight long since acquired. (Leopold acknowledges a similar wealth in "Red Legs Kicking," as does Thoreau, in his journals, where he laments its loss.)

I find in Gary Nabhan's "A Child's Sense of Wildness" (in *Orion Nature Quarterly*, Autumn 1990) that Nabhan, who cites Edith Cobb's study, verifies its truth in terms of his recollection of experience as a "toddler" in the Indiana Dunes. I mention this because the question this prompts him to ask involves some of the profound issues of the relation of nature (and nature writing) to civilization: "What will be the fate of those who become adults unable to conjure up a single memory of nature from their childhood?" This question suggests the value of Muir's book and of his fidelity to the "pagan" child, who, in spite of punishment, followed to good purpose "the natural inherited wildness in *our* blood" (my italics).

The child, as Muir presents him, is already a naturalist, but his eye is innocent and his wonder never-failing. As with Huck Finn, whom he sometimes calls to mind in his speech ("The Yankee explained that they [deer] traveled and fed mostly at night . . . and how the Indians knew all about them and could find them whenever they were hungry"), this vouchsafed innocence measures our loss as adults, a national loss as well because Muir's childhood—the paradise nature afforded him—represents a similar stage in our history. Muir has few harsh words for his father and needn't condemn him because, in taking up the perspective of childhood, we do.

And we do so again at the end of the story, when Muir presents himself as a provincial seeking to enter the world who must do so without the financial help of the father who had worked him almost to death. (Snyder says that "of all moral failings and flaws of character, the worst is stinginess of thought, which includes manners in all its forms.") Yet the final chapter, in which Muir tells of leaving home for the capital city of Madison with his inventions as a conspicuous passport, is buoyant, its characterizations and speech worthy of Twain and the best American humor. Since we know him as a naturalist, it is surprising to find him writing about his inventions at the expense of almost all that nurtured his genius at the university. The chapter, it seems to me, is woefully truncated, but we must allow Muir the pleasure he still feels in having achieved at great odds such a splendid Franklinian success. He does not speak of the way to wealth but of the inventions he made both to steal time from his father ("time-wealth," he calls it, precious time in which to read and improve himself) and to regulate his life, and he is as proud of them as Franklin was of the less successful scheme by means of which he hoped to acquire virtue.

Perhaps the equanimity of Muir's story is owing to the fact that he writes in the assurance of having found and followed his vocation. His self-authorizing books are essentially an account of vocation, of a spiritual, if not a Christian, calling, the vocation in his case, as often in the case of other nature writers, a singular problematical one for the very reason that no other is consonant with the self. Now he gives his inventive genius its due because, though it was rare, it was not problematical; it was very much in the American grain. At this early stage of his life the naturalist and the inventor marched together, the latter, it might be said, in the service of the former, having brought him to the university—and, as he finds later, having kept alive the fame he achieved there. But Muir, who makes light of Emerson and himself when he says that he "hitched [his] dumping-wagon to a star," does not forsake the naturalist his story has all along brought forward, and in the episode with Griswold, the student who awakens his "wild enthusiasm" for botany, states the fundamental articles of his mature transcendentalist faith.

Natural things, he says, reveal "glorious traces of the thoughts of God." (*Traces*: inscriptions in the Book of Nature, *correspondences* to be interpreted, since Nature, in Emerson's teaching, is the symbol of spirit.) As Griswold demonstrates with the pea vine and locust tree, "'the Creator'" made them with "'the same idea in mind.'" ("The Maker of this earth" is indeed the supreme inventor in Thoreau's account of the thawing railroad cut, having "but patented a leaf.") This being so, the cardinal aspects of Nature are the "'essential unity with boundless variety'" and the "'harmony of their relations'" educed for Muir initially in the study of botany.

It is characteristic of Muir to say that he was "charmed" by Griswold's teaching—teaching that sent him "flying to the woods and meadows" and that encouraged him to wander in search of the "inner beauty" of things. Defined here by the appreciation of relationship, harmony, and unity, beauty is the result, as Wordsworth says, of seeing into the life of things; it is, Muir claims in his journal, the perfect synonym for God. And just as characteristic, made so by long usage, are *flying* and *wander*, which conjoin here to express liberation, *flying* not only suggesting *fleeing* but *flight*, the ascent that belongs to Muir's vertical imagination.

And so, at the end, his college education incomplete but having prepared himself in his wayward way in the necessary sciences, Muir makes short work of the much longer story of his life by saying that he "wandered away on a glorious botanical and geological excursion, which has lasted fifty years and is not yet completed." This is in keeping with the claim that all of his life he has been growing fonder of wild things and encloses the book thematically even as it keeps it open. So does the concluding statement, that in leaving the University of Wisconsin he was entering the larger world of the University of the Wilderness, that is, the universe itself (from the Latin *universum*, the whole world turned into one). This is another way of saying, as he had earlier, that once

Griswold opened his eyes (more than a metaphor to one who had known blindness), he was led "on and on into the infinite cosmos."

University of the Wilderness. For Muir, this is not the oxymoron it would have been for Bunyan. On the contrary, it is coextensive with the University of Wisconsin. It is a place as beautiful and a seat of learning, advanced learning certainly, higher learning. By setting out as a student (the probationary vocation par excellence), Muir certifies his natural piety and justifies his "lifelong wanderings."

Muir's lifework reverses that of his youth, which was literally spent—he was "put to the plow at the age of twelve"—in the pioneer labor of turning wilderness into arable land. He expresses no self-pity but commiseration for the many who were "made slaves through the vice of over-industry," those driven by the zeal to make "better use" of the "unproductive wilderness" than had the Indians they dispossessed—the Indian way *now* unquestionably salutary, fitted to the wilderness he considers "fertile" and "hospitable." The pioneers, he says, "toiled and sweated and grubbed themselves into their graves" and, as a result, "in a very short time the new country [the "new world" he tells us he entered as a child] began to look like an old one." (In an autobiographical fragment, Muir describes in detail, quietly but it seems in fascinated horror, the way the "beautiful trees [in Canada] were simply slashed down" in order to open a bit of ground to meager cultivation.)

Muir wasted under this over-industry and, again, we remember, when he imposed it on himself as a fruit farmer at Martinez. At one point in the narrative, he lets us know that he now looks out of the study window (of his fine house) at the linnets bathing in the dew. He has the not uncommon ambivalence of denying and approving the same thing and appreciates productive as well as idle land. Most of *Steep Trails*, a collection of essays and letters to newspapers reporting his exploration of the western states, is promotional, full of descriptions of the bountiful natural resources of the wilderness that resourceful people, good Scots perhaps, can turn into money.

Muir was asked to do many "heavy jobs" at the expense of his physical growth, but the deepest (advisedly) in his memory and the most important in establishing the vertical axis of his imagination is the digging of the well that nearly cost him his life. This experience caps the story of the ploughboy. Muir tells it with remarkable restraint and follows it with an extended account of the open-air homing flight of bees, to which in other writings he happily likens himself. He reminds us that at Fountain Lake Farm water was taken from a spring (immemorially, a holy source). The spring-fed lake, moreover, is a small glacier lake, his Walden but not a walled-in pond, where he notes that he "drifted about . . . for hours" and in learning to swim first mastered himself in combat with death. For him this pond is as inalienable, as much a part of himself, as Walden, the landscape of infant dreams, was for Thoreau. The immediate point, of course, is that the lake, as Thoreau says of Walden, is a "well ready dug," or better, as its name tells us, a fountain, the veritable fountain of Muir's youth, its water, as Bachelard claims of such water, linked with the hope of cure by virtue of its own dynamic and energetic nature. Fountain Lake is surely the literal source of *fountain*, one of Muir's obsessive words—and rightly so, since *source* and *flow* are at the heart of his generous, generative vision.

But at Hickory Hill Farm there was "no living water, no spring or stream or meadow or lake" (for *living water*, see *John of the Mountains*, Muir's journals, page 121), and the incredible task of chipping a well through nearly ninety feet of limestone fell to Muir. Day after day he descended into the three-foot hole of his own making, until near the end of his digging he was overcome by chokedamp and hauled up only in the nick of time. Muir calls the well a "dreary bore" but somehow overlooks another pun: *immured*. (When I told the story of the well to a friend, he immediately adduced Poe's "The Cask of Amontillado," for which, incidentally, I wrote another ending in the tenth grade. Poe, who knew about the pit, the great poet of dead water!) Imagine being confined in such a small space at such depth and always to have to rely on others to bring one up. And consider what Muir tells us earlier, how his pride in his skill in climbing nullified the servant girl's warnings of hell: "I always insisted that I would climb out of it. I imagined it was only a sooty pit with stone walls." The equivocal *imagined* anticipates his discovery that hell is the bottom of a well, the inability to move, a noisome gas, darkness, death.

A journal entry ("By the Grand Crevasse") recovers this experience in telling the story of the dog Stickeen: "No sunbeam ever sounded its depths. Death seemed to lie brooding forever in the gloom of the chasm—a grave ready made. . . . The poor child, Stickeen, was left alone on the side of that awful abyss, unspeakably lonely, so pitifully helpless and small, overshadowed with darkness and the dread of death." Finally, hushing his fears and "mak[ing] firm his trembling limbs," Stickeen "slipped down into the shadow of death" and, as we know, succeeded in crossing the ice-sliver bridge, his cries of joy rendered by Muir as "'Saved, saved, saved!'" Muir, who believed that Stickeen heralded a new gospel, concludes that "he was indeed a fellow-creature—a little boy in distress in guise of a dog."

Muir's recognition of animal rights, a pervasive theme of *The Story of My Boyhood and Youth*, is grounded in his own suffering, in the injustice of his own childhood. When Nob, a horse driven too hard by his father, falls ill, Muir notes that "all the dreadful symptoms were just the same as my own when I had pneumonia." When he extols mountain air, isn't this because he remembers and perhaps still suffers from the effects of pneumonia and chokedamp? The signature here ("I lay gasping for weeks") is repeated when he says of the experience of the well, "I was dragged out, violently gasping for breath." Muir died of pneumonia.

Colette Gaudin cites the following in behalf of Bachelard's ethic of joy and vertical axis of reverie: "*Anguish is artificial: we were meant to breathe freely.*" A motto for Muir, who in his journal read out the experience of the well as the fable of civilization and nature, lowland and mountain, "death exhalations" (smog) and "pure air." "Our bodies," he says, "were made to thrive only in pure air, and the scenes in which pure air is found." What he has learned from the experience of the "deep well" and his recent experience in San Francisco prompts his warning: "Go up and away for life; be fleet!"

Glaciers, so important to Muir, assured him that there were fountains in the sky, where vertical reverie tells us they should be and where Muir put them when developing the conceit of the "Love fountains of God" in a letter to Catherine Merrill: "We all flow from one fountain [an overflowing oversoul "saturating all and fountainizing all"]. All are expressions of one Love. God does not appear and flow out, only from narrow chinks and round bored wells here and there in favored races and places." We see that Muir finds the vertical axis of imagination, as Bachelard claims, the most liberating and that for him "every valorization is a verticalization." He seldom journeys downward, choosing instead to live vertically, to ascend steep trails. As he sees it, you either go to high places or stay below, and he advises us to go to the mountains because, as he notes in his journal, "Of all the upness accessible to mortals, there is no upness comparable to the mountains." What he says in another entry would surely have delighted Bachelard, whose reverie on "maternal water," the "milk of Mother nature," would as surely have delighted Muir: "The higher we go in the mountains, the milkier becomes the Milky Way." Which is to say, as so much in Muir's work does, that up—the high places where "young glaciers are nursed"—is a nurturant direction.

The experience of the well is present everywhere in Muir's work because it informs the way his imagination works, but it is most conspicuously present when extreme danger recalls it. The episode of his blinding is linked with it because he was cast in darkness. In this instance, his slow recovery has its duplicate in the aftermath of the dreadful night on Mount Shasta, where the fumarole was indeed infernal, its carbonic gases those that once before had threatened his life. Then there is the account of climbing Mount Ritter, where he was "nerve-shaken for the first time since setting foot on the mountains." His mind, he says, "seemed to fill with a stifling smoke"; and not to be overlooked is the fact that when "this terrible eclipse" was over and he repossessed himself, his "trembling muscles became firm again" (see Stickeen, above) and he made his way effortlessly to the "blessed light" of the summit. "Had I been borne aloft upon wings," he says, choosing the freest ascensional image, "my deliverance could not have been more complete."

But vertical valorization isn't always easy, not when Muir finds the well/hell above, near the top of Mount Shasta, and the home he associates with mountains is more readily placed below. The article in which he recounts this experience in *Harper's New Monthly Magazine* (September 1877) is called "Snow Storm on Mount Shasta," where another version in *Steep Trails* is called "A Perilous Night on Shasta's Summit," *perilous* and *night* much to the point. These articles differ considerably. The latter pairs the experience with another on Mount Shasta in which Muir happily waited out a snowstorm in a nest he had made and was displeased when Sisson came to rescue him. And since he groups it with other accounts of "rambles" at Shasta, it benefits as well from his description of the Modoc Lava Beds, a forbidding volcanic landscape that prompts him to speak of a "darkness like death." Michael Cohen, in *The Pathless Way*, says of the article in *Harper's* that Muir "described a kind of journey to the underworld," and he cites Muir's statement, much amended in the other version, that "the weary hours wore away like a mass of unnumbered and half-forgotten years, in which all our other years and experiences were strangely interblended." During these weary hours Muir may have lived through the geological history of mountain building, as Cohen claims, but in doing so he relived his own history and discovered a fiery creation of the dread kind Blake evokes in "The Tyger."

Muir often reported his exploits to Mrs. Ezra Carr, but in this instance was notably brief, suggesting the extremity of the experience at the same time as he minimized it—or read out its compensation in "valuable experiences." In both versions, Muir tells how he and Fay, after the terrible night, managed to reach their rescuers and were "soon mounted and on [their] way *down* into thick sunshine—to 'God's country,' as Sisson calls the chaparral zone" (my italics). But according to Linnie Marsh Wolfe, who consulted Muir's journal, Muir was "unshaken in his loyalty to nature's wholeness" and made this reply to Sisson: "Yes, this is God's country—all these grand forests, and sunny fields where the mountain apples grow, and the strawberries and the violets. But they all depend upon the benefactions of the mountain itself that you call desolate and God-forsaken!" Muir ends both versions with a bedroom scene reminiscent of the dark days in Indianapolis: "How fresh and sunful and new-born our beautiful world appeared! Sisson's children came in with wild flowers and covered my bed, and the sufferings of our long freezing storm period on the mountain-top seemed all a dream." (*Seemed* in the *Harper's* is truer than *vanished* in the other version.) Linnie Marsh Wolfe, who provides still another version, unwittingly calls up Muir's recovery from blindness when she writes, "How sweet life appeared, as if he was seeing it anew!"

Muir doesn't wholly disagree with Sisson, whose remark about the chaparral country calls attention to his own lavish description of the circumambient landscape of Shasta in "Summer Days at Shasta." This introductory essay, with its guidebook aspects, is a set piece in which Muir shows his skill as a nature writer and expresses his now popular sentiments about nature's curative value; and he might have referred Helen Hunt Jackson to it, when in answer to her letter he told her that without inconvenience she could "circle away all summer around Mount Shasta." The essay is worth mentioning because its circular complements the vertical imagination and, even though the vertical may be read cosmologically (as heaven, earth, and hell), Muir needs both to be true to his sense of cosmos, that is, to what he actually sees when he reaches the summit and realizes his reverie of the terrestrial paradise, of home. Though the vertical ascent may be read as "masculine," both linear in its drive and hierarchical in its valuation, it is better read in psychological terms that accord with climbing out of a pit, or, as Muir puts it in his journal, the "lowlands, where hidden dangers destroy without calling forth any strength to resist or enjoy." For him climbing is the supreme exercise in alertness and enables us at the summit to "see . . . better" the "grand outlook—all the world spread below." The top views he enjoys, often of great tree-form rivers and glaciers as well as imposing forests, are networks declaring a vital unity secured by *balance* and *integration* rather than *dominance*. I take these words, of such significant currency now, from Ursula Le Guin, another notable California writer, whose essays provide a way of understanding Muir that explains his popularity not only with mountaineers but with a reading public whose sensibility may be said to be "feminine."

The circle Muir describes has Shasta for its center, and Shasta, unlike the God who made and still makes the world, is a maternal presence, the immediate fountain-source of all good. Muir approaches Shasta perspectively, plane by plane, as in landscape painting (in summary: "meadow, forest, and grand icy summit harmoniously blending and making one sublime picture evenly balanced"), paying homage here, if not in his excursion to Mount Ritter, to William Keith and other painter-friends. But once entered in this way, he spatializes the landscape in ever-widening circles of benefit and beauty. Instead of a pictorial landscape, we find ourselves within an areal-scape that in size and scope evokes the cosmic. Muir reads its brief historical development in terms of the progressive inhabitation by Indians, miners, cattle-raisers, hunters, trappers, and farmers, but, more significantly, he explains the existing zones in geological-orogenic terms. He thereby reminds us of the living energy at the heart of things. Perhaps to awaken the fitting sense of the sublime as well as to suspend us in the eternity of earth-time, he notes in closing the still present danger of volcanic eruption.

To return to *The Story of My Boyhood and Youth*. Most of the adumbrations are present understandings, the love of storms, for example, told on the first page in terms of his later appreciation of the elimination of boundaries: "when the sea and the sky, the waves and the clouds, were mingled together as one." And soon he tells us of his earliest acquaintance with animals, as instances of "the capacity of a child's heart for sorrow and sympathy with animals." The story of "Llewellyn's Dog" is surely intended to recall and point up the usefulness of his own "Stickeen," the most popular of his writings, and the discovery of the mother field mouse feeding her young is intended to recall Burns' "To a Mouse" (mentioned by Muir in the eloquent commemoration of Burns in which he describes himself)—to recall not just the familiar line about "the best-laid schemes o' mice an' men" but the following stanza:

> I'm truly sorry man's dominion
> Has broken Nature's social union,
> An' justifies that ill opinion
>   Which makes thee startle
> At me, thy poor, earth-born companion
>   An' fellow mortal!

The recollections of his daring and skill at climbing and of playing travels around the world are obvious in intention. Less so is the chapter "A Paradise of Birds," which may represent the extent to which Muir, the farm boy, wished to be paired, and compared, with John Burroughs, an equally popular nature writer.

For good reason the most telling recollections hide the most, those of Muir's arguments and conflict with his father, whose dogmatic beliefs correspond with the beliefs of Professor J. D. Whitney. Whitney's catastrophism, his violent "engulfment hypothesis," as Muir calls it in *Studies in the Sierra*, remarking in his scientific repudiation of it that it "furnishes a kind of Tophet for the reception of bad mountains," is comparable to his father's dire fundamentalism. Both belong, as Muir makes out, with beliefs, now discarded, in such things as phrenology and spirit rapping. In dramatizing the dialectical skill of his coming-of-age, Muir shows us another aspect of his early education and enjoys, I suspect, a double victory in remembering how, where it counted most to all he believed, he had studied the Book of Nature, explained the origin of Yosemite on uniformitarian principles, and brought down another formidable opponent.

      Walk in the world. Williams' injunction in *Paterson* might well be Muir's, for *walk/walking* is one of his master tropes, the necessary *turn*, *way*, and *manner* already defined by *tropos* and appropriate alike for poet and naturalist, or anyone who goes afield. *Walk* and *walking* belong to the conceptual metaphor of life as a journey; they evoke a *path* or *way*, and by virtue of the fact that a vocation is "one's walk in life," a way of life intrinsic to the self, determined by its tropism, and walking itself sometimes becomes a vocation, we may speak of a *pathless way* (as Michael Cohen fittingly entitles his book on Muir). Charles Olson, perambulating Gloucester toward the end of his life, takes note of "the last walking period of man," thereby using walking to define something we once did and seldom do now. At best, our walks are short, a matter of quick trips, supporting Muir's coupling of *unwalked* and *unseen* in *A Thousand-Mile Walk to the Gulf*, the positive version of which is Vernon Carstensen's statement in the foreword of *The Story of My Boyhood and Youth*, that "throughout his life [the journey of his life] he would be a looker and a walker." However much we walk, we most likely do so unmindful of the sense of destination conveyed by Daniel Muir ("the Bible," he told John, "is the only book human beings can possibly require throughout all the journey from earth to heaven") and by Muir himself ("Ramble to the summit of Mount Hoffman . . . the highest point in life's journey my feet have yet touched").

These quotations suggest the extent to which Muir, in his wayward way, kept in mind the salvational goal of life's journey. Though the key words at the beginning of *A Pilgrim's Progress* are also Muir's ("I walked through the wilderness of this world"), they no longer convey Bunyan's meaning. Muir did indeed walk; he is probably our greatest walker—and, as Tom Lyon says, "our wildest writer." His words for *walking* include *ramble, drift, saunter, wander, rove*, and *stroll*, all of them coincident with what he called, when worrying over his vocation, "my pathless, lawless thoughts." Muir didn't walk *through* (out of) the wilderness-of-this-world, he walked *in* its still remaining wilderness, *wilderness* by his time having acquired the salutary meaning he did so much to foster. His transitional work depends on, at the same time as it advances, the transvaluation of these terms already under way during the 1850s and 1860s—terms, it should be noted, that belonged to long-established conservative, patriarchal thought.

The richest gloss on this radical change is David C. Miller's *Dark Eden: The Swamp in Nineteenth-Century American Culture*, an iconological, iconographical, and phenomenological study that provides a context enabling us to see both the historical dimensions of Muir's identity crisis (significant because it intersects history) and the most likely reason for the ready reception of his work. In fact, Muir's work, much of it published in newspapers and magazines, carries on the conversation ("the 'unending conversation,'" according to Kenneth Burke, "that is going on at the point in history when we are born") that Muir found in magazines like *Atlantic Monthly* and *Harper's Monthly*. These national maga-

zines, begun in the 1850s, were available in Madison during his years there—
magazines, incidentally, for which he later wrote.

Muir's early letters place him in the conversation of his time, not those to Emily
Pelton that tell of exuberant adventure on the Wisconsin and Mississippi rivers
(these especially please me because I know this landscape) so much as those to
Mrs. Ezra Carr, his tutelary confidante, to whom he began to write when he
went to Canada during the Civil War. Muir strikes his essential note, as William
and Maymie Kimes point out in their indispensable bibliography of his work, in
his first publication, the report of finding the *Calypso borealis* that Mrs. Carr
gave to Professor J. D. Butler, who submitted it to the *Boston Recorder*, where
it appeared in 1866. Writing of this forty-five years later, Muir failed to remember Mrs. Carr's first intervention in the making of his career, perhaps because
by this time he felt some embarrassment over this most important of his correspondences and wished to withhold some of his letters from publication, particularly those in which he mentions Mrs. Elvira Hutchings and perhaps some
of those that expose his feelings for Mrs. Carr.

The *Boston Recorder* is not available to me to check, but it seems to me that in
his recollection of the event he conflates it with his subsequent experience of
swamps on his walk to the Gulf. The recollection of "this first grand excursion"
in Canada (in William F. Badè's *Life and Letters of John Muir*) tells of "wading
in bogs and swamps that seemed more and more extensive and more difficult to
force one's way through." There are bogs of this kind here, but I suspect that
Muir's account of "struggling through drooping branches and over and under
heaps of fallen trees" belongs as much to later experience if only because when
he fears that he must pass the night there he remembers the nests that Humboldt said the Indians built in the trees of "the flooded forests of the Orinoco."
The swamp that he describes is still the traditional dark and fearful waste,
though the allusion to the jungles of South America has (as had the exotic travel
articles of the time) begun to transform it, and the rare orchid he finds, "when
the sun was getting low and everything seemed most bewildering and discour-
aging," redeems it.

In the recollection, Muir says that this white flower, which belongs to romantic
quest and is described in a way that to readers now seems explicitly sexual, was
"the most spiritual of all the flower people I had ever met" and that "I sat down
beside it and fairly cried for joy." In the letter to Mrs. Carr, from which Badè

cites only the remarks on the beauty and usefulness of all plants, including weeds, Muir's rapture is extravagant:

> I never before saw a plant so full of life; so perfectly spiritual, it seemed pure enough for the throne of its Creator. I felt as if I were in the presence of superior beings who loved me and beckoned to me to come. I sat down beside them and wept for joy. Could angels in their better land show us a more beautiful plant? How good is our Heavenly Father in granting us such friends as these plant-creatures, filling us wherever we go with pleasure so deep, so pure, so endless.

The letter continues, with a rising (rousing) rhetoric of the kind popular in sermons—and Muir has found the text of one of the sermons he ever afterward preached. But enough has been cited to show the extent to which the sensibility he expresses so well was shaped by literary conventions, that is, by what he heard and read, and by expectations, notably those of Mrs. Carr, who represented the highest culture and the transcendentalist, advanced yet genteel, aspirations of the time.

Stephen Fox is surely right when he says that "aside from his family, Jeanne Carr exercised the most significant influence on his early life." She opened the intellectual world to him and sustained him over many years by her loving approval of his determination (often expressed as indecision) to pursue self-culture and find his own vocational way. She was Muir's good angel. And since she was an enthusiastic botanist, who told him that "it is only from our Great Mother that we really learn the lessons of our Father's love for us," it may not be farfetched to think that he botanized as much because of her as because of Griswold's lesson. He once addressed her as "My Dear Mother Carr" and said, "You helm my fate more than all the world beside." Their correspondence is full of flowers not only because of scientific interest but because flowers at this time spoke the language of sentiment—made for a kind of "amatory botany," to employ a phrase of S. Hall Young used in another context. It takes nothing from Muir to acknowledge the aegis of Mrs. Carr and how much his work was nurtured by and contributed to a "feminization of American culture" of a positive kind not considered by Ann Douglas.

I take the demonstrably psychic aspect of the account of finding the *Calypso borealis* as evidence of the changing intellectual climate even though swamps, as in the example of the Slough of Despond, had long been used to represent the psyche. It is not so much the symbolization of the swamp that matters now as the fact, established in Thoreau's "Walking," that the swamp has become a chosen place, a *"sanctum sanctorum,"* a place of joy, not sorrow. Here we search for "the springs of life." And just as important is Thoreau's belief that instinctively we turn in this direction: that the self, relying on "instinct" ("there is a subtle magnetism in Nature . . . if we unconsciously yield to it"), will find a path to the wilderness that more fully accords with the symbolic path which "we love to travel in the interior [psychic] and ideal [spiritual] world." We are told that Muir first read Thoreau during his Yosemite years, at the urging of Mrs. Carr and Emerson, but it is altogether possible, since "Walking" was published in the *Atlantic Monthly* in 1862, that he read this essay while at the University of Wisconsin and found in this stirring apologia a directive and warrant for his own life.

So much tallies, not the least the reference to Humboldt that speaks for Muir's intention on his "long walk": "Humboldt came to America to realize his youthful dreams of a tropical vegetation, and he beheld it in its greatest perfection in the primitive forests of the Amazon, the most gigantic wilderness on the earth." Muir, of course, may have read Humboldt at Hickory Hill, for even then, he claims, he wished to emulate Humboldt, one of the great popular heroes of the age. According to Linnie Marsh Wolfe, he read Humboldt during his stay in Canada. In the editions I have, *Aspects of Nature,* Humboldt's first book, was published in Boston in 1850 and *Cosmos* in 1851, the later monumental work perhaps inspiring the inscription in Muir's travel notebook: "John Muir, Earthplanet, Universe." But attributions of this kind are not as important as what the publication of such books tells us about the climate of opinion at the time when "Walking," "Song of the Open Road," and Emerson's *Essays* were written, all of them having come to mind in reading *A Thousand-Mile Walk to the Gulf.*

Enough has been said of Thoreau's essay, and all that needs to be noted in Whitman's poem is the first verse:

> Afoot and light-hearted I take to the open road,
> Healthy, free, the world before me,
> The long brown path before me leading wherever I choose.

Another inscription in the journal of Muir's walk to the Gulf—it accompanies a sketch of himself on his knees in the woods studying a map—is "the world was all before them where to choose" ("their place of rest" omitted here but not in the earlier citation from *Paradise Lost* in a letter to Emily Pelton announcing his departure for Canada). Later on, probably in 1878, in a notebook entry that Robert Engberg and Donald Wesling, the editors of *John Muir: To Yosemite and Beyond,* say is especially important in understanding "the young man Muir" (see Erik Erikson), Muir speaks of this time of vocational indecision as "the time . . . when all the world is said to lie before us for choice." (The skepticism here confirms the fact that for him there was nothing to choose, only one calling to follow.) By 1878, the crisis this involved—Emerson, speaking from experience, says that vocational choice is the crisis of one's life and that "the call of our calling is the loudest call"—seems to have been forgotten. Muir depicts himself as indeed "light-hearted," ready, he tells us, "with plant press and small satchel on my back" and rich in "visions of tropic lands," to be off on a "grand Sabbath day three years long," a Sabbath much like the one that young man Thoreau proposed to enjoy in Nature, "of the affections and the soul." And he could do this "feeling free and conscience calm," as he claims after the fact, because Emerson's essays, addressed as they are to the sanction of the "soul's emphasis," assured him that what he had done was right. In indexing the copy of *Essays* that Emerson gave him, Muir paraphrases Emerson to suit himself. Emerson's "only by obedience to his genius, only by the freest activity in a way constitutional with him, does an angel seem to arise before a man and lead him out of the wards of the prison" becomes Muir's succinct "in your own path there is always an angel guiding gently."

Emerson, who recognized Muir by adding him to the select list of "My Men," also gave him Sampson Reed's *Observations on the Growth of the Mind* (1826, but probably in the revised edition of 1838), which had served him well in his own vocational crisis and confirmed his reliance on correspondential vision. Reed spoke of human development in terms of organic growth, that is, from an inner, self-determining principle; and he demanded that this *peculium* of the mind be allowed to grow freely, to absorb (by the imaginative assimilation that "correspondence" enables) what it needed from the sustaining world. Muir told Mrs. Carr, in 1872, that he had received this "profound little book" and had found it "full of the fountain truth."

Recollection distances and lightens the protracted crisis of vocation that Muir endured and paradoxically overcame by walking away, into his destiny. He would have us believe that America and walking are somehow equated, that his walking in the wilderness of nature, with only insignificant interruption, began with his arrival in America. By the time he writes this autobiographical note he has read "Walking" and incorporated it in what is beginning to be a legendary account of himself, a pleasing, genial self-representation. We find him almost effortlessly "strolling off into the woods botanizing," "wandering at will in bog and meadow," and "sauntering free and alone [not lonely, but singly, unencumbered by the duties of settled social existence] in a constant state of [ecstasy]." I supply the blurred word in the manuscript, falling back on Muir's frequent use of the word and on echoes of Thoreau's confession of the glory he experienced in his youth and (not so strangely) on Jonathan Edwards' personal narrative of the delight and affection he found in his "great and glorious God." The "soul-hunger" that Muir admits had tormented him is a kind of spirituality he now dismisses as belonging to the time when he "was *on* the world but [not] really *in* it."

This certifying statement—a touchstone he applies to others—brings us to the heart of Muir's work. It tells us how much he was impelled by the desire to be in the world, to have his being there by participating bodily in it. His envy of "happy reptiles that had advantage of so much body in contact with earth" explains the primacy of his perception (I borrow in my fashion from Merleau-Ponty) and the otherwise curious statement in his recollection that science was of secondary importance, not his vocation but a way to legitimate it: "Nature [personified] held me afield. I lingered in woods and bogs in pursuit of science. Botany and geology led me on, or rather I allowed these sciences to pursue me, for though I studied hard, all kinds of wild beauty was allowed to come to me, to draw and hold me as they were able." Muir's perceptions, fostered by unusual attentiveness and receptivity, are almost always accompanied by the sensation of being filled (and of *being* fulfilled) by the pervading physical presence of elemental things. And this justifies his lingering: "The beauty and harmony of sunshine and crystal water filled every faculty [sense] with intense joy." His world is "Godful," his God is "warm."

Muir exhilarates us because he speaks the language of pleasure. This is why he seems childlike. There is much in his work to be grateful for, but nothing, I sometimes find, as his restoration of the body and testimony to the joy of bodily being. This comes of his *worlding* (*this* worlding, you might say) and his discovery, in walking, that "our body is not in space like things; it inhabits or haunts space . . . [and] through it we have direct access to space." Merleau-

Ponty says this, and Muir anticipates him when he remarks of an early trip to Yosemite that "the scenery was enchanting, and we allowed our bodies ample time to sponge it up." (It takes time to come into space.)

This sentence tells the transition from spectator to participant. There are innumerable instances of this essential experience. Of the beautiful days he enjoys in Yosemite, Muir says that they "do not exist as mere pictures" but "saturate themselves into every part of the body and live always." A noteworthy instance, because at the same time as he moderates it in *My First Summer in the Sierra*, he makes it one of his versions of Emerson's transparent eyeball, is the ecstatic journal entry on entering the mountains for the first time. The mountains he enters enter *into* him, not *in* him, as in the revision, and the "bright seething white-fire enthusiasm" bred in him by the mountains is not reduced to "kindling enthusiasm." In the journal, there is the present sense, the very quick and texture of experience: "A perfect influx into every pore and cell of us, fusing, vaporizing by its heat until the boundary walls of our heavy flesh tabernacle seem taken down and we flow and diffuse into the very air and trees and streams and rocks. . . . Responsive, we are part of nature now. . . . Nature like a fluid seems to drench and steep us throughout, as the whole sky and the rocks and flowers are drenched with spiritual life—with God." The oversoul has become a fountain. And the "flesh-and-bone tabernacle" that in the revision "seems transparent as glass" is not limited to sight in its experience of the circulations of being. For Muir, to cite Merleau-Ponty once more, "the perceiving mind is an incarnated mind."

(A sentence in Muir's recollection—"shortly after leaving college I began to doubt whether I was fully born"—sends me back to *Love's Body*, where Norman Brown says that "the real birth is the second birth." Leafing through Brown's provocative book, I find a remark, supported by Matthew 10:39 but as readily supported by the lives of Thoreau and Muir: "The solution to the problem of identity is, get lost." Further on, there is an applicable word, *mundification*, which is what occurs when the world is Godful, "the divine *substantia*," as Brown explains, "in all creatures," all creatures now "full of divinity." And perhaps, since Muir took the New Testament with him on his walk to the Gulf and long afterward became a cultivator of grapes, I might add for good measure another sentence from Brown: "At any rate he [Jesus] calls us to come outdoors; Dionysus calls us outdoors.")

Thoreau reports in his journal a recurrent dream, a variant of the rough and the smooth, that concerns the ascent of a mountain (its summit "unhandselled, awful, grand," like Katahdin). His way involves "a dark and unfrequented wood," the gate to which, he realizes, is "Burying Hill." From the top of the mountain, he discovers that "there are ever two ways up: one through the dark wood, the other through the sunny pasture." In keeping with what he had written of the rough way (among other things, he has "an indistinct remembrance of having been out overnight alone"), he asks, "Why is it that in the lives of men we hear more of the dark wood than of the sunny pasture?" It seems that he would have it otherwise, though this is not the case when, in "Walking," he mentions Dante and Bunyan. Here he decides for tragedy—a "divine tragedy," to be sure. But Muir, whose *A Thousand-Mile Walk to the Gulf* is mostly the record of traveling in the dark wood and the selva oscura of the self, omits from his recollection anything to suggest that the journey with which he began his "three year's *Sunday*" was not the "glorious walk" and "floral pilgrimage" that he expected it to be. This may explain why he began his essential autobiographical work at the highest pitch, with *My First Summer in the Sierra*, and didn't follow the chronology of his experience. As a matter of fact, though he had it typed, he never edited the journal of *A Thousand-Mile Walk to the Gulf*. Considering the easy way in which he opened the future at the end of *The Story of My Boyhood and Youth* and that *A Thousand-Mile Walk to the Gulf*, in Herbert Smith's view, is "perhaps the most revealing of Muir's work" ("a classic of Transcendental introspection . . . dealing with the most crucial period of his life"), he would have found doing this troublesome.

A Thousand-Mile Walk to the Gulf, so named by Muir to indicate the length and destination that made it special, is the record of what the French call the crisis-of-the-thirtieth-year, that is, of an unusually severe trial of vocation and faith. The longest of Muir's "long lonely excursions" (his characterization in the autobiographical sketch of his wanderings in Canada), this journey in his twenty-ninth year is also the darkest. It is framed by death. He said of the blinding in Indianapolis that preceded and prompted this journey that "in that terrible darkness I died to light," and he was brought near death in Florida by malaria and typhoid fever. This journey, which might have death and resurrection for its theme, also tells of Muir's "graveyard life" in Bonaventure Cemetery near Savannah, this life indeed life, in keeping with his transvaluation of traditional notions of death. He speaks here, as Whitman does, of "the beautiful blendings and communions of death and life, their joyous inseparable unity," death itself part of the "divine harmony." Among the many sketches in the journal, there are two of the graveyard, one in which Muir, hatless, is lying on the ground beneath a live oak, a grave at his feet, two owls in a tree, the other (entitled "My Bonaventure Home") of Muir seated by the little shelter he had built, a grave on one side, birds in flight and on branches on the other.

There is a delightful comic quality to these homespun sketches and several others in which he depicts himself. Self-representation is of crucial importance to him at this time, for it effectively dramatizes his experience to himself in much the same way as his letters, often written on the instant, do—only in the letters, where he has an audience, he often presents himself in a heroic way absent in the sketches. His letters, with his journal entries the freshest of his writing, are engaging because of the urgent need he has to complete his experience by telling it. The sketches also reenact his experience and give it back to him (they anticipate Polaroid photography and its gratification), and they should be published because they lighten the journey in a contrapuntal way, make light of it. There is one sketch in which Muir depicts himself pulling himself with grapevines out of the Chattahoochee River and another in which he depicts himself flat on his back in a swamp, a "dainty," he whimsically says in the text, for the open-jawed alligator on a log. (Snyder: "We are all edible.") The sketches reveal a Muir equal to, not yet subdued, by his experience. One measure of the journey is that after he falls ill he no longer includes himself in what he sketches. The only drawing that relates to him is the most objective, the graph he keeps at Cedar Keys to chart his recovery. And this is curious because he places full health at 0, at the bottom of the vertical, and death at 100, at the top.

In another unpublished note recovered by Engberg and Wesling, Muir rebukes Thoreau for counseling us, in "Walking," to go forth "in the spirit of adventure," prepared, that is, to leave all behind, family and friends, our affairs settled and our wills made. Muir remembers this because he took it literally. In still another note, this one published by Badè in the introduction to *A Thousand-Mile Walk to the Gulf*, Muir recalls how determinative this walk was, how, as a result of his blinding, he decided henceforth by studying nature to dwell in "heaven's light" and how, before setting out, he went home to bid everyone a "formal good-bye." Badè also cites the explanation, later crossed out, with which Muir opens the journal: a portentous analogy to the tides in nature that in the unsatisfied soul are "constant," "cumulative," and "overmaster[ing]." And he was overmastered, driven, as he told Mrs. Carr at the time, intent on going south but uncertain of where he was going, "doomed [he attitudinizes] to be 'carried of the spirit into the wilderness.'"

It hardly matters that Muir thought to suppress the psychic burden of the journey. *A Thousand-Mile Walk to the Gulf* offers little of the rich natural lore of Bartram's *Travels* (the Romantic source of swamp imagery) or the acute sociological observation of Olmsted's antebellum investigations of the South. Coming to this book as we probably do, already acquainted with Muir, we read it for Muir himself, to discover the out-setting naturalist, to see him adventuring and seeing what he saw, and to find out how the journey, as journeys are purported to do, changed him.

Muir is already a skilled writer—why, we wonder, didn't he think of writing as a career? Herbert Smith, whose early study of Muir is chiefly literary, considers Muir, in this, his first journal, to be inexperienced as a writer, when, in fact, he has been well schooled by writing letters and writes, not unselfconsciously, as Smith believes, but consciously, aware of an audience. Even as he adds to the journal, Muir edits it and remarks on what he has written, the following, for example, in respect to the blacksmith: "Poorly told. Give this story in full," (This is not, I think, a later editing.) His "apparent casualness," to cite Smith, is just that—apparent.

The transcendental strain, already conspicuous in his letters, is of course conspicuous here: Muir would not be Muir without it. But he is also adept at depicting picaresque incidents (the robber, the guerrilla band, the threatening black man in the swamp) and rendering some of them (the crossing of the Rolling Fork River on a horse with a black boy mounted behind him; mountaineers going downhill in a ramshackle wagon) in the broad strokes of frontier humor. His prejudices are also those of the frontier, albeit of the northern backwoods. He is not unwilling to eat with blacks but tells of it humorously, at his own expense; and though in this instance he doesn't express his aversion to dirt, he notes that he slept outdoors. "Little Nig" is his designation for the boy on the horse; the blacks in the cottonfields are "Sambos and Sallies." His provincialism surprises us. He measures society and scenery, economy and plants, by what he knows of Wisconsin, and in his regard for civilization and progress is not a primitivist. He has the assurance of what he believes is a superior point of view.

His characterizations are also often broad, as they will be in *My First Summer in the Sierra*. Those people he portrays, like the blacksmith, the Georgia planter, and the clerk in Savannah, are foils for himself. As he caustically says early on of a Kentuckian, they are "the useful, practical men—too wise to waste precious time with weeds, caves, fossils, or anything else [they] could not eat." (*Eating* is an economic key word, as is *bread*.) These people enable him to dramatize the problem of vocation and, characteristically, to argue the case. Even in the recollection cited earlier, Muir presents the problem dramatically, probably because he frequently encountered it as an agon to be won by speech:

> "Young man," they said, "choose your profession—Doctor, Lawyer, Minister?"
> "No, not just yet," I said.

The conversation with the blacksmith (the manliest of men: "hammer in hand, bare-breasted, sweaty, and covered with shaggy black hair") is the longest and most to the point and suggests how far Muir has come from Longfellow's exemplary village blacksmith. When the blacksmith tells him that "picking up blossoms doesn't seem to be a man's work at all in any kind of times," Muir argues, as he did with his father, by turning the Bible to his advantage. Muir, it should be noted, never loses an argument and, in this instance, besides establishing his cleverness (a Yankee trait?) establishes the fact that he is "a very strong-minded man." These arguments, notably the one in which he proves his identity as John Muir–the–botanist, always center on this unusual vocation, and though they show how strong-minded he is also show how ingratiating he can be (as always in his letters), how appealing he is in his openness, harmlessness, and *talk*.

It strikes me now that ingratiation is a hallmark of his art. In this book, not only because the sketches of himself with his hat and satchel and plant press bring it to mind, he endears himself as Chaplinesque. And why not? He claimed to be a "self-styled [indeed] poetico-trampo-geologist-bot . . . etc." (his take on a similar self-description by Thoreau) and he once said that he might have become a millionaire (the least of his brags) but "chose to become a tramp." *Tramp*: not, I think, as we find it defined by Eiseley's experience, but perhaps by the *vagabondia* that Bliss Carman and Richard Hovey, Muir's contemporaries, made famous.

Walking, according to John Stilgoe in *Common Landscape of America, 1580 to 1845,* vanished in the eastern United States in the 1840s with the coming of the railroad. By 1867, when Muir set out, he was able to go by rail from Indianapolis to Jeffersonville and begin his walk on the southern side of the Ohio River. Choosing the "wildest, leafiest, and least trodden way" (not Whitman's "paths untrodden" but a way into "the wild, happy land" that as a boy he imagined America to be), he began what Stilgoe calls "self-paced travel." This kind of travel belonged to colonial New England, where "out-of-town travel never began as passive submission to an inviting road but as a deliberate breaking of centripetal orbit." This reminds me of Emerson's "Circles" and how much Muir's walking answers to its figuration of "the heart's refusal to be imprisoned" and its "immense and innumerable expansions"—how much his walking stirs us because it figures the very urging of life. Muir intended this walk to make good his boyhood dream, to allow him the freedom to wander that had been denied him. The motto he inscribed in his journal expresses his illimitable desire even as "Universe" evokes the ordered, beautiful, and harmonious cosmos he celebrates.

Muir simplifies when he admonishes us, as he often does, to walk in the wilderness. Thereby, he believes, we "escape the tyranny of custom and confusion . . . [are] born again and make a new beginning." This healing, as he usually represents it, happens without the journey-work of the psyche that travel initiates. The notable exception, of course, is this long lonely walk, with its critical illness and travail of spirit, the latter, acknowledged in passing, but best told when, on the voyage north, Muir recapitulates and reflects on his experience. This reflexivity is the most significant formal aspect of the book. Using the sky and the sound of the wind as indices, Muir charts a journey from the familiar to the strange, from being at home in the world to being estranged from it. In Kentucky and Tennessee, he does not feel himself "in a strange land," but in Georgia, to cite the motif from Exodus 2:22 that he develops, he begins to be "'a stranger in a strange land,'" and when he reaches Florida, he is "a stranger, indeed."

Strange and *stranger* are heavily invested words, one attributed to what he sees, the other to what he becomes as a result of this. These words make us realize how much our being and well-being depend upon the *familiar* (its etymology going back to *family*) and how very much this was true for Muir. When he enters "an impenetrable cypress swamp" in Georgia, he notes the following, some of it in sentence fragments:

> Am made to feel I am now in a strange land. I hardly know any of the plants, but few of the birds, and I am unable to see the country for the solemn, dark, mysterious cypress woods which cover everything.
>
> The winds are full of strange sounds, making one feel far from the people and plants and fruitful fields of home. Night is coming on and I am filled with indescribable loneliness. Felt feverish; bathed in a black, silent stream; nervously watched for alligators.

Strangeness and loneliness, to which in subsequent work Muir seldom admits, figure the beginning of a "night-journey," to use a Jungian term, which soon brings him to the "Tombs" of Bonaventure Cemetery. Here his affirmation of life prefigures the outcome, not of the present journey, for there is further darkness to traverse, but of his passage to California, where he enters into the light.

Florida, which had been the land of paradisal dreams, quite overwhelms him, it is "so watery and vine-tied." His initial response is again one of loneliness: "Not a spirit whisper of sympathy came from anything about me." Fearful of alligators, he immediately imagines one, only to find instead a white crane, which, it should be noted, he reads as a talisman of spirit. At this point in the journey, having admitted that he was not brave, he writes a paragraph, later deleted, on the character attributes of cowardice and courage, cleverly dismissing his concern. Though he saw only one alligator, he calls the swamps through which he waded and wallowed and extricated himself from clutching vines and briers, "this alligator wilderness," perhaps acknowledging in this way that swamps represent an "older creation." Even more estranging than these dark places is the palmetto that "so strangely toned" the winds. "These palms and these winds," he says in reviewing the journey, "severed the last strands of the cord that united me with home," and the wind, heard at night, had the "power to present the distance from friends and home, and the completeness of my isolation from all things familiar." His illness and long, incomplete convalescence among the palms of Cedar Keys undoubtedly contributed to this music. But his illness goes unmentioned, its place taken here by what for him is the most remarkable experience of his journey: the recovery of childhood that signals his rebirth.

In the entry for 23 October, the first in the chapter on Cedar Keys, Muir records that, while still distant from the Gulf, he scented the salt air and instantly envisioned his childhood world in Dunbar, Scotland. The telling line here is: "My whole childhood, that seemed to have utterly vanished in the New World [*manuscript version*: "which appeared to die in the presence of the new life in the new world"] was now restored amid the Florida woods [*manuscript version*: "while yet amid the vines and sunless forests of Florida"] by that one breath from the sea." The later reflection, almost as long as the entry, fills it out and adds to its significance:

> When I was a day's journey from the Gulf, a wind blew upon me from the sea—the first sea breeze that had touched me in twenty years. I was plodding along with my satchel and plants, leaning wearily forward, a little sore from approaching fever, when suddenly I felt the salt air, and before I had time to think, a whole flood of long-dormant associations rolled in upon me. The Firth of Forth, the Bass Rock, Dunbar Castle, and the winds and rocks and hills came upon the wings of that wind, and stood in as clear and sudden light as a landscape flashed upon the view by a blaze of lightning in a dark night.

Restoration is a gift of the spirit, of the dove evoked by "the wings of that wind"—an ascensional image even though the dove usually descends. Muir is passive, the recipient of this "one *breath* from the sea" (my italics). The dark swamp from which he is suddenly liberated (lifted) recalls the well in which he nearly died, for the "long-dormant associations" are not only of Scotland but of Wisconsin, where his childhood died. He remembers the ploughboy in the present recollection of weary, feverish plodding, and he remembers the well in figuring the flood (fountain) of associations that restores his childhood as a "blaze of lightning in a dark night."

Among Muir's papers there is a note, "Flashes of Light," which is interesting for two reasons that seem to me to originate in this experience. Muir attributes to such flashes of light the evocation of "latent memories of our youth" and the power to make the untrodden wilderness "familiar." (I am indebted to Kathleen

Anne Wadden, "John Muir and the Community of Nature," *Pacific Historian* 29 [1985]: 98–99.)

Muir's journey, in Kenneth Burke's terms as set out by Bill Rueckert, is purgative-redemptive, employs the rhetoric of rebirth, and follows the dialectic of the mystic or upward way. This is not established so much by the vivid memory that restores the childhood self (as Muir would have it by not going beyond it in his reflections) as by the illness that followed it. This illness, so totally reducing him, is necessary to cancel the guilt he feels in following his daemon (demon) and perhaps in having had the experience of recovered childhood with its implicit rebuke of his father and in writing in his journal the otherwise anomalous sermons, the interior dialogues with himself and his father in which he uses his father's formal means to transvalue his beliefs and deny him. No one knew better than Emerson that the repudiations of the self-reliant have a cost, that, as he says of the American Scholar, "he takes the cross of making his own [road], and, of course, the self-accusation, the faint heart, the frequent uncertainty and loss of time, which are the nettles and tangling vines in the way of the self-relying and self-directed." Muir's obsession with dirt and cleanliness also figures here because he probably viewed his illness as the result of pollution and impurity, that is, of the moral laxity that was said to predispose people, as David Miller points out, to infection, especially that due to the miasma of swamps. And before Muir departed he had been warned that "the swamps in the South were full of malaria."

In stating his beliefs, Muir justifies his vocation and sanctions it with religious significance. These beliefs, I think, were not formed but elicited and confirmed by the journey. The world he sees about him already *flows*. His top views, as in the Cumberland Mountains, are indeed sublime but chiefly because he sees the totality of the divine order. The plants he sees are "flower creatures" who, he maintains, feel as we do and have every right to a happy place in the creation, as do animals, whose rights he eloquently defends against human dominion—enslavement, greed, use. His ear is already tuned to the harmonies of natural things, instructed perhaps by Carlyle, who said that "the heart of Nature [is] everywhere music." He removes the sting of the "death orthodoxy" and attacks the current establishment and its prejudices in a long set piece on anthropocentrism that breaks the narrative but is symptomatic of his recovery from illness. A storm at sea inspires him with a sense of "nature's beauty and harmony." And, finally, he reflects on the Book of Nature, "the one grand palimpsest of the world," the reading of which validates his botanical studies and (for us) prefigures his reading of glacial writing, the very language of the creation of the world.

Muir wisely relinquished his "Amazon plans" and never again went South until, late in life, he visited the southern states and even traveled to South America. He doesn't seem to belong in the tropics and is only at home there when, as in Cuba, he is happily free on the fringes of the jungle. By contrast with what precedes it, the sojourn in Cuba is idyllic, of unusual equanimity, soft and subdued. Captain Parsons of the *Island Belle* is a good father who provides the convalescent every comfort and furthers his studies by taking him ashore every day. Muir explores the edges of the forest and rambles on the beach and seems better able to cope with Havana than, subsequently, New York. (The disorientation and revulsion he claims he feels in cities seems to me to some extent to be an affectation.) In Cuba, and even more in Panama, where he views the "riotous exuberance" of the jungle from the train, he at least sees a token of the vegetation he had come so far to study—vegetation that pleases him because it holds its "rightful kingdom" against the "enslavable plants" introduced by man.

The journal ends with Muir's passage in steerage from New York to California, an immigrant's passage to make good the earlier one, this one insuring the freedom that fosters new birth. Some material on Panama, much of it on dirt, has been omitted, and Badè, who divided the journal into chapters, completes its partial purgative-redemptive narrative. He adds a letter to Mrs. Carr in which Muir tells of his arrival in the flowery Eden of the San Joaquin valley ("here, here is Florida!," the flowers, moreover, not "entwined," as in Cuba, but "free and separate"). And he properly closes the narrative by adding Muir's essay on "Twenty Hill Hollow."

This descriptive essay ends with the uplifting assurance that nature heals, that those who are "choked in the sediments of society" will "breathe deep and free in God's shoreless atmosphere of beauty and love." In witness of this, Muir tells of his own "baptism in this font" (fountain of light) and what a "resurrection day" it was for him. The landscape is sunny, fragrant, and bright, not a bare, wintry common, but the certifying experience is (remarkably) similar to Emerson's: "You cannot feel yourself out of doors; plain sky, and mountains ray beauty which you feel. You bathe in these spirit-beams, turning round and round, as if warming at a camp-fire. Presently you lose consciousness of your own separate existence: you blend with the landscape, and become part and parcel of nature." *Part and parcel of nature.* These are Emerson's words in *Nature* and Thoreau's in "Walking." Muir makes them his own (his *you* allowing us to share his experience) and in a long life filled with resurrection days may even be said to surpass his masters in describing them.

> When I came to California from the swamps of Florida, full of malarial poison, I crawled up the mountains over the snow into the blessed woods about Yosemite Valley, and the exquisite pleasure of convalescence and exuberant rebound to perfect health that came to me at once seem still as fresh and vivid after all these years as if enjoyed but yesterday.
> —Letter to Helen Hunt Jackson, 16 June 1885

Though Muir's recollection of illness and recovered health was prompted by solicitude for Mrs. Jackson and simplifies his spiritual autobiography, it dramatically points up the transition, the resurrectional moment, in the journey of his life. The imaginative liberties he takes anticipate *My First Summer in the Sierra*, the first of the self-authorizing books, published in 1911, for they underscore the *exuberant rebound* that characterizes this most exuberant and lyrical of all his books. When Muir arrived in California he was neither so full of malarial poison nor so sick that he crawled up mountains, and, in any case, he didn't make his way over snow. Even so, what matters in this recollection is the vertical disposition of his experience. Florida, as he recalls it, is defined by swamps, which the two-way appositive suggests are also full of poison, the substitution of *poison* for *fever* doing much to evoke the traditional noisome place. *Crawled* contributes to this at the same time as it confers on Muir the swamp's baleful associations. For it might be said that Muir belongs to the swamps just as later he belongs to the "blessed woods" of the mountainside—that in both instances geography figures the condition of the self after the fashion, say, of Hawthorne, for whom the outer figures the inner.

Hawthorne comes to mind because Muir was partial to his work. This, it seems to me, is curious considering Hawthorne's preoccupation with hidden sin and guilt. Muir mentions Hawthorne in "A Strange Experience," the chapter he devotes to telling of the realization of the presentiment of Professor Butler's presence in Yosemite Valley. "Hawthorne," he says, "could weave one of his weird romances out of this little telepathic episode, the one strange marvel of my life, probably replacing my good old Professor by an attractive woman." Readers of Muir's letters to Mrs. Carr as well as familiar with what is known of his relationships with Elvira Hutchings and Thérèse Yelverton will readily make the replacement that Muir, it seems, wishes to make.

But this is not as Hawthornesque as the deception of *the one strange marvel of my life*, for by the time Muir prepared his journals for publication he had had another presentiment, a foreboding one of his father's death, which the happy recollection of *my good old Professor* may have enabled him to hide. (After leaving home to walk to the Gulf, Muir visited his father only once, in answer to the summons of this presentiment.) *Hawthorne*, of course, is not out of place in a chapter—an interlude—in which Muir, in finding Professor Butler in his valley, recovers the liberating intellectual world of his youth and adds to his characterization the distinction of having had a college education. Muir knows his audience. Yet it may be that Muir mentions Hawthorne in order to confess himself, to provide the reader who recalls Hawthorne's burrowing into the self a clue to the self that Muir had undoubtedly plumbed in the trials of strangeness and sickness—the self that Calvinism teaches us always harbors pollution in its deep, dark caverns. *Snow*, accordingly, is not adventitious but the sign (a Muir hallmark) that the arduous journey upward, out of the swamp, is one of purification. Muir's obsession with uncleanliness also testifies to this and should be remembered when he claims, as he does in this book, that "nothing truly wild is unclean," that nature, "serenely wild," as he now finds it, is clean and pure.

With slight tampering, Emerson's epigraph to *Nature* serves Muir as well: "And, striving to be [purified] man, the worm / Mounts through all the spires of form." Yes, not just the worm, but man-the-worm, for whom evolutionary striving is an emblem of spiritual aspiration and the onward work of self-perfection. The healing that Muir tells us that people from the lowlands find in the mountains also involves purification—of the *low* aim, among other things, that prefers use to beauty. And purity is the spiritual accompaniment of health, for health is simply what occurs when we seek nothing from nature but enjoyment. In going to nature, Muir matches Thoreau in following a vocation of purity; Thoreau, who says in *A Week on the Concord and Merrimack Rivers* that "we need pray for no higher heaven than the pure senses can furnish, a *purely* sensuous life." Because Muir knew this, he practiced "a complete ascesis," as Tom Lyon says in "John Muir's Enlightenment" (*Pacific Historian* 25 [1981]).

It might be said that illness is a swampy, impure condition that by our own efforts we must try to crawl out of, where health, consequently, is something given us: works and faith. Muir says that "perfect health came to me at once." This gift is forever afterward associated with Yosemite, his chosen place, the place of the richest season of his life and of his most notable scientific achievement. In acknowledging this, Muir speaks for the wonder at and gratitude for Being he recovered there. *Wonder and gratitude for Being*: I owe this concept to Hannah Arendt (by way of George Kateb's fine book, which I am now reading), and in view of the world alienation of our time, consider exemplary those people, like Muir, who confirm wonder and gratitude for us.

This book, the sunniest in our literature, would be more exactly titled if a comma were inserted: *My First Summer[,] in the Sierra*. There is something initial and initiating about the rambles he reports in journal form, this evident in the freshness and candor of the entries and the clarity of their expression. The several summers Muir made into one comprise the veritable summer of his life. The reasons for this are many, for one, the sense that every day was a new creation and that he had come into "a new heaven and a new earth." An equally important reason, to cite Stephen Fox, is "the degree of psychic integration previously unknown to him" that accompanied this. (Fox adds, and I want to keep it in mind, that "after years of wandering he felt as though he belonged up there"—or, to put it in Muir's way, that in the mountains he was at home *and*, as we say, had come home to himself.) Muir's ebullience—"enjoying wild excitement and excess of strength," as he often does—is a measure of his "perfect health," of his being *hale* and *whole*, and wholly, unselfishly involved with nature. This is to say that the deepening of his ecology comes from the recovery of a vivid sense of cosmos. "We and the cosmos are one. The cosmos is a vast living body, of which we are still parts. The sun is a great heart whose tremors run through our smallest veins. The moon is a great gleaming nerve-centre from which we quiver forever." Muir knew this before D. H. Lawrence declared it in *Apocalypse*, and Muir knew (the contrastive structure of his book confirms this) that "what we want is to destroy our false, inorganic connections, especially those related to money, and re-establish the living organic connections, with the cosmos, the sun and earth." I omit "with mankind and nation and family" because at this time Muir was only "start[ing] with the sun." The rest, as Lawrence believed, inevitably followed.

Open the book almost anywhere and you discover his sentiment of being.

July 19   Watching the daybreak and sunrise. The pale rose and purple sky changing softly to daffodil yellow and white, sunbeams pouring through the passes between the peaks and over the Yosemite domes, making the edges burn; the silver firs in the middle ground catching the glow on their spiry tops, and our camp fills and thrills with glorious light. Everything awakening alert and joyful; the birds begin to stir and innumerable insect people. Deer quietly withdraw into leafy hiding-places; the dew vanishes, flowers spread their petals, every pulse beats high, every life cell rejoices, the very rocks seem to thrill with life. The whole landscape glows like a human face in the glory of enthusiasm, and the blue sky, pale around the horizon, bends peacefully down over all like one vast flower.

Everything awakening alert and joyful: Muir, too, verifying the great truth of awakening, as primary in Thoreau's experience as in Muir's, that, as Maritain puts it, "We awake in the same moment to ourselves and to things." Wakefulness (alertness) gives us the world and denies the dualism of estrangement. For we not only awaken *to* things but *among* them. Shunryu Suzuki says that "when you are there, everything else is there." Muir's awakenings, day after day, prove that the experience of the real presence of the world is not anomalous.

Copying out this passage on the sunrise makes me appreciate even more than I had when marking it Muir's literary mastery, especially his evocation of process and things-in-relation (the "event" of sunrise that restores the cosmos) and expression of ecstatic states of feeling in terms of the transformation of the landscape. As often with Muir, participles convey the sense of process, in this instance both his, of *watching*, and that of the *changing* natural world around him, this twofold unitary action accounting for the *blending* he sometimes mentions. That Muir's landscapes are in motion confirms Bachelard's observation that when things begin to move they are no longer alien to the subject but "move in us by arousing our latent desires and needs"—confirms, too, the "dynamic imagination" that "puts seemingly unrelated objects 'into the same motion,' not 'into the same slot,' and suddenly a world forms and becomes one before our very eyes."

Muir is so secure in his art that he doesn't question the flourish of *fills and thrills*. Both *fill* (influx) and *thrill* (response), frequently used by him, are true, after all, to his complete experience of the fountain-flow of light, the unity he achieves certified by rhyme. *Fills and thrills* is also the hinge of the passage, the participles adding up to the present tense and present sense of fullness. (At dawn, on another day in the Sierra, Muir notes in his journal, "We live in the present and are full," *full*, here, speaking also for the fullness of time.) Now each thing, Muir among them, participates in its own way, yet in concert, in the sunful (not sinful) world. And the world, seen initially in a painterly fashion, becomes a "whole landscape," made whole by the blue sky that "bends peacefully down over all like one vast flower." This "azure dome," he says a few pages later, is "over all like a bell-flower," the flower, in this instance, evoking a protective, transparent (parent?) bell jar, his oversoul.

Muir effortlessly achieves the egoless stance within the field that some poets and naturalists now value. He is the exemplary "schoolboy under the bending dome of day" who foregoes Emerson's promise in "The American Scholar" of self-aggrandizement by means of sympathetic correspondence. He eliminates the personal pronoun in order to enact the central fact of his experience: that the "I" has merged with the "eye" to become, as Robert Creeley says of Louis Zukofsky (an "objectivist" poet), "a locus of experience, not a presumption of expected value." Muir doesn't glow with enthusiasm, though this is implied and felt, reflected as it is from the face of things; the whole landscape does. He brings the world to significant life by anthropomorphizing it, but he himself is not anthropocentric. His happy use of the blue sky reminds me of how troubled Olson was in an early poem when the declaration "over all / the sun" failed to compose a whole landscape of the fragments of his observation. And the blue sky reminds me especially of Snyder's selfless art and of his great poem "The Blue Sky," a meditation on healing and wholing in which the azure dome of the sky confirms our sense that being is round.

With Muir, of course, the activity of the body, in being in the world, bestows being-in-the-world.

> Drinking this champagne water is pure pleasure, so is breathing the living air, and every movement of limbs is pleasure, while the whole body seems to feel beauty when exposed to it as it feels the campfire or sunshine, entering not by the eyes alone, but equally through one's flesh like radiant heat, making a passionate ecstatic pleasure-glow not explainable. One's body then seems homogeneous throughout, sound as a crystal.

The final phrase replaces the transparent eyeball with the transparent body and is certainly telling in a visual culture like ours that perhaps because of this limitation seldom experiences the manifold pleasures of "bodily elation" (Engberg and Wesling's phrase) that Muir enjoys. (Or any pleasure at all, if Trilling's "The Fate of Pleasure" truly states the case.) Pleasure is the keynote of Muir's summer—*glowing* pleasure, cognate with beauty, a sensuous, not a sensual, pleasure, easily aestheticized and spiritualized. It is thus made acceptable to an audience that believes, as Muir does, that nature ("pure wildness") is God's first temple. The fitting conclusion to Muir's "wonderful summer journey" is the account of Cathedral Peak, where, reminiscent of finding the *Calypso borealis*, he finds the cassiope. "Here at last," he says, "every door graciously opened for the poor lonely worshiper." This signal experience reminds me of Ginsberg's "Transcription of Organ Music" in which he, too, is overwhelmed by how much *out there* graciously stays open for him; and it corroborates Muir's belief that "in our best times everything turns into religion." *Here at last*: By summer's end he proves worthy.

Nothing in Muir's first summer bewilders him. In the Sierra, nature seems to be a splendid park, cared for by "some master landscape gardener." "Who would ever guess," he says early on, "that so rough a wilderness should yet be so fine, so full of good things. One seems to be in a majestic domed pavilion in which a grand play is being acted with scenery and music and incense. . . . God himself seems to be always doing his best here, working like a man in a glow of enthusiasm." But as much as anything, it is Muir, working in a glow of enthusiasm, whose art domesticates it—and whose art is more than a "trick of the rhetoric," to cite Emerson's criticism of "A Winter Walk," in which he says that Thoreau makes "a wilderness *domestic* (a favorite word)."

The door that opened for Muir is one instance of what Bachelard calls *cosmicity*, that is, of the way Muir dreams the world in a single image. *Home*, to which the door admits us, becomes the indispensable cosmological word, the image of what we want the world to be especially when we find ourselves estranged from it. And given all the evidence, this is what Muir wishes it to be. He makes himself at home by speaking of "Nature's carpeted mountain halls," by frequently considering landscape and natural phenomena in terms of rugs, lacework, and embroidery. He reminds us that nature, even though God makes it, is "feminine," with all that this has immemorially meant for our dwelling there.

And then the familiar, which is not so much what his rambles achieve as what he *finds*, bespeaks the family: "The whole wilderness seems to be alive and familiar, full of humanity, the very stones seem talkative, sympathetic, brotherly. No wonder when we consider that we all have the same Father and Mother." To him the landscape is as expressive as a human face, "so human it is, every feature and tint of color goes to one's heart. . . . in a place like this, we feel ourselves . . . kin to everything." *Other* is now br*other* and m*other*, and father, too.

Even more resonant than *door* in opening the world as home is *nest*.

> July 1   Summer is ripe. Flocks of seeds are already out of their cups and pods seeking their predestined places. Some will strike root and grow beside their parents, others flying on the wings of the wind far from them, among strangers. Most of the young birds are full feathered and out of their nests, though still looked after by both father and mother, protected and fed and to some extent educated. How beautiful the home life of birds! No wonder we all love them.

The fledglings are immediately present in *flocks*, their nests in *cups* and *pods*. Like Muir himself, they seek "their predestined places," having, like seeds, their destiny coded within them; and some, like Muir, will not strike root, stay in the natal place, but fly on the *wings* of the wind. The easy though abrupt transition from seeds to birds follows from these submerged images, but the description of the nest and parental care (even the detail, "to some extent educated") is owing to, and wishfully answers to, *far from them, among strangers*. This prompts the exclamation on the beautiful *home life* of birds—that is, the home life Muir fancies he once knew (for the ploughboy was protected and fed, and had brothers and sisters) and now, in his predestined place, longs to have again, as the last sentence tells us we all do.

In making this entry, Muir, I'm sure, remembered that in his boyhood he had raided the nests of larks (their imprisonment and liberation figure his own youth) but also was moved by the memory of the childhood he didn't have. Bachelard tells us, in the wonderful chapter on nests in *The Poetics of Space*, that "the discovery of a nest is always a source of fresh emotion," for "it takes us back to our childhood or, rather, to a childhood; to childhoods we should have had. For not many of us have been endowed by life with the full measure of its cosmic implications." The reverie toward childhood so conspicuous in Muir's writing tells the great loss that subsequently he tried to make good—and does make good for all of us by filling out what Bachelard charts in moving from the fact that "being starts with well-being" to an imagination of the world as "the nest of mankind." When "we examine a nest," Bachelard says, "we place ourselves at the origin of confidence in the world, we receive a beginning of confidence, an urge toward cosmic confidence." This is so with Muir, in this ripe summer.

"The best gains of this trip," Muir says of climbing Mount Dana, though *trip* may stand for the summer's ascent, "were the lessons of unity and interrelation of all the features of the landscape revealed in general views." The glacial history he also reads in the landscape (the revelation of the Book of Nature) confirms his intuition of cosmos, and the conclusion of this entry, following from his wish to build a cabin here, secures the identity of cosmos and home: "No other place has ever so overwhelmingly attracted me as this hospitable, Godful wilderness."

In *My First Summer in the Sierra*, Muir makes the difficult passage from home to home. This is why his self-characterization differs markedly from that in *A Thousand-Mile Walk to the Gulf* (where the absence of a possessive in the title may be significant): "Early in the morning I tied my notebook and some bread to my belt, and strode away full of eager hope, feeling that I was going to have a glorious revel." Now he walks *in*, not *to*, a place, for having arrived he is not compelled by the linear insistence of a destination. Though he makes light of it, we should not discount the fact that the journey this summer is made in company, that he has a base camp and, except for a brief bread famine (treated humorously, as food often is), is never without bread. Nor should we discount the extent to which his sheepherding solution to the "bread problem, so troublesome to wanderers" joins him with those whose economic activity destroys the very world he finds himself presently liberated to enjoy. His characterizations of Mr. Delaney ("Don Quixote") and Billy (Sancho Panza) are broadly comic, intended again as foils for himself, to separate himself from them *and* purge himself of their work. Billy, especially, puts us on Muir's side, for we wouldn't want to be thought indifferent to the Gospel of Nature nor a "dullness in the rays of God's beauty." Yet it may be that their company and even sheepherding spare him the introspection of his long lonely walk. They and the "silly sheep" may have been as welcome to him as modulation as they are to us for whom an unbroken succession of entries at ecstatic pitch would be too much, even tedious. This was Muir's formal problem, and he knew how to solve it.

The entry of 21 August, from which I cited above, comprises all of chapter 9, on Muir's not untroubled excursion to Bloody Cañon and Mono Lake. Muir begins with high hopes, "sauntering enchanted, taking no heed of time," reminded even of his boyhood when newly arrived in Wisconsin. But when he enters "the gate of the pass" (Bunyan again), he meets a band of dirty Indians who besiege him and, he confesses, revulse him. Following this, having at sundown "crept into a hollow by the side of a small lake," Muir spends a sleepless night made glorious, however, by a visitation of the moon.

> As I lay recalling the lessons of the day [that the wild may be wilder than he likes and no longer pure?], suddenly the full moon looked down over the cañon wall, her face apparently filled with eager concern, which had a startling effect, as if she had left her place in the sky and had come down to gaze on me alone, like a person entering one's bedroom. . . . she seemed to be just on the rim of Bloody Cañon and looking only at me. This was indeed getting near to Nature. [Muir trusts a cliché to tell his intimacy.] I remember watching the harvest moon rising above the oak trees in Wisconsin. . . . With these exceptions I might say that I never before had seen the moon, and this night she seemed so full of life and so near, the effect was marvelously impressive and made me forget the Indians, the great black rocks above me, and the wild uproar of the winds and waters making their way down the huge jagged gorge.

Forget? The landscape described at the end of this passage is sublime, after the fashion, say, of Salvador Rosa, and heightens the effect of the moon's benign appearance (like the nurse in Duncan's poems who lights the light). Poet that he is, Muir acknowledges the White Goddess, for without her presence the hospitable cosmos would be incomplete.

This episode, coming late in the book, emphasizes the fact that Muir's achievement—his high season—is temporary, that ascent is followed by descent as surely as summer is followed by autumn. (Recall Thoreau's A Week on the Concord and Merrimack Rivers, in some ways a comparable book.) The journey up and back corresponds with the seasons, with the rhythm of life, with the creative and destructive processes of nature; and this seasonal journey is punctuated by and recapitulated in the daily journeys from and to camp, the return unfailingly reminding Muir of the lowlands, the busy world of enslavement, dust, and din. The structure of the book, accordingly, figures Muir's vocational dilemma, the need for bread (the contrapuntal motif) that keeps him low. This is the structure he sees in clouds (and correspondingly in the mountains beneath them), the structure of the psyche answering to his experience of death and resurrection.

> July 23   Another midday cloudland, displaying power and beauty that one never wearies in beholding, but hopelessly unsketchable and untellable. What can poor mortals say about clouds? While a description of their huge glowing domes and ridges, shadowy gulfs and cañons, and feather-edged ravines is being tried, they vanish leaving no visible ruins. Nevertheless, these fleeting sky mountains are as substantial and significant as the more lasting upheavals of granite beneath them. Both alike are built up and die, and in God's calendar difference of duration is nothing. We can only dream about them in wondering, worshiping admiration, happier than we dare tell even to friends who see far-thest in sympathy, glad to know that not a crystal or vapor particle of them, hard or soft, is lost; *that they sink and vanish only to rise again and again in higher and higher beauty.* As to our own work, duty, influence, etc., concerning which so much fussy pother is made, it will not fail of its due effect, though, like a lichen on a stone, we keep silent.

What I have italicized declares Muir's faith in the goodness of the natural process: "Ripe and ready death [is as] beautiful as life," this confirmed even by his anxious dream of falling into Yosemite Valley. He believes that he participates in an ever-renewed and higher ascent. That this is the burden of the passage is indicated by the otherwise curious comment on work, duty, and influence, which, along with "friends who see farthest in sympathy," is owing to the presence in his thought of Mrs. Carr, to whom he once wrote in reply to her admonitions, "My horse and bread are ready for upward. . . . I will fuse with spirit skies."

In effect, Muir says that by doing what he's doing he will get his work done in God's good time. Keeping a journal (there are sixty extant journals) is part of this work and calls in question the adequacy of art, which comes to mind because Mrs. Carr ceaselessly urges him to mint his experience in words. Yet even as he deplores his skill he manages well enough to describe the midday clouds, to evoke them as "sky mountains" before establishing their aesthetic correspondence with the mountains below. In turning to nature to express its spiritual correspondence with himself, Muir's chief concern here is with transience and loss ("visible ruins" is the Romantic clue), neither of which need trouble him, he realizes, because he has all the time in the world and nothing is lost to change, only transformed. This props his cosmic faith. And what he now says of crystal and vapor particle, he says again definitively in a more elaborate figure, circular and efficacious, in *Studies in the Sierra*, the series of essays on glacial action that he finally wrote and that, if justification were needed, justified his rambles in the mountains.

Linnie Marsh Wolfe speaks of Muir's "life's business of studying the Cosmos." This suggests to me that the most explicitly relevant text, *Studies in the Sierra* (the essays published in the *Overland Monthly* in 1874 and 1875, the book in 1950), might have been called *Studies in the Cosmos*. Thoreau told his dream of cosmos in the fable of the artist of the city of Kouroo, found himself at the railroad cut in "the laboratory of the Artist who made the world and me" (*and me*: how wonderfully telling!), and saw in the flowing clay "the principle of all the operations of Nature." In the larger flowing landscape of the Sierra, Muir saw the "Master Builder" at the work of earth making, his chosen tool "the tender snow-flowers . . . the offspring of the sun and sea." Thoreau's Artist follows the organic aesthetic, where Muir's, sculpting mountains, follows the classic, like Michelangelo, releasing the form inherent in the material, "disinter[ing] forms already conceived and ripe." I cite Muir for the sake of *disinter*, its primary meaning *exhume* and its secondary meaning *to bring from obscurity into view*, both of considerable significance to someone who had been raised from the darkness of the pit. And I note this rare subscription to classic principle because it is, I think, Muir's way of acknowledging the majesty of the Creator, for whom the most innocent and seemingly evanescent thing, a tender snow-flake, is the instrument of stupendous power.

The snow-flowers may be said to join Muir's sciences, geology and botany. They belong, he explains, to a circle of phenomena that has the power to wear down mountains: "Ocean water is lifted in vapor, crystallized into snow, and sown broadcast upon the mountains. Thaw and frost, combined with the pressure of its own weight, change it into ice, which . . . immediately begins to flow back toward the sea whence it came." Muir writes serviceable scientific prose, but where it counts, employs metaphors, here those of birth and death: *sown broadcast, whence it came.* A sketch shows a "wheel . . . constructed of water, vapor, snow, and ice," a sun-whirled wheel that, moving against the side of a mountain, functions as a grindstone. Elliptical in shape, it is, even so, Muir's cosmic wheel, his most important figure, one whose axis is essentially vertical. By virtue of all this wheel does (that is, by virtue of all God does, "'He [who] hath *builded* the mountains'"), the earth we know has been made habitable and has become home.

This figure comes to mind when Muir, at the end of his journals, thinks of death: "The rugged old Norsemen spoke of death as *Heimgang*—home-going. So the snow-flowers go home when they melt and flow to the sea, and the rock ferns, after unrolling their fronds to the light and beautifying the rocks, roll them up close again in the autumn and blend with the soil." I cite the entire entry to show that whether the annular movement is vast or merely seasonal, the common fact of descent, its initial vertical meaning now transformed by the circle, is the flowing and the blending, the endings in which, Muir assures us, we too will find ourselves at home in the fertile places of the world.

From home to home: from the Bible, the revealed word of God, to the Book of Nature, the revealing work of God; from a sinful to a sunful world, its palpable beneficent light the veritable Light; from a cosmology grounded in fear of the world to a cosmology of confidence in the world. Muir substantiates the belief of Marx (in a critique of Hegel, as I learn from Stanley Cavell) that "the criticism of religion is the presupposition of all criticism." Like Emerson, he begins with religion, the focus of the considerable argument in *The Story of My Boyhood and Youth* and *A Thousand-Mile Walk to the Gulf*, and of course never relinquishes the deepest incentive of what, in view of his study of creation, might be called his pilgrimage to origins, to the fountains of the rivers that run through us and make them "part and parent of us."

Thoreau, in saying that "it is impossible for the same person to see things from the poet's point of view and that of the man of science," says nothing of the man of religion because for him religion is subsumed in poetry—poetry nothing less than the great art of cosmos, the expression of the beauty that Muir said was the perfect synonym for God. Muir, I think, proves Thoreau wrong, that is, the Thoreau of 1852 who said this and not the Thoreau who eventually relied more on the certainty of empirical law (discovered in the science of phenology) than on unpredictable epiphany to sustain his faith in the redemptive power of nature. William Ellery Channing considered Thoreau a poet-naturalist, which is exact enough if we recognize that the poet has priority and that what the hyphen joins it holds in tension. This characterization serves as well for Muir, though for him there is no longer any tension. In blending terrestrial and celestial—in effect, bringing heaven to earth—Muir was not troubled by the questions Thoreau asked himself in his youth: "May we not *see* God? . . . Is not Nature, rightly read, that of which she is commonly taken to be the symbol merely?" At one point in *My First Summer in the Sierra*, Muir says that "the place seemed holy, where one might hope to see God," in this tentative way (and unguardedly elsewhere) telling us that in ascending the Sinai of the Sierra he did see God.

Now it is important to note that Thoreau himself made Muir's affirmation possible by what may be his greatest achievement, given that it was the lifelong experiment to which all he did contributed: the revision of Emersonian "correspondence" to the end of restoring the reality and presence of the world and establishing its reciprocity with the perceiving mind. (For the definitive study, see H. Daniel Peck, *Thoreau's Morning Work*.)

When Muir remarks in his journal that "Nature is not a mirror for the moods of the mind," he is not repudiating the idea of correspondence but only Emerson's version, in which mind is sovereign and subjectivity is privileged to "put nature under foot." In *Nature*, Emerson says of the exemplary case, that of the poet: "He uses matter as the symbol of it. The sensual man conforms thoughts to things; the poet conforms things to his thoughts." (The emphasis of *his* implies that the sensual man has no thoughts of his own, no originating mind.) Muir, on the contrary, has no use for *use*, perhaps because he had been used; except as he beholds its beneficence in nature, power does not exhilarate him. Donald Worster, in the chapters on Thoreau in *Nature's Economy*, distinguishes the Emersonian from the Goethean doctrine of correspondence in which mind and nature are co-equal: "For Emerson the human mind [is] central to the cosmos, not merely a coordinate sphere with physical nature." This is the imbalance to which Thoreau and Muir object, Thoreau, in a journal entry of 2 April 1852, imputing it to egotism. The universe, Thoreau says, "is not a chamber of mirrors which reflect me. When I reflect, I find that there is other than me."

Muir subscribes to the idea of correspondence both as a cosmological and literary doctrine, inevitably so because he took the Book of Nature for his text and set out to read or interpret it. His art, accordingly, always has a religious resonance. When, in the calamity of his blindness, Mrs. Carr told him that God had given him the "eye within the eye, to see in all natural objects the realized ideas of His mind," she defined in correspondential terms a religious vocation that was agreeable to Muir. Symbolic reading, to be sure, is conveyed by reference to spiritual sight, but there is no aggrandizement in its use, and since Muir's seeing inclined that way he was willing to let natural objects, in predicating themselves, declare not only the ideas but the very presence of God.

For Muir, reading nature is not limited to observation but demands participation, a total bodily activity that Tom Lyon, in his pamphlet on Muir, calls "immersion." It is an experience always fuller and richer than writing, symbolic or otherwise, can convey. When Muir deplores his literary skill, he speaks once more for the absence of ego, the lesser place he assigns himself in the encounter with nature. For, as Thoreau learned, he stands in reciprocal relation to what he experiences and must grant reality to what so affects him, these things that Thoreau called *phenomena* not because they were merely phenomenal but because they were real, were events, things-and-their-relations, as with wonderful regularity they presented themselves to him, stood forth out of the flux of the seasons, out of the process that is reality. And daily in the Sierra, where for Muir the days (never to be regretted as with Emerson) were truly an epitome of the year.

Muir's large debt to transcendentalism may be gauged by the following prospect in Sampson Reed's *Observations on the Growth of the Mind*:

> The imagination will be refined into a chaste and sober view of unveiled nature. It will be confined within the bounds of reality. It will no longer lead the way to insanity and madness by transcending the works of creation and, as it were, wandering where God has no power to protect it; but finding a resting place in every created object, it will enter into and explore its hidden treasures. . . . When there shall be a religion which shall see God in everything, and at all times, and the natural sciences not less than nature itself shall be regarded in connection with him . . .

Muir's debt to Emerson is not, as it is to Thoreau, so much one of how to study nature as one of psychology, of the liberation of the spirit, the call of "The American Scholar" and the reassurance of "Self-Reliance," which enabled him to follow his vocation and fulfill its obligation to raise and cheer. Muir does this, as Thoreau does, because he restores the primacy of the world and places us within it, as part and parcel of the cosmos.

Thoreau observes that "anciently, the faith of a philosopher was identical with his system, or, in other words, his view of the universe." This reminds us, among other things, that there are many faiths and cosmologies, among them Thoreau's and Muir's, which, given their dependence on divinity, may not be as readily endorsed now as they were in the nineteenth century. Thoreau anticipates this loss, if loss it is, by suggesting that perhaps we may be heartened by biography—and, I would add, the patent autobiography of nature writing. "The fact that interests us most," he remarks, "is the life of the naturalist"—the life of a naturalist, say, for whom the love of the world itself would now of necessity be relied on to insure its indispensable integrity and health.